Computer Science, Technology and Applications

Computational Mathematics and Analysis

nova
science publishers
www.novapublishers.com

Computer Science, Technology and Applications

Digital Twins: The Industry 4.0 Use Cases: The Technologies, Tools, Platforms and Application
Kavita Saini, PhD (Editor)
Pethuru Raj Chelliah, PhD (Editor)
2023. ISBN: 979-8-89113-057-9 (eBook)

Situational Modeling: Definitions, Awareness, Simulation
Alexander Fridman, PhD (Editor)
2023. ISBN: 979-8-88697-590-1 (Hardcover)
2023. ISBN: 979-8-88697-725-7 (eBook)

More information about this series can be found at
https://novapublishers.com/product-category/series/computer-science-technology-and-applications/

Computational Mathematics and Analysis

Higgs Boson: A Mathematical Survey with Finite Element Method
Harun Selvitopi, PhD (Editor)
2023. ISBN: 979-8-88697-785-1 (Softcover)
2023. ISBN: 979-8-89113-063-0 (eBook)

Fundamental Perceptions in Contemporary Number Theory
J. Kannan, M.Sc., M.Phil., PhD (Editors)
Manju Somanath, M.Sc., M.Phil., PhD (Editors)
2023. ISBN: 979-8-88697-794-3 (Hardcover)
2023. ISBN: 979-8-88697-864-3 (eBook)

More information about this series can be found at
https://novapublishers.com/product-category/series/computational-mathematics-and-analysis/

Abhaya Kumar Sahoo
Chittaranjan Pradhan
Bhabani Shankar Prasad Mishra
and Brojo Kishore Mishra
Editors

Building Intelligent Systems Using Machine Learning and Deep Learning

Security, Applications and Its Challenges

nova science publishers
www.novapublishers.com

Library of Congress Cataloging-in-Publication Data

ISBN: 979-8-89113-342-6

Published by Nova Science Publishers, Inc. † New York

Contents

Preface

Data science is a growing field that involves various applications using statistical and machine-learning techniques applied on large dataset. As technology continues to advance, data scientists are able to mine more information from ever-larger sets of data, making it easier to analyze patterns in the world around us. This book presents an overview of different primary models in intelligent systems using machine learning and deep learning. It begins by defining the concepts and principles of machine learning, including supervised, unsupervised, and reinforcement learning models. This also explains how deep learning extends these models through the interference of Artificial Neural Networks (ANN), and discusses popular deep learning architectures such as Convolutional Neural Networks (CNN) and Recurrent Neural Networks (RNN). The book indeed explores how the different models would be useful in various real-world applications, like, computer vision, natural language processing, and robotics. Finally, it concludes by discussing some of the challenges and future benefits of intelligent systems with reputed machine learning models and models in deep learning. In technical words, Intrusion detection system (IDS) refers to them as packets, and large packets are transferred across an internet network in a second's time. Intrusion detection system uses machine learning techniques to detect any potentially harmful network activities. These packets might include data that is encrypted or not. The essential concept here is that the system detects any interruption in the network excluding the decryption of packets. Most popular algorithms like Naïve Bayes, SVM, KNN, and Random forest are used in the field of IDS.

Intelligent system can also be applied in software testing. In order to reduce the cost of regression test suites and increase the effectiveness of regression testing, requirement-based test case prioritization (RTCP) is adopted by most of the research practioners to prioritize the test cases. The objective of this field is to rank the requirement-based test cases as higher priority by selecting the relevant features. For this, the machine learning classifier k-Nearest Neighbor, Decision Tree, Random Forest, Bagging,

Support Vector Machine algorithms are being used to evaluate the features for the test case prioritization. In the field of security, we provide a thorough analysis of the various OSNs security and privacy threats and their detection and prevention along with predicted the phishing threats by implementing the approaches of machine learning. In this book, a brief summary of current solutions that can better protect the OSN users' privacy, security, and protection is discussed. The experimental result demonstrates that after implementing the feature selection techniques like Information Gain (IG), Chi-square and ANOVA test on the phishing dataset, the significant features so created able to evaluate the machine learning classifiers such as k-Nearest Neighbor (KNN), Logistic Regression (LR), Decision Tree (DT) and Naïve Bayes (NB) efficiently and obtained the performance in terms of accuracy as 99.7% in KNN classifiers for detecting the phishing threat.

In the field of agriculture, apple disease has caused a considerable loss and is a major concern in countries with the biggest production. In this study, a deep learning and transfer learning models are developed to recognize objects from a dataset of approx 10000 pictures separated into 4 classes: healthy, black rot, cedar apple rust, and apple scab. This book also explains about designing and implementing a novel sigmoid butterfly optimization algorithm with a deep learning model for big data classification in an Apache Spark environment. Intelligent system uses Natural Language Processing (NLP), which is a sub field under artificial intelligence that deals with the communication languages between computer and human. A major process in NLP is machine translation which is the conversion of input text from one source language to target language without affecting the meaning. The input and output for NLP is natural language text. To implement the system, a new model for machine translation using Optical Character Recognition (OCR) is employed. The system also uses Bidirectional Recurrent Neural Network (BRNN) and dictionary based approaches for English to Kannada and Marathi language translation. Artificial Intelligence is increasingly used in various healthcare-related applications ranging from diagnostics to therapeutics and prosthetics. A new class of Artificial Intelligence (AI) models, known as Generative AI, has emerged in recent years. Generative AI has been used extensively in image reconstruction and augmentation. This is particularly helpful in healthcare systems to produce substantial synthetic data which could be used for analysis and devising personalized therapeutics. Generative Adversarial Networks have earned notoriety for producing synthetic data which are virtually indistinguishable from real data. This book presents a comprehensive overview of existing generative AI models and how they can be used in healthcare applications to perform data augmentation of Electroencephalogram (EEG) data and image regeneration of visual stimulus from EEG signals.

In the healthcare sector, a thorough analysis of the current state of deep learning technologies used in diabetes research indicates better performance by deep learning methods for closed-loop diabetes management. Several DNN architectures and learning methods have been employed in different fields and have produced experimental results that are superior to those of earlier traditional machine learning methods. In this book, it presents about geospatial-artificial intelligence (GeoAI) which provides enormous opportunities and challenges to active earth research. Theoretical advances, big data, computer hardware, and high-performance computing platforms that enable the creation, training, and deployment of GeoAI prototypes quickly are the driving forces behind its rapid development. The automation of geospatial studies and artificial intelligence, particularly computer vision techniques and the most recent intelligent systems including both research and industry, have made significant strides in recent years.

Dr. Abhaya Kumar Sahoo, Ph.D.(CSE)
Dr. Chittaranjan Pradhan Ph.D.(CSE)
Dr. Bhabani Shankar Prasad Mishra Ph.D.(CSE)
Dr. Brojo Kishore Mishra Ph.D.(CSE)

Chapter 1

Intelligent Systems for Future Applications Using Machine Learning

Anil Kumar Meher[1,*]
Abhaya Kumar Sahoo[2,†]
and Rekhanjali Sahoo[3,‡]

[1]Department of Computer Science & Engineering, Centurion University of Technology and Management, Bhubaneswar, India
[2]School of Computer Engineering, KIIT Deemed to be University, Bhubaneswar, India
[3]Department of Computer Science Engineering, GITA Autonomous College, Bhubaneswar, India

Abstract

Data is a collection of raw facts and figures that can be generated from various sources such as social media, health, agriculture, stock markets, weather forecasts, etc. Data from different means of communication is increasing every day, such as Facebook, Twitter, Amazon, LinkedIn, etc. Dealing with the massive amounts of data generated from these sources is now a very difficult task. So, in order to maintain the 5'V concept, we have to use modern tools to process the data. Extracting meaningful data from large amounts of data uses data processing, which uses statistical techniques and algorithms, scientific techniques, different techniques, etc. Data science is a multidisciplinary field that uses scientific methods, processes, algorithms, and systems to extract knowledge and insights from structured and unstructured data. Data science is released in the market to process large amounts of data and discover unseen patterns,

* Corresponding author's Email: anil.meher@cutm.ac.in.
† Corresponding author's Email: abhaya.sahoofcs@kiit.ac.in.
‡ Corresponding author's Email: rekhanjalisahoo23@gmail.com.

In: Building Intelligent Systems Using Machine Learning and Deep Learning
Editors: A. Kumar Sahoo, C. Pradhan, B. Shankar Prasad Mishra et al.
ISBN: 979-8-89113-342-6

gain meaningful insights, make business decisions, etc. Most of the tools used in the data science industry are Python, Machine Learning, NoSQL, MongoDB, Hadoop, Spark, etc. Fields directly or indirectly related to data science include statistical learning, machine learning, deep learning, machine learning, image processing, signal processing, natural language processing, predictive modeling, etc. If we see a trend of faster global data growth, then we have to consider data science with many tools. Data science provides a method of collecting, cleaning, integrating, analyzing, visualizing, and processing data to create data products. Due to the high availability of data, data science roles such as data scientist, data engineering, data analyst, process owner, business analyst, etc. constantly emerging. Now the demand is even greater. Data science careers are currently among the highest paying careers in the world. Due to its wide application in various industries, there is a growing demand for data scientists who can analyze complex data and communicate the results effectively.

Keywords: data science, intelligent system, big data, machine learning, deep learning

Introduction

Data Science is the area of study which involves extracting insights from vast amounts of data using various scientific methods, algorithms, and processes. It is also the application of computational and statistical techniques to address or gain insight into some problem in the real world. In other words, we have a lot of data with us, but we are not trying to find out any insights from it. And this need to understand and analyze data to make better decisions is what gave birth to Data Science. At a high level, data science is a set of fundamental principles that support and guide the principled extraction of information and knowledge from data. Possibly the most closely related concept to data science is data mining-the actual extraction of knowledge from data via technologies that incorporate these principles [1]. We think that data science is lying at the intersection of Mathematics, Data and Technology, where mathematics includes linear algebra, statistics and probability; data includes its types like structured, semi-structured and unstructured data; technology includes machine learning, big data, business intelligence, predictive analytics etc. The past two decades have seen a proliferation of data generation and collection. This trend has been driven by several developments, including the emergence of social media, e-commerce, smart phones, wearable technology, and the internet of things (IoT). The potential of data science and analytics to enable data-driven theory, economy, and professional development is increasingly being recognized. This involves not only core disciplines such as computing, informatics, and statistics, but also the broad-based fields of business, social science, and health/medical science [2]. The below Figure 1 here describing the core components of data science formation and the intersection between the all three like data, mathematics and technology.

An intelligent system is an advanced computer system that collects, analyzes and responds to data collected from the surrounding environment. It can work and communicate with other agents such as users or other computer systems. A growing number of ICT-based systems rely on so-called "operational intelligence" to derive important facts from heterogeneous human-generated data sources, such as vehicle mobility, occupation of space in smart buildings or via connected data sources. Sensing devices in smart cities, autonomous driving, and smart digital health scenarios, to name a few. This data is used to analyze complex processes and systems in the physical world and to make critical social and business decisions. For these reasons, intelligent data analysis and decision-making tools are becoming the most important assets of cutting-edge ICT-based companies and organizations. The Machine Learning for Intelligent Systems course provides training in advanced AI/ML theory and tools, efficient big data processing, software implementation, and real-world problem solving techniques.

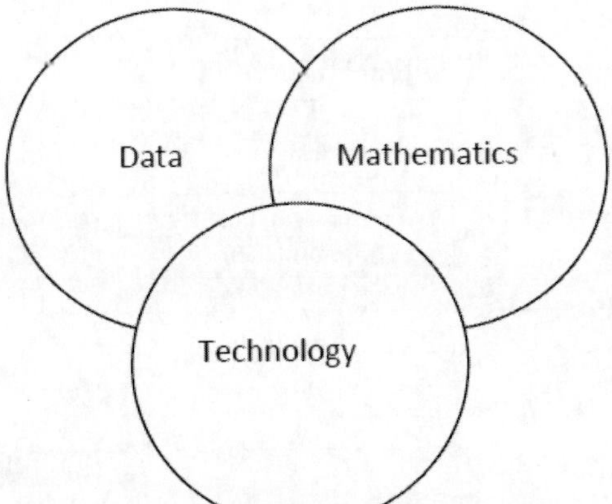

Figure 1. Data Science: An intersection of Data, Mathematics and Technology.

A data science lifecycle is defined as *the iterative set of data science steps required to deliver a project or analysis*. A general data science lifecycle process includes the use of machine learning algorithms and statistical practices that result in better prediction models. Some of the most common data science steps involved in the entire process is business understanding, data exploration and preparation, data representation and transformation, data visualization and presentation, train, validate, deploy, feedback etc. *Business understanding* phase understands what customer exactly wants from the business perspective. *Data exploration* means data requirements and data collection where requirement means the chosen analytical approach to determine data requirements and collection means identify, gather and curate available data resources relevant to problem domain. *Data preparation* means we have different types of data like incomplete data, corrupted data, noisy data, irrelevant data, unfriendly data etc. to prepare for use. *Data representation* includes statistical analysis and exploratory visualization of data. *Data transformation* means algorithm alignment and data formatting. *Data Visualization* phase significant patterns and trends are filtered by statistical methods. Cognitive bias can occur in the data visualization phase [3]. After visualization we have to train our data using model building techniques and after that we need to validate the models and lastly we have to deploy the models. Then finally we have to collect feedback from clients. The below Figure 2 is describing about the life-cycle of data science process in real world scenario.

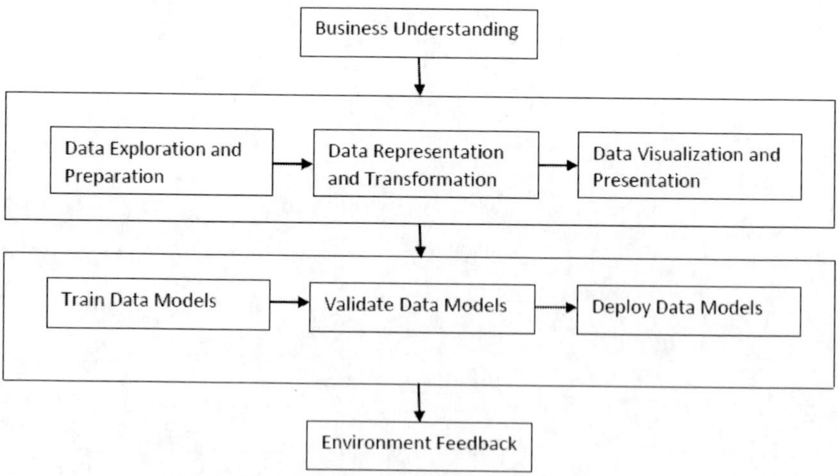

Figure 2. Data Science life-cycle.

It has been calculated from a survey that 90% of today's data are created in last 5 years. Every day we create 2.5 quintillion bytes of data. The estimated global internet traffic rate is 50000 GB/Sec. A person generates 1100 TB of data in their life span. In a minute 300 hours of video uploaded to YouTube, 204 M e-mails are sent and 500000 comments posted in Facebook. Among 6000 planes one airplane can generate 2.5 TB of data per day. 680 million smart meters producing 280 Petabytes of new raw data. That means we are surrounded with data everywhere, every time because we all are connected digitally in real time. Data science was originated in 2001 to handle these kinds of huge, structured, semi-structured and unstructured data. Multifaceted and huge datasets have various types of different and important features that are closely in resemblance with "Big Data" andto administer the datasets is troublesome with the traditional information preparing frameworks and hence data storage, data transition, data visualization, data penetrating, data analysis, data security, data privacy violations and sharing propose different uphill challenges that the "Big Data" reinforces [4].

Data science helps to access resilient distributed dataset (RDD) which is the combination of different formats of data. These RDD helps to recognize type of data files processed through spark cell. Spark is a data processing tool especially used under big data for huge data science operation using Python or R or Scala tool. RDD is Spark's primary abstraction and is also a fault tolerant collection of elements that can be parallelized. There is no doubt, nevertheless, that the potential of data science and analytics to enable data-driven theory, economy, and professional development is increasingly being recognized. Using two types of RDD operations namely transformation and action we can parallelize the data across cluster. This is important with large amounts of data (big data), because we do not want to duplicate the date until needed, and certainly not cache it in memory until needed. As data is very important for data science, so types of data should be taken into care as data science supports various types of data to be processed. *CSV* files are familiar to everyone as input/output to spreadsheet applications where rows correspond to individual records and columns of plain text are separated by comma or some other delimiter (tab, |, etc.). *JSON fie* (JavaScript Object Notation) is an open standard format that uses humanreadable text to transmit data objects consisting of attribute-value pairs and it is used primarily to transmit data between a server and web application, as an alternative to XML.ORC file (Optimized Row Columnar) introduces a lightweight indexing that enables skipping of complete blocks of rows that do not match a query. It comes with basic statistics, min, max, sum, and count, on columns. Parquet files are a columnar storage format suitable for any project in the Hadoop ecosystem, regardless of data processing framework, data model, or programming language chosen. Flat files or text files may need to be parsed into fields/attributes where fields may be positional at fixed offset from the beginning of the record or text analytics may be required to extract meaning. The below Figure 4 describes the classification of structured, semi-structured and unstructured data under RDD.

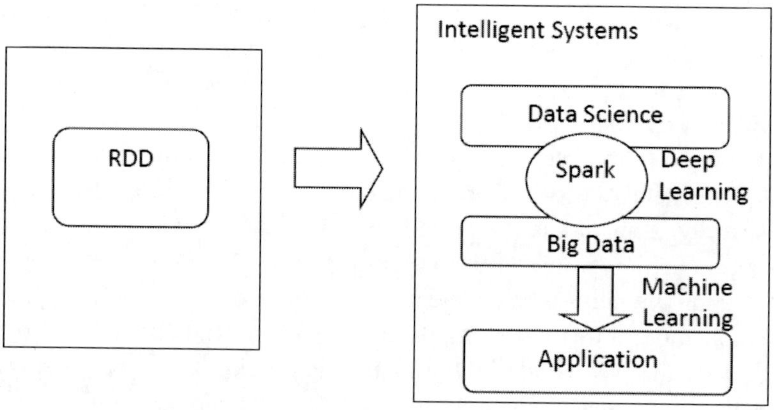

Figure 3. Intelligent System application workflow.

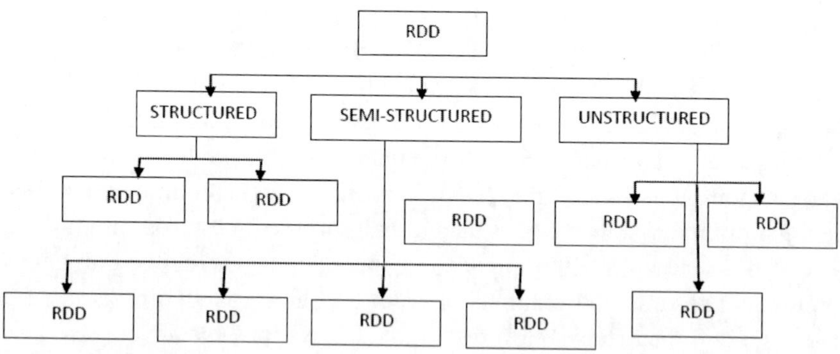

Figure 4. RDD Classification.

In most cases we use Scala for data processing using spark. But sometimes it has seen that python can also be used for the same. If we are using python, then the shell available for Scala is "spark-shell" and if we are using python then the shell available for python is "Pyspark." Apache Spark introduced a new approach for data science and engineering where wide ranges of data problems can be solved using a single processing engine with general-purpose languages [5]. Above Figure 3 is describing about the workflow of different technologies to fulfill the requirement of Intelligent System.

Domain distribution along with tools required for data science operations are many. But we can choose according to our requirement. For example, Python, R and Scala all are supporting spark to process the data, so we can choose anyone. Here we think python will be the best as it provides huge amount of library as compare to others. Spark provides parallel distributed processing, fault tolerance on commodity hardware, scalability, etc. Spark adds to the concept with aggressively cached in-memory distributed computing, low latency, high level APIs and stack of high evel tools. Spark has four libraries namely Spark SQL, Spark Streaming, MLlib and GraphX for processing of data. Those who are work in domain of data science solve problems and answer questions through data analysis every day. They build models to predict outcomes or discover underlying patterns, all to gain insights leading to actions that will improve future outcomes. And the tools and technologies used in data analysis are evolving rapidly, enhancing data scientists' abilities to reach the goal. The below Figure 5 is describing about the domain tools distribution for data science operations.

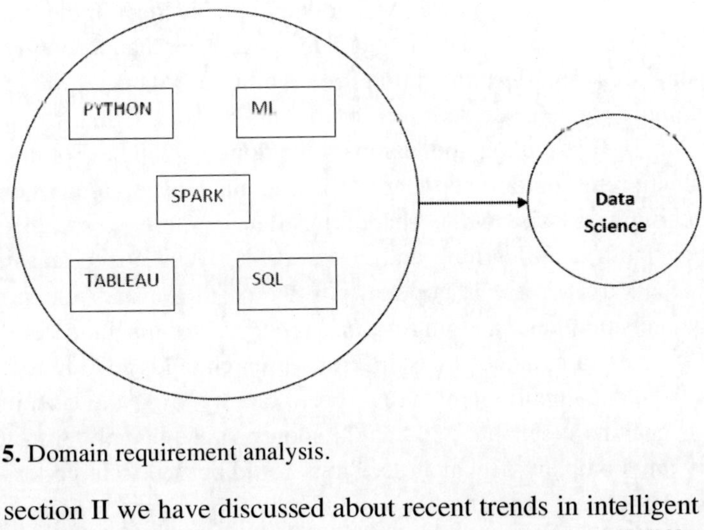

Figure 5. Domain requirement analysis.

In section II we have discussed about recent trends in intelligent system, in section III we have discussed about key responsibilities of different data science roles in industries, similarly in section IV we have discussed about the literature review of the paper in which we have focused about different methods with comparisons, in section V we have discussed about the application of machine learning and deep learning in the area of data science for intelligent system. In section VI we have discussed about the future study and in section VII we have the conclusion about this paper.

Trends in Intelligent System

There are decades when nothing happens, and there are weeks when decades happen. We live in a world where AI and data science are shaping and complimenting the future of humanity across nearly every industry. The rapid adoption and focus on data science has led to accelerated change and expansive growth in top areas including AI as a Service, AutoML and TinyML, data regulation, data governance, and a continued boom in cloud migration. The term data science is very popular now a day. The study, processing and storage responsibility of data is all under the control of data science. Data science itself is a combination of many tools and technologies. The global enterprise focus and expectations have shifted radically in the last few years as data science is increasingly augmenting human potential to reimagine business fundamentals and drive paramount value.

Artificial intelligence is perhaps the single technology trend that will have the greatest impact on the way we live, work and do business in the future. AI allows businesses to analyze data and gain insights faster than through manual means, using software algorithms that improve in their work as they receive more and more data. Deep learning represents a subcategory of machine learning that is focused on the parameterization of DNNs. For enhanced clarity, we will refer to non-deep-learning-based machine learning as classical machine learning (classical ML), whereas machine learning is a summary term that includes both deep learning and classical ML. While deep learning has seen a tremendous increase in popularity in the past few years, classical ML (including decision trees, random forests, support vector machines, and many others) is still very prevalent across different research fields and industries [6]. As datasets and computing resources grew rapidly over the ensuing two decades, it became clear that ML would soon power not only Amazon but essentially any company in which decisions could be tied to large-scale data [7]. AI can help firms predict what customers will buy, using AI should lead to substantial improvements in predictive ability and AI algorithms probably have good predictive ability for incrementally new products [8]. Deep Learning provides the opportunity to use a simpler model to accomplish complicated Artificial Intelligence tasks, Although Deep Learning algorithms have been used for some Big Data domain like computer vision and speech recognition [9].

Experts have said that 80% or more of a data scientist's job is getting data ready for analysis. McKinsey once predicted that there will be an acute shortage of Data Science Professionals in the next decade and impact on various sectors like Web development, Digital advertisements, Ecommerce, Internet search, Finance, Telecom, and Utilities [10]. We shall create and cultivate a large number of data science professionals who "understand data, and can analyze and implement the measures." Accurate understanding of connotation, research direction, and methodology of data science is required [11]. "Data science" as a scientific term was initially proposed about 15 years ago, and has since increasingly attracted attention and debate within statistics, analytics, computing, social science, and other scientific domains and disciplines [12]. Data science is an interdisciplinary field aiming to turn data into real value like data may be structured or unstructured, big or small, static or streaming where value may be provided in the form of predictions, automated decisions, models learned from data, or any type of data visualization delivering insights [13]. The purpose of this article has been to share an overview of the conceptualization, development, observations, and thinking about the age of data science initiatives, research, innovation, industrialization, profession, competency, and education [14].

Popular AI techniques include machine learning (ML) and deep learning (DL) methods, natural language processing (NLP), as well as knowledge representation and expert systems (ES), can be used according to their data characteristics, in order to make the target applications intelligent [15]. Machine learning and artificial intelligence algorithms can assist human decision making and analysis tasks. While such technology shows promise, willingness to use and rely on intelligent systems may depend on whether people can trust and understand them [16]. ML has become an extremely popular topic within development organizations that are looking to adopt a data-driven approach to improve their business by gaining useful information from the data they collect [17]. The field of intelligent systems also focuses on how these systems interact with human users in constantly changing and dynamic physical and social environments. The first robots had little freedom of decision: They imagined a predictable world and performed the same actions over and over at the same time. Today, a robot is considered an autonomous system that recognizes its environment and can move around in the physical world to achieve certain goals.

Key Responsabilités in Data Science towards Intelligent System

Data science now a day is one of the best emerging technologies in market. As the amount of data are increasing unexpectedly day by day we are dependent more on data science tools for processing and storing of these huge amount of data. And for this we have different roles in organizations to gather, analyze, filter, curate, and aggregate, process, represent, and deploy all the datasets. So following are some of the roles which are currently assigned by the software companies for data science operations. The below Table 1 is created to describe the different types of users in data science operation and their roles and responsibilities, problems facing and expected solutions for them.

Table 1. Roles of Data Science Users

Roles	Responsibilities	Problems	Challenges	Solutions
Data Analyst	Analysis and visualization	Organizations are trying to predict fraud or suspicious activities and their patterns to help drastically reduce losses due to frauds.	How to make the sense of the structured data? Where is the signal and where is the noise?	Data refinery tools.
Data Scientist	Analysis and modeling	Now that we have sanitized and curated the data.	What predictions can we make?	Data models.
Data Engineer	Integration and refinement	Vandalized incidents are often submitted as legitimate accident claims	How to predict fraudulent behavior.	Deep learning.
Business Analyst	Understands business needs, build plans, and generate actionable insights.	Conflicts due to various factors such as team members proposing a new idea for the project, arguing over its implementation, timelines and more.	Changing requirements or business needs, conflicts with stakeholders.	SRS, wire framing
Product Owner	Define the problem and build a hypothesis	Lack of information and analysis before planning.	Forecasting delivery and timeliness, decision fatigue.	decision trees, decision matrices.
Business Sponsor	Plan, define KPIs and provide feedback	Focusing on own needs not company, their processes are ineffective.	No proper communication, delegating role.	Market research, consumer insights.

Literature Review

ML has become a very popular topic among development organizations looking to take a data-driven approach to improving their business by deriving useful insights from the data they collect. With ML models, organizations can continuously predict changes in their business and make decisions accordingly. Machine learning uses algorithms that iteratively learn from data to improve data, describe data, and predict outcomes. Once an ML model is trained, it can predict new data provided as input. The output of the model on new data will depend on the data used to train the model. Machine learning and deep learning are now two areas where we can explore more different applications like health, agriculture, social media, etc. All of these areas contain huge amounts of data that can be generated every day, whether labeled or not. So we can think accordingly and apply different kinds of machine learning and deep learning algorithms. Based on the data we discuss in this article, which application areas are some supervised algorithms, some unsupervised algorithms, and some augmented algorithms best suited. We have also collected information about these algorithmic techniques, as well as the areas in which they are used and the challenges we still face in these areas. The below Table 2 describing about the use of intelligent system in various sector. Some concepts and ideas from information science and computational intelligence are rapidly being integrated into many areas of electrical and computer engineering (ECE), particularly through the use of development innovations in machine learning. Fields such as computer and robotic vision, image processing and biometrics have benefited greatly from recent advances in deep learning. So the bellow Figure 6 is describing about the relationship between AI, ML, DL, DS and IS.

Table 2. Use of Intelligent System in various sector

Use Sectors	Use Areas
Education sector	Learning management system
Healthcare	Biomedical engineering
Human identification	Biometric monitoring
Manufacturing	Robotics and automation
Retail management	Recommendations for e-commerce
Weather and climate	Satellite imaging and analysis

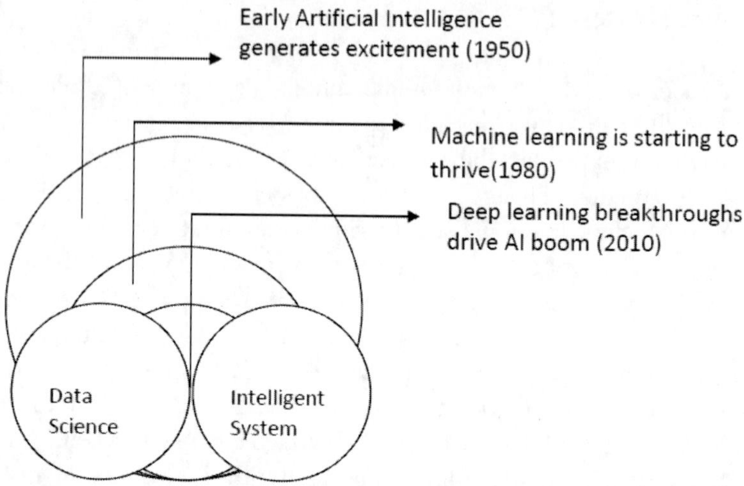

Figure 6. Related technological relationship.

Table 3. Feature comparison between different ML & DL methods

	Regression	Classification	Clustering	Reinforcement
Type	Supervised learning	Supervised learning	Unsupervised learning	Decision making
Data	Labelled/training data	Labelled data	Unlabeled data	Automatic
Output	Continuous	Discrete	Not-given	Depends
Task	Prediction	Computation	Grouping	Exploitation and exploration
Variables	Numerical	Categorical	Both	NA
Example	Linear regression	Logistic regression	K-means	Q-learning

Apart from this we have taken some methods frequently used for machine learning and deep learning process and made some differences based on some key features and some previous articles or paper references. The above Table 3 is describing about various types of ML and DL methods available in data science and further how they will help to design an Intelligent System it will tell.

Applications of Machine Learning and Deep Learning Methods Used in Data Science and Intelligent System

There are various types of machine learning methods available to apply in data science. The two categories are supervised and unsupervised learning methods. *Supervised* machine learning creates a model that, in the presence of uncertainty, makes evidence-based predictions whereas *Unsupervised* learning method detect hidden patterns or internal structures in unsupervised training data and also used to eliminate datasets that contain input data without labeled responses. Supervised learning methods are regression and classification whereas unsupervised learning methods are clustering and association. The applications of intelligent system involve in the areas like healthcare, robotics, education, character and face recognition, factory automation etc. and for this we can apply different methods of machine learning and deep learning.

Regression in Healthcare

Regression is a supervised learning technique which helps in finding the correlation between variables and enables us to predict the continuous output. There is a huge usage of regression in healthcare system like it is used to predict an individual's health care costs based on certain variables. Predict total surgical time for efficient operating room (OT) utilization. It is also used to predict Length of Stay (LOS) at the hospital. It is also used for risk prognosis to the cases of individual patients. The below Figure 7 is describing about the data representation of data while we are applying linear regression to the dataset.

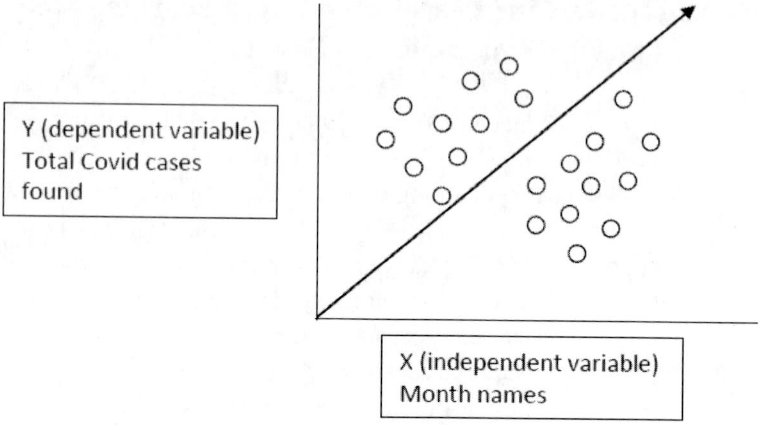

Figure 7. Data representation for healthcare.

Future Challenges

It is assumed that the cause and effect relationship between the variables remains unchanged. This assumption may not always hold good and may lead to misleading results. It involves very lengthy and complicated procedure of calculations and analysis. It cannot be used in case of qualitative phenomenon like honesty, crime etc.

Classification in Agriculture

Classification algorithm is a supervised learning technique that is used to identify the category of new observations on the basis of training data. It is a very important application of remote sensing. There are so many platforms like GEE (Google Earth Engine), are exploring the multiple satellite data with different high level and advanced classification techniques. One technique is random forest algorithm that has an ability to analyze crop growth related to the current climatic conditions and biophysical change. Random forest classification has the ability to predict crop yield. The below Figure 8 is describing about the classification technique dataset representation.

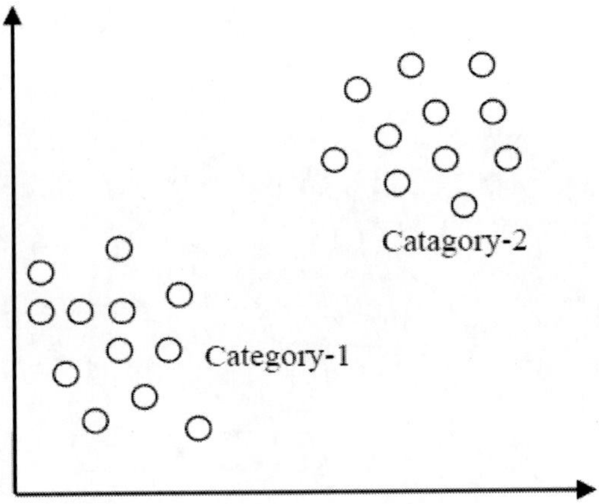

Figure 8. Data representation for agriculture.

Future Challenges

Challenges include various data sources, low precision, and low performance in real time, long collection cycles, high complexity, diversification and lack of appropriate data. So the main aspect of challenges includes data cleaning, data consolidation and persistent storage.

Clustering for Speech Recognition

Clustering or clustering analysis is a machine learning technique which groups the unlabelled datasets. It is a task of dividing the population or data points into a number of groups such that points in the same groups are more similar to other data points in the same groups and dissimilar to the data points in other groups. It is used to segment and cluster the speaker speech. Speech segmentation is essential in speech recognition and speech synthesis. Its quality has a huge impact on the follow-up speech recognition. K-means clustering based on HMM (Hidden Markov Models), is used for various operations like signal processing and speaker recognition on living beings. The below Figure 9 here describing the concept of data clustering representation for the dataset we have.

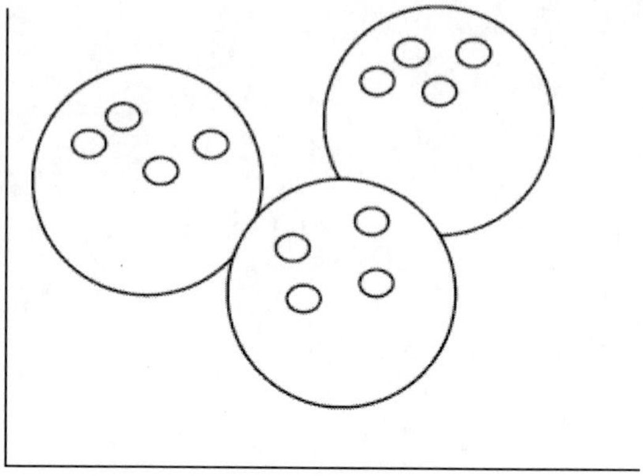

Figure 9. Data representation for speech recognition.

Future Challenges

Outliers are always affecting clustering results. Data sparsity is also another challenge due to missing information. Large datasets are difficult for clustering like hierarchical clustering.

Various techniques or methods proposed for deep learning to deal with real world development. Some of the techniques are like reinforcement learning, CNN, RNN etc.

Reinforcement in Self Driving Cars

Deep reinforcement learning is a subfield of machine learning that combines reinforcement learning and deep learning. RL considers the problem of a computational agent learning to make decisions by trial and error. Some of the autonomous driving cars applying the concept of deep learning using reinforcement algorithms for dynamic pathing, controller optimization, motion planning etc. for example parking can be achieved using learning automatic parking policies where as lane changing can be achieved using Q-learning while overtaking can be implemented by learning overtaking policies. The below Figure 10 is describing about the reinforcement process used for large datasets in real world.

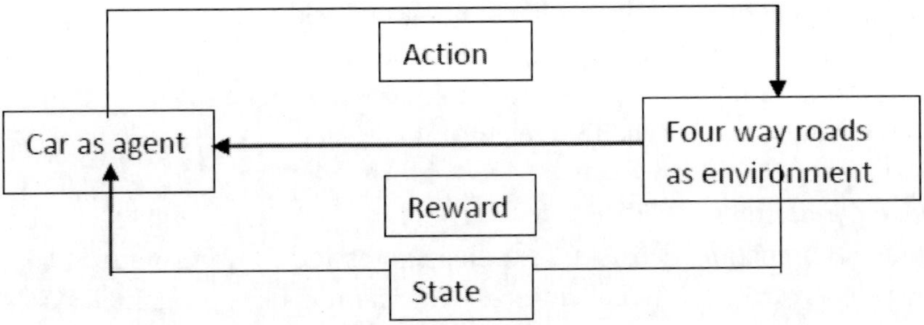

Figure 10. Data representation for reinforcement.

Future Challenges

Sample efficiency is the major challenge of reinforcement learning. Apart from this reproducibility issues, sparse rewards etc are the major areas of challenges we are facing in real world.

CNN in Facebook

With deep learning, a Convolutional Neural Network or CNN is a type of artificial neural network, which is widely used for image/object recognition and classification. Deep learning thus recognizes objects in an image by using a CNN. It is a very popular technique which is frequently used. The most popular CNN used in Facebook is image tagging. Generally image tagging describes the images and makes them easier to find using visual search technique. Tagging involves recognition of objects and even sentiments of the image tone.

Future Challenges

The challenges include over fitting, exploding gradients, class imbalance, need of large datasets.

RNN for Face Detection

A Recurrent Neural Network (RNN) is a kind of artificial neural network mainly used in speech recognition and natural language processing (NLP). RNN is used in deep learning and in the development of models that imitate the activity of neurons in the human brain. It makes the use of known features to make sense of the image and put together a proper description of the input image. It also used as streaming tool to make it easier for the customer to operate with the service and find relevant image etc.

Future Challenges

Extreme illumination, occlusion, extreme expressions, low resolution and in-plane rotation are the key challenges of deep learning face recognition system.

Future Study and Challenges

As data are growing day by day, data scientists are unable to process these huge amounts of data for the companies. So we need to focus more on this so that data will be properly handled. Future of Data Science 2030 is estimated to bring opportunities in various areas of banking, finance, insurance, entertainment, telecommunication, automobile, etc. A data scientist will help grow an organization by assisting them in making better decisions. The work of a data scientist, often hired to automate business processes and activities, could be largely "automated" in the future. We are entering an era where data science is more than ever a team sport. It's no longer about building the model; it's about what we do with the model once we have it. Being a data scientist is generally considered one of the most secure jobs in the world today. At the same time, we need to add a lot of network security to it.

Data scientists may be challenged by the growing popularity of cloud computing. A data scientist's job will become more "operational," in part as organizations use new sets of tools that capture a data scientist's workflow and best practices, and quickly and easily train company on these best practices. As coding and artificial intelligence become more important, the skills data scientists use to do their jobs will change. At the same time, they also need to be more business-oriented. Finally, some data scientists will have the opportunity to make a "quantum leap."

The electronics market is at the beginning of a technology-driven shift towards data-driven insights provided by intelligent systems. Today, analytical models are already built for them using ML and DL levels, and further dissemination is planned. For any real-world application, intelligent systems are not only faced with the tasks of model building, system specification, and implementation. They tend to solve a variety of problems rooted in the operation of ML and DL that pose relevant challenges to the information systems community. They require not only technical knowledge, but also human and business aspects that go beyond the constraints of the system to consider the environment and the ecosystem of the application. Certain challenges we are facing while using intelligent systems are:

1. Data mapping
2. Uncertainty in action
3. Data computation is very time consuming process.
4. Physical world decisions are not static.

Conclusion

This paper is based on the relationships between machine learning, deep learning, artificial intelligence, data science and intelligence. Also it focuses on the application areas and the methods specifically used for them to achieve the goal. The data science field is exploding in popularity. More than ever, companies are recognizing the need for data science and data analysis to succeed. And in this new digital age, having a firm grasp on how to process information is critical. It's even more important now that it's easier than ever before to obtain large amounts of data as well as get your hands dirty with programming and machine learning techniques. Data science is a growing field that involves the application of statistical and machine-learning techniques to large sets of data. As technology continues to advance, data scientists are able to mine more information from ever-larger sets of data, making it easier to analyze patterns in the world around us. Data scientists are on the front lines of every major technological development, helping companies understand and respond to changes in their industry and customer behavior. Machine learning and deep learning concepts are used to predict calculate and aggregate data using different methods. When it comes to data representation, everyone has their own opinion and use. The purpose of these methods is to automate the construction of analytical models and allow computers to learn from data without being explicitly programmed. In order to make accurate predictions, it is important to use high quality data that is representative of the real data that the algorithm will use.

References

[1] Provost, F., & Fawcett, T. (2013). Data science and its relationship to big data and data-driven decision making. *Big data,* 1(1), 51-59.

[2] Harris, H., Murphy, S., &Vaisman, M. (2013). *Analyzing the analyzers: An introspective survey of data scientists and their work.* "O'Reilly Media, Inc."

[3] Ho, D. A., &Beyan, O. (2020). Biases in data science lifecycle. *arXiv preprint arXiv*:2009.09795.

[4] Memon, M. A., Soomro, S., Jumani, A. K., &Kartio, M. A. (2017). Big data analytics and its applications. *arXiv preprint arXiv*:1710.04135.

[5] Salloum, S., Dautov, R., Chen, X., Peng, P. X., & Huang, J. Z. (2016). Big data analytics on Apache Spark. *International Journal of Data Science and Analytics,* 1(3), 145-164.

[6] Raschka, S., Patterson, J., &Nolet, C. (2020). Machine learning in python: Main developments and technology trends in data science, machine learning, and artificial intelligence. Information, 11(4), 193.

[7] Jordan, M. I. (2019). Artificial intelligence—the revolution hasn't happened yet. *Harvard Data Science Review,* 1(1), 1-9.

[8] Davenport, T., Guha, A., Grewal, D., &Bressgott, T. (2020). How artificial intelligence will change the future of marketing. *Journal of the Academy of Marketing Science*, 48(1), 24-42.

[9] Sohangir, S., Wang, D., Pomeranets, A., &Khoshgoftaar, T. M. (2018). Big Data: Deep Learning for financial sentiment analysis. *Journal of Big Data,* 5(1), 1-25.

[10] Nadikattu, R. R. (2020). Research on data science, data analytics and big data. *International Journal of Engineering, Science And,* 9(5), 99-105.

[11] Xu, Z., Tang, N., Xu, C., & Cheng, X. (2021). Data science: connotation, methods, technologies, and development. *Data Science and Management*, 1(1), 32-37.

[12] Cao, L. (2016). Data science and analytics: a new era. *International Journal of Data Science and Analytics*, 1(1), 1-2.

[13] Bichler, M., Heinzl, A., & van der Aalst, W. M. (2017). Business analytics and data science: Once again?. *Business & Information Systems Engineering,* 59(2), 77-79.

[14] Cao, L. (2017). Data science: a comprehensive overview. *ACM Computing Surveys (CSUR)*, 50(3), 1-42.

[15] Sarker, I. H., Hoque, M. M., Uddin, M. K., &Alsanoosy, T. (2021). Mobile data science and intelligent apps: concepts, AI-based modeling and research directions. *Mobile Networks and Applications*, 26, 285-303.

[16] Nourani, M., Kabir, S., Mohseni, S., & Ragan, E. D. (2019, October). The effects of meaningful and meaningless explanations on trust and perceived system accuracy in intelligent systems. In *Proceedings of the AAAI Conference on Human Computation and Crowdsourcing* (Vol. 7, pp. 97-105).

[17] Injadat, M., Moubayed, A., Nassif, A. B., & Shami, A. (2021). Machine learning towards intelligent systems: applications, challenges, and opportunities. *Artificial Intelligence Review*, 54, 3299-3348.

Chapter 2

Fundamental Models in Intelligent Systems Using Machine Learning and Deep Learning

R. Rathi[1]
E. P. Ephzibah[1,*]
V. Mareeswari[1]
P. Visvanathan[1]
R. Kanchana[2]
and E. Deepakraj[1]
[1]School of Information Technology and Engineering, VIT, Vellore, India
[2]Vel Tech Rangarajan Dr. Sagunthala R&D Institute of Science and Technology, Avadi, India

Abstract

In the current scenario, we hear news about robots, Artificial Intelligence (AI), or autonomous drones. Some of them are killer drones in the military, destructions caused by AI, joblessness in the future due to robots, and statements that project a negative of AI and its effects on human lives. But there are many cases where we see the benefits of machine learning and deep learning models outweigh these drawbacks, especially in healthcare, human activity monitoring and caring, etc. Despite the vast technological growth and usage of the same, one must know the fundamental models behind such advancements. This chapter presents an overview of different primary models in intelligent systems using machine learning and deep learning. Supervised, unsupervised, and reinforcement models are the basic models that come under machine

---

* Corresponding Author's Email: ep.ephzibah@vit.ac.in.

In: Building Intelligent Systems Using Machine Learning and Deep Learning
Editors: A. Kumar Sahoo, C. Pradhan, B. Shankar Prasad Mishra et al.
ISBN: 979-8-89113-342-6

learning principles. This chapter also explains how deep learning extends these models through the interference of Artificial Neural Networks (ANN) and discusses popular and widely known architecture on deep learning using Convolutional Neural Networks (CNN). The chapter indeed explores how the different models would be useful in various real-world applications, like, computer vision, natural language processing, and robotics. Finally, in the conclusion, a discussion on some of the challenges and future benefits of intelligent systems with reputed machine learning models and models in deep learning is given.

Keywords: intelligent systems, machine learning, deep learning

Introduction

Intelligent systems have become an essential part of our daily lives, from personal assistants to autonomous vehicles. These systems are designed to learn from data, make decisions, and interact with the environment. Intelligent systems are built basically with the help of high-end technologies like machine learning and recently, deep learning has been added to it. Machine learning involves the process of inculcating or imparting knowledge to the machines with the help of learned data and improving performance in a real-time scenario without an explicit program. Deep learning is a subcategory of machine learning with artificial neural networks that learns the data.

An overview of fundamental models in intelligent systems using machine learning and deep learning has been framed. It starts with an introduction to the basic concepts and principles of the learning undergone by the machines which includes unsupervised learning, supervised learning, and reinforcement learning. It's followed by an explanation of how deep learning extends these concepts through the use of ANN and discusses popular deep learning models such as CNN and RNN.

Natural Language Processing (NLP), computer vision management, and robotics automation are some applications of deep learning systems. Discussions on how these models are used in these applications and the challenges faced when implementing them are also provided. Finally, some of the challenges and future directions in the wider area of intelligent systems using emerging advanced deep learning techniques are also addressed. This chapter is written to provide the readers with a deeper understanding of the above-mentioned reputed models and their applications.

Related Work

The authors [1] provide a comprehensive survey of neuroevolutionary techniques, which combine neural networks and evolutionary algorithms to evolve neural network architectures and parameters. The authors [2] provide a comprehensive survey of transfer learning techniques, which enable the transfer of knowledge from one domain to another. Transfer learning has become an important technique with limited labelled records for training deep learning networks. The authors [3] provide a comprehensive survey of meta-learning techniques, which enable the learning of algorithms. Meta-learning has become an important technique for enabling intelligent systems to learn from a small number of examples. The authors [4] explore the limits of transfer learning for natural language processing tasks using the transformer architecture. The authors show that a large pre-trained model can achieve good performance with minimal specific fine-tuning. The authors [5] proclaim that the traditional notion of generalization in machine learning may not be sufficient to explain the performance of deep neural networks. The authors propose a new framework for understanding generalization in deep learning based on the geometry of the learned representations. The authors [6] Suggested the ResNet architecture, which makes residues connectivity for the training of deep neural networks. This has become a popular architecture in computer vision applications. The authors [7] have proposed an architecture that already has become the standard transformer architecture for NLP tasks. The authors [8] have proposed and made known the new architecture called Generative Adversarial Networks commonly known as GANs, which have become one of the best methods for generating more realistic images and other types of data. The authors [9] have framed a model on Deep Convolutional GAN also called DCGAN architecture, which uses GANs to learn unsupervised representations of images. DCGAN has become a popular method for generating high-quality images. The authors [10] introduced the concept of deep reinforcement learning, which has become a popular method for training agents to play games and control robots. The authors [11] introduced a mechanism that enables neural networks to specifically focus on a part of the input sequence while generating the output sequence. Attention has become a standard component of many neural network architectures.

Artificial Intelligence and Intelligent Systems

Before getting into the details of the different models, let's understand the fundamentals of AI and Intelligent Systems (IS). Artificial Intelligence (AI) is a human brain-like system or model that has activities in machines that understand the data to make decisions like humans. The algorithms were developed to undergo some activities as humans like learning, reasoning, and perception eventually with decision-making tasks. From the existing literature, on a wider aspect, the two major types of AI are narrow and general AI which are also commonly termed weak and strong AI respectively. Specific tasks can be accomplished by the first type and intellectual tasks can be performed by the second type. AI has numerous applications across a range of industries, including healthcare, finance, transportation, and manufacturing. Some notable examples of AI include virtual assistants, image and speech recognition systems, self-driving cars, and predictive analytics.

IS directs us to a brighter and hope-filled future. As machines gain knowledge and understanding, they thrive in the e-space almost everywhere around the world and in all sectors of life. Everyone can witness machines playing vital roles in underwater, in outer space, in any location on earth, and even in cyberspace. They help people to do things that they cannot or are unable to do using assistive technologies. The power of IS is unimaginable. These systems are built based on an objective to accomplish the task and the algorithms that are written for implementation have all the specifications of the objective.

Machine Learning

Machine Learning concentrates on building models that learn and understand data with frequent or adequate training. In other words, it is a technique where computers try to learn the available data and find hidden patterns which enable them to take meaningful decisions depending on the learned patterns.

The models that are available in machine learning can be categorized as supervised (data with input and output attributes), or unsupervised (data with only input attributes). The machine learns the data with both the input and output attributes provided during the training phase. The data without output labels are quite common in real-time scenarios. For applications of this type, an unsupervised learning technique enables the machine to find out the patterns and associations between the attributes. Image recognition, speech recognition, fraud detection along with self-driving cars are some of the wide ranges of applications that can be implemented using machine learning techniques. Its ability to automatically recognize patterns and make predictions based on data makes it a valuable tool in many fields.

Deep Learning

To be more precise, deep convolutional neural network learning has emerged as a subset or sub-type of machine learning that can build ANN capable of learning followed by making decisions on their own with the help of examples. This deep learning in machines helps in identifying a stop sign board, differentiates different pedestrians, and understanding the climatic conditions, especially in driverless cars. It enables a unique learning process for better classification of objects using images, sound, or even text. Sometimes the performance of such models even overrides human expertise and proves to be a vital source of knowledge management and effective decision-making. These neural networks consist of layers of interconnected nodes that process and analyze data and learn to identify meaningful and interesting patterns in the data.

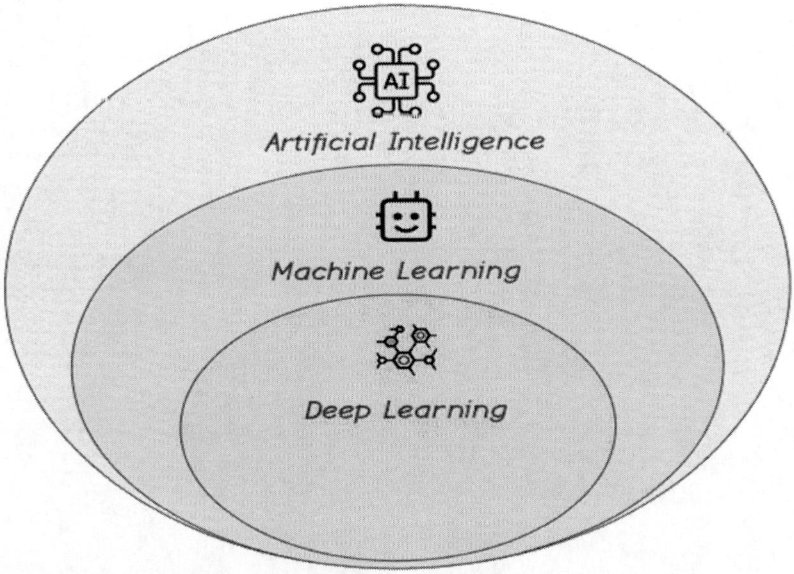

Figure 1. Hierarchy of learning systems.

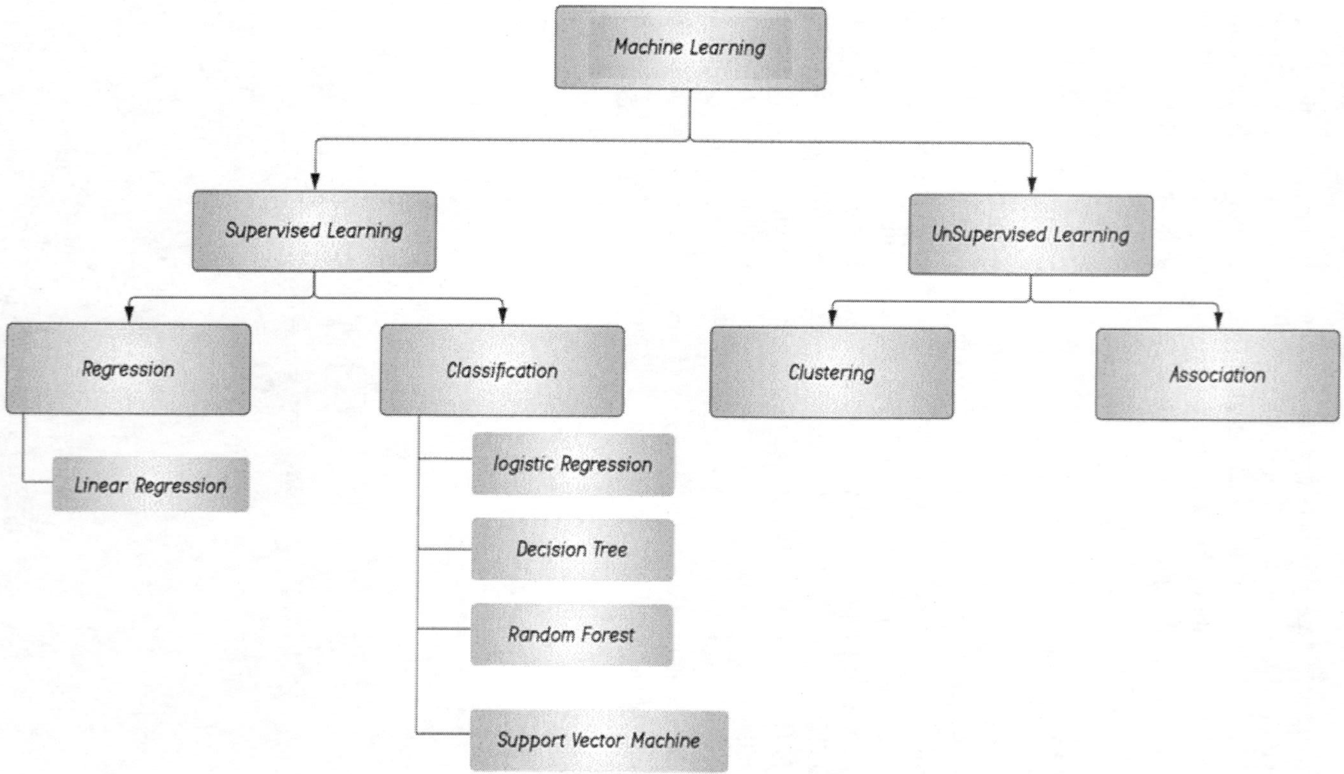

Figure 2. Techniques of Machine Learning.

Even though there are vast areas of applications that prove the importance and effectiveness of deep learning techniques, computer vision management, natural language processing, and image processing are to be mentioned. As it deals with a large volume of labelled data, most probably of type image, it requires even higher computing power to accomplish the task. Therefore, a Graphics Processing Unit (GPU), which is a parallel processing unit for image and video rendering is needed for intelligent systems. Despite its impressive capabilities, deep learning is still an area of active research, with ongoing efforts to improve its performance, scalability, and interpretability.

Figure 1 shows a hierarchical setup of the learning methodologies in artificial intelligent systems.

Figure 2 is given to get an idea about the different models in machine learning and the various techniques available in each type.

Understanding the basics of each technique provides a helping hand for further study and research. The insight that people gain from the fundamentals enables them to explore more with clear knowledge and understanding. There are mathematical backgrounds to be known in all these techniques.

1. Linear Regression

In a dataset where we have the dependent and independent variables, the relationship between them is very important to frame meaningful rules. Linear regression is an efficient mathematical procedure that helps researchers to find the association between the predictor(independent) and response (independent) attributes. The goal of linear regression is to find a linear relationship between the input features and the output variable such that the prediction made by the model is as close to the true value as possible. The algorithm works by finding the function for the best-fit straight line through a set of data points. This line is defined by a slope and an intercept, which are estimated using a process called "ordinary least squares." This creates a minimization process that reduces the variation that is produced between the projected and the actual values.

In general, a linear regression involves generating a straight line that accommodates the data points with a single independent variable called simple linear regression. When there are more independent variables, the model developed to provide the relationship is called a multiple linear regression model. The input data for linear regression can be continuous or categorical and can be scaled or transformed as needed. The dependent variable is always continuous. The dataset taken for consideration is initially segmented into training data and test data. The training data train the model with a straight line framed or computed to fit the model. The test data evaluate the performance of the model.

Next, the appropriate model for the data is selected, and the values or parameters suitable to the model are estimated with the data called training data. This involves finding the values of the slope and intercept. The object is to minimize the error which is nothing but the sum of the squared differences that exist between the targeted and the obtained values of the attributes. The gradient descent optimization algorithm helps us in improving the performance of the generated model. Only when the model parameters are estimated, the model is ready to be used for prediction. Given a set of new input features, the model predicts the value of the output variable using the estimated slope and intercept. There are certain evaluation metrics available in the literature to check the efficiency and quality of the predictions. Linear regression is widely used in various applications such as finance, economics, and science for predicting values and understanding relationships between variables. It is a powerful and flexible technique that can be easily extended to include more complex models and additional variables. Figure 3 projects the formula for linear regression and figure 4 depicts the pictorial representation of the same.

Formula:

$$y = \beta_0 + \beta_1 X_1 + \cdots + \beta_n X_n + \in$$

y = obtained /predicted value
β_0 = y-intercept
$\beta_1 x_1$ = the regression coefficient (β_1)
(for multiple independent variables/ attributes)
$\beta_n x_n$ = nth regression coefficient
$\in$ = error value of the model

Figure 3. Formula for Linear regression.

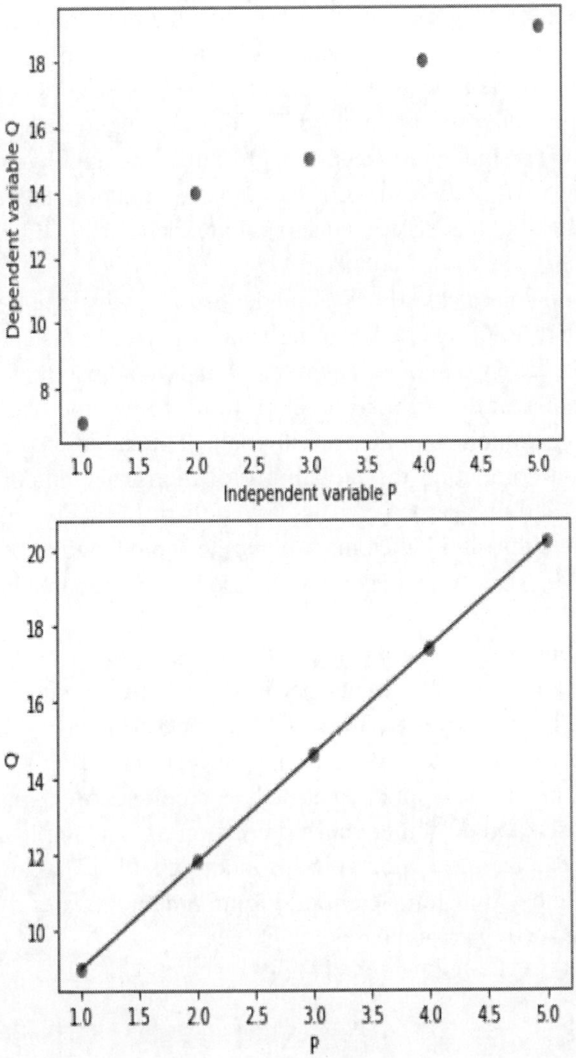

Figure 4. Linear Regression.

2. Logistic Regression

Machine learning is made possible with the help of another regression technique called Logistic Regression that is suitable for classification problems. The objective here is to classify a binary class label. (1 or 0). It is a type of supervised learning technique that works by finding the absolute relationship that exists among the variables and the probability of a binary or two-value class. In this method of classification, the response variable can be of type binary and the independent variables can be categorical or numerical values. The logistic regression model estimates the result based on the probability value of the binary class label by fitting a sigmoid function to the input variables. The end result of the sigmoid function is nothing but a probability value that lies between 0 and 1 that represents the likelihood of the binary outcome.

A system that has a classification model using a logistic regression model is trained using a set of labelled training data, where each instance is labelled with the correct binary outcome. The model learns to adjust the coefficients of the input variables in the sigmoid function to maximize the likelihood of the observed binary outcomes in the training data. The value or predicted value for the test data computing the probability of the binary outcome using the input variables and the learned coefficients. If the probability value is greater than a predefined threshold, the binary outcome is predicted to be 1, and if the probability value is less than the threshold, the binary outcome is predicted to be 0.

The efficiency or the performance of this model can be evaluated and assessed depending on the various performance metrics such as F1 score, precision, recall, accuracy, etc. These metrics help to measure how well the model predicts the binary outcome on new unseen data. Logistic Regression is widely used in various applications such as credit scoring, spam detection, disease diagnosis, and customer churn prediction. It is a simple and effective algorithm that can handle a wide range of input variables, making it a popular choice in the field of machine learning. Figure 5 demonstrates the formula to be used for logistic regression cases.

Formula:

$$y = \frac{1}{1 + e^{-(a + b_1 X_1 + b_2 X_2 + \cdots + b_n X_n)}}$$

y = the estimated output

$b_1 x_1$ = b_1 is the regression coefficient and x_1 is the independent variable (for many variables that are independent)

$b_n x_n$ = b_n is the regression coefficient and x_n is the last predictor

Figure 5. Formula for Logistic regression.

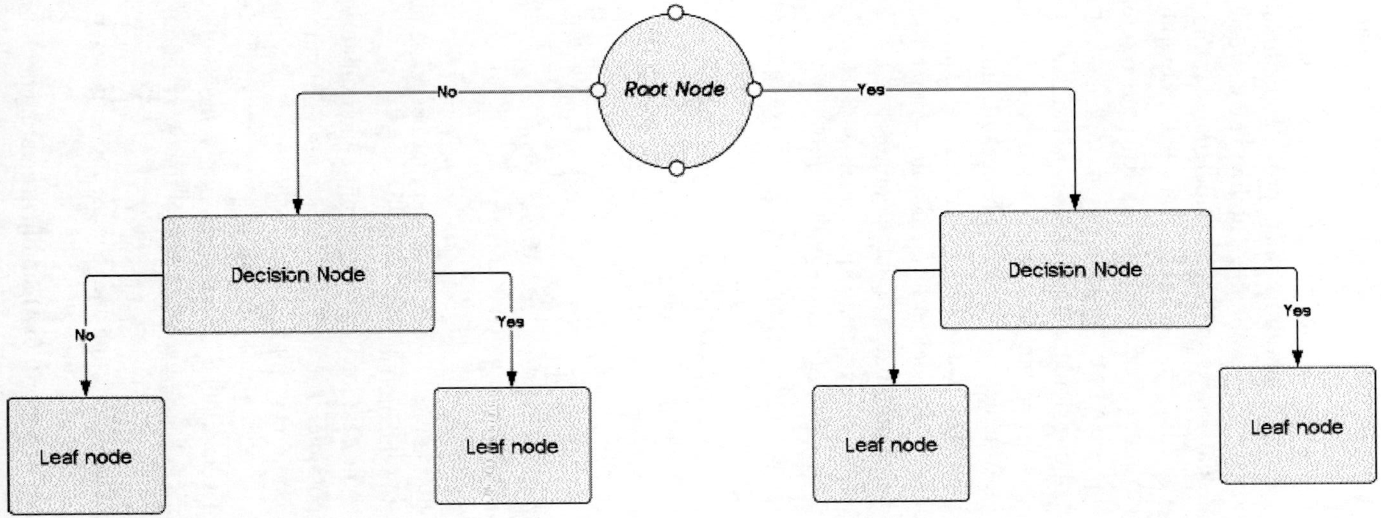

Figure 6. Decision Tree.

3. Decision Tree

A well-known and most commonly used method called decision tree is one of the efficient machine learning algorithms that provides solutions for classification and regression types of problems. The tree is constructed with features available in the internal nodes and the class label in the leaf node. The rule generated can be framed through the nodes from the root to the leaf. Decision Trees are used to build predictive models for both discrete and continuous variables, making them a versatile algorithm.

The primary objective of decision tree algorithms is to build a model that can make decisions based on a set of input features. These features are used to split the data recursively into smaller sub-groups, where the splitting criteria are based on the most significant feature that separates the data with the highest purity or homogeneity. The idea is to create sub-groups that are as homogeneous as possible based on the dependent variable.

The decision tree is capable of generating class labels and also numerical outputs. Thus, there are two types of trees called classification trees and regression trees. The classification trees generate categorical output that maps input variables of any type to class labels. The regression trees are the ones that generate continuous or numerical output and the goal here is to predict numerical output using the different input variables or independent variables. Figure 6 is a graphical representation of the decision tree with its root node, decision node and leaf node.

3.1. The Process of Building a Decision Tree Model Involves the Following Steps

1. Select a variable that is most informative and that best separates the data into groups of high homogeneity or purity.
2. Recursively divide the data into sub-groups until each subgroup is as homogeneous as possible.
3. Then a stopping condition is applied with less observations in a deep tree.
4. At every leaf node a class label or final prediction of the label is given based on the majority class or average value of the observations in the subgroup.
5. Prune the tree to reduce overfitting and increase model generalization.

Some of the commonly used algorithms that help in creating decision trees are

1. Iterative Dichotomiser3 - (ID3)
2. C4.5
3. Classification And Regression Tree - (CART)
4. Chi-square Automatic Interaction Detection - (CHAID)
5. Multivariate Adaptive Regression Splines – (MARS)

Decision Trees are interpretable models and can be visualized easily, making them ideal for use in business and other applications. They are easy to use, and their performance is relatively good, even for large datasets. Consider the tree that is very deep and the label that projects the stopping criteria is also weak, then the model can have an overfitting problem, which can be mitigated by pruning the tree or using a perfect combination of the methods such as Random Forests or Gradient Boosting.

4. Random Forest

The random forest machine learning is similar to decision tree algorithm that generates output as either categorical or numerical. It is an ensemble method, which combines multiple models not only to increase prediction accuracy but also to reduce overfitting. In a random forest approach several decision trees are built. The final outcome is obtained by combining their predictions. Based on the chosen subset of features and samples the trees are built. The trees produce multiple rules, and these rules help in appropriate prediction of the test data. Thus, repeating the process several times leads to the development of a forest with multiple decision trees.

The information gain is the measure that helps in choosing the input feature by reducing the entropy value which is nothing but the impurity in the data. A method that recursively split the data from the dataset in the form of attribute selection that identifies irrelevant and redundant data. The tree generation stops with the condition that the tree has maximum depth. After training the model in which multiple trees are constructed, the testing phase starts. The process of classification is performed by all the trees and the output of the test data is confirmed by the output generated by more trees or in the other case depending on the average with classification or regression type of problems respectively.

It has many advantages over other machine learning algorithms. First, it is very flexible and can handle a wide range of input features, including categorical, numerical, and ordinal features. Second, it is less prone to overfitting compared to single decision trees. Thirdly, missing data and irrelevant data can be easily and effectively handled. Fourthly, the feature selection process is very vigilant and paves a way to understand the data and identify most importantly the relationships that exist between input and output attributes.

In summary, amongst the various machine learning algorithms, random forest is efficient and powerful that works by taking into account the decisions from multiple trees to improve prediction accuracy and also reduce overfitting. It is flexible, robust, and can handle a wide range of input features. Finance, healthcare, and natural language processing are the various applications in which Random Forest is widely used.

5. Support Vector Machines (SVM)

SVMs are influential and widely used learning algorithm that comes under the supervised machine learning type. SVMs are primarily used for classification tasks, where the objective is to classify the new data into its corresponding type according to the set of input features. In other words, it searches for a boundary that can differentiate the data elements of the classes. The margin identified is the gap between the hyperplane and the data points from the different classes that are closer to each other among different classes.

Support Vector Machines are capable enough to handle data that can be linearly separable as well as non-linearly separable. It finds a hyperplane that separates the data when it deals with data that can be separated linearly. When handling data that cannot be linearly separated, SVM transforms the data to a higher dimensional space that makes it possible to linearly separate it. Thus, SVM methodology provides effective measures to differentiate the data belonging to different classes.

As SVM deals with data in two different ways, there are two types of SVM. They are linear SVM and KERNEL SVM. Linear SVM projects the data on a hyperplane where they can be linearly separated. Data mapping to a higher dimensional space is done with the help of the kernel function framed which enables the separation easier and more effective. SVMs are also used in deep learning for tasks in various fields and in real-time applications. In the last layer of the artificial neural networks, SVM is used so as to perform classification with enough content and knowledge about the data. In deep learning, SVMs are typically used as a final layer in the neural network, to make the final classification decision based on the features learned by the network.

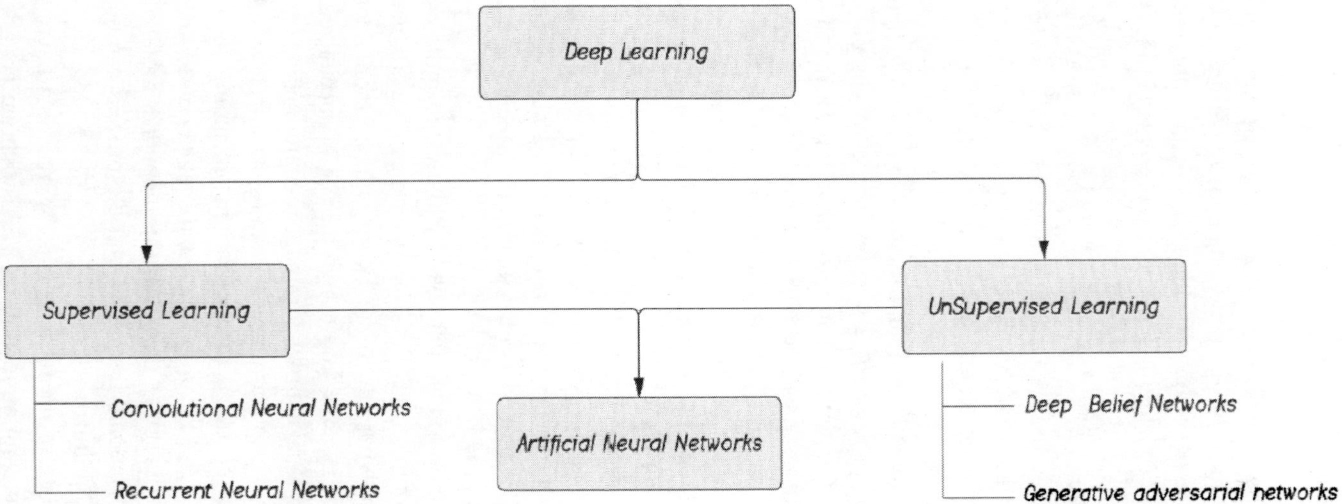

Figure 7. Techniques of Deep Learning.

In summary, for both deep learning and machine learning SVM proves to be the best and the most effective classifier. A hyperplane that separates the data between data belonging to different class labels. SVMs can be used for linearly separable and non-linearly separable data and are particularly useful for tasks such as image classification and object detection with prediction. Significant techniques for deep learning have been represented in Figure 7.

6. Artificial Neural Networks

Artificial Neural Networks (ANNs) is a learning algorithm that is an imitation of the working and structuring of the human brain. It is a broader category of learning that encapsulates machine and deep learning algorithms that can handle complex data representations. Neurons in ANN like human neurons receive the input signals, process them, and finally produce the output as a resultant signal. As there are different layers present in the system, the signals are passed on from one layer to another layer. The input layer is the first layer that receives the input from the user and lets the signal to other layers in a sequential manner, and the output layer eventually produces the final signal. There are multiple layers hidden between the input and output layers where the computation of the network takes place. During the training phase, the weights and biases of the neurons are adjusted to bring down the differences between the actual output and the obtained output. The process of training the network with multiple input-output pairs and adjusting the weights along with the biases are the primary tasks involved in machine learning that can be optimized using an optimization algorithm using the stochastic gradient descent method.

Deep learning takes ANNs to the next level by allowing for the creation of much deeper and more complex networks. Deep learning networks can have many hidden layers, allowing them to learn much more complex representations of data. This is achieved through the use of specialized types of neurons, such as convolutional neurons for image recognition and recurrent neurons for sequential data. Deep learning has been used to achieve state-of-the-art performance in a wide range of applications, including image and speech recognition, natural language processing, and even playing games such as Go and Chess. However, training deep learning networks requires large amounts of data and computational resources, and the process can be time-consuming and difficult to optimize.

In summary, ANN is one of the important techniques that have a wide scope and tremendous success in almost all the fields that are complex and need high performance. As they are imitating the human brain, they use complex mathematical models for learning the data and use the knowledge for classifications and predictions. ANN requires data in large volume with more computational resources for better performance which totally depends on data quality and the type of network architecture.

7. Convolutional Neural Networks

Convolutional Neural Networks (CNNs) belong to the type of deep neural network that are considered to process and analyse data which is a grid-like structure. For example, data in the form of images, video, or speech. These networks are capable of performing tasks like image classification, object detection, and facial recognition. CNN performs the operations using different layers where each and every layer performs a specific task on the data received as input. The convolutional layer extracts the features like edges and textures using a set of filters on the input. This input layer produces the output in the form of feature maps, which are essentially a set of 2D matrices that represent the activations of the filters across the input image.

The size of the feature maps is reduced by the pooling layer, the layer next to the input layer, by performing a down-sampling operation thus reducing the parameters in the network which can ultimately make the training process efficient. Max pooling and average pooling are the different types of pooling layers, which can be used depending on the task at hand. After the pooling layer, there are typically several more convolutional and pooling layers, each of which extracts more complex features from the input image. The fully connected layer is the final layer in CNN which takes the output of the convolutional and pooling layers and maps it to a set of output classes. Based on the probability distribution of the output classes, the final layer produces the output.

The main advantage of CNN is its ability to learn spatial hierarchies of features. Because the filters in the convolutional layers are learned through the training process, the network can automatically learn to recognize more complex patterns in the input data. Thus, CNNs are highly effective for image classifications, where the objective is to identify the presence of certain objects or features in an image.

Overall, CNNs have become a critical tool in the field of machine learning and deep learning and are used to reach and gain state-of-the-art accuracy on a wide range of real-time applications. The CNN performance is unbeatable for processing and analysing grid-like data, such as images and video. The different phases in CNN are represented pictorially in Figure 8.

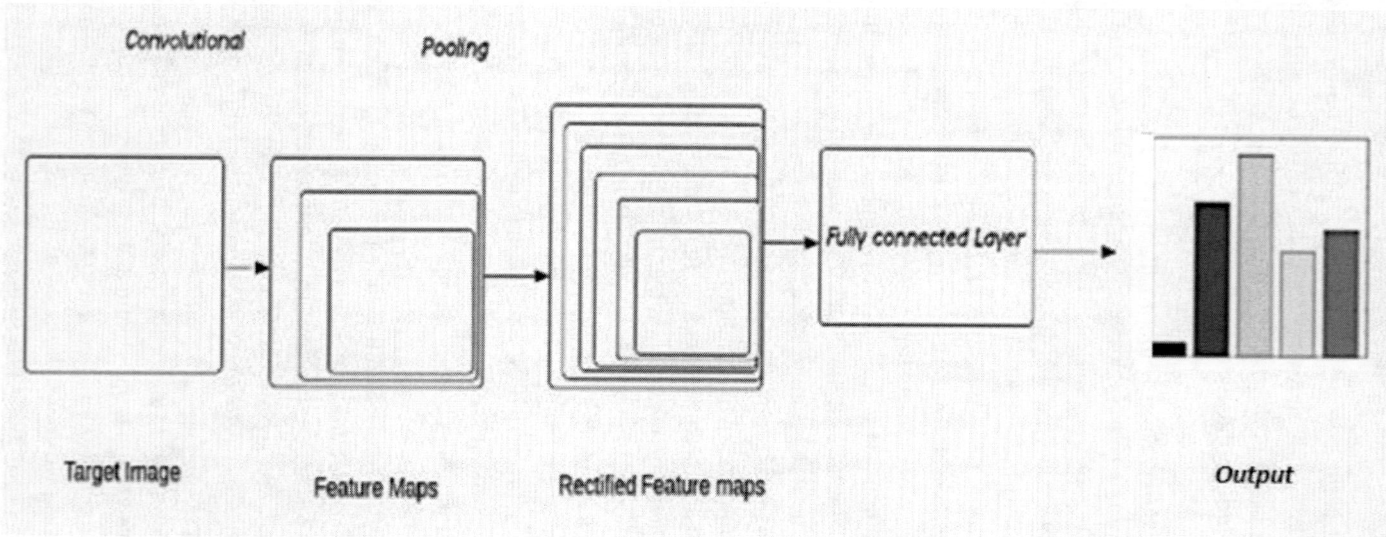

Figure 8. Convolutional Neural Network.

8. Recurrent Neural Networks (RNN)

One of the important deep networks that is framed to process sequential data that comes in applications related to speech, text and time series is the Recurrent Neural Networks. A feedforward neural network processes input data in a single pass, whereas RNNs maintain a state that can be updated and reused across multiple time steps. This allows them to model temporal dependencies in the data and capture long-term dependencies that may be difficult to model with other types of neural networks. At a high level, an RNN consists of a series of cells that has a state called hidden state which at each time step is updated. The signal at the current time step and the input from the previous hidden state are the inputs to each cell. The output of each cell is a prediction for the current time step, as well as the hidden state that is updated and passed on to the next cell in the sequence.

Handling variable-length input is one of the benefits of this type of network because the updates in the hidden state are updated at each time step. The network can process input sequences of any length. This makes RNNs highly effective for tasks such as speech recognition that have variable lengths in the input sequence that can vary depending on the length of the spoken words. There are several types of RNNs, including the vanilla RNN, the Long Short-Term Memory (LSTM) network, and the Gated Recurrent Unit (GRU). The LSTM and GRU networks arc designed to address the issue of vanishing gradients, which can occur when training RNNs on long input sequences. They are controlled by the additional gates for the flow of information that passes through the network.

In summary, RNNs are great at handling applications on a wide range of tasks that include speech detection, machine translation, and natural language processing. Their ability to handle sequential data and model temporal dependencies makes them highly effective for tasks that involve processing and analysing time series data.

9. Generative Adversarial Networks

Deep learning and machine learning are both subsets of AI that train the machine to understand the data. This type of network falls under the extensive category of learning. These models are good at learning from data by adjusting the weights of the model parameters to minimize a loss function. The output generated by this model depends on the input data. Labelled examples of input-output pairs are provided in supervised learning, while there are only input attributes given in unsupervised learning to identify patterns and structures in the data. GANs are a specific type of deep learning model that is designed to generate new data that is similar to a given dataset. They are mainly of two neural networks: a generator network and a discriminator network. The generator network takes a random noise vector as input and produces a sample of data that is similar to the training data. The discriminator network takes a sample of data as input and produces a binary output indicating whether the input is real or generated. The generator network is trained to generate data that fools the discriminator network, while the discriminator network is trained to correctly classify the input data as either real or generated.

GANs are a powerful tool for generating new data, such as images or videos, that is visually similar to the training data. They have been used for a variety of applications, including image and video generation, text-to-image synthesis, and music generation. In contrast to GANs, other types of deep learning models, such as convolutional neural networks (CNNs) and recurrent neural networks (RNNs), are designed for specific tasks, such as image classification or sequence prediction. CNNs are commonly used for computer vision tasks, such as object detection and image segmentation, while RNNs are often used for natural language processing tasks, such as language translation and speech recognition.

Overall, GANs are working well in the deep learning and machine learning toolkit, allowing for the generation of new data that is similar to a given dataset. While GANs can be difficult to train and prone to mode collapse, they have shown great promise in a wide range of applications and continue to be an active area of research in the field.

10. Deep Belief Network

A Deep Belief Network (DBN) is a type of artificial neural network that is composed of multiple layers of Restricted Boltzmann Machines (RBMs). RBMs are probabilistic models that can learn a probability distribution over the input data by using a layer of hidden units. The weights of the RBM are learned by minimizing the difference between the data distribution and the model distribution, which is achieved by using a technique called Contrastive Divergence. A DBN is typically composed of several RBMs stacked on top of each other. The input layer of the DBN is connected to the first RBM, which is trained to learn a set of low-level features from the input data. The output of the first RBM is then used as input to the second RBM, which learns a set of higher-level features based on the features learned by the first RBM. This process is repeated for each subsequent layer, with each RBM learning a more abstract representation of the input data.

Table 1. Short Overview of All Fundamental Models

S. No	Technique	Pros	Cons
1.	Linear Regression	➢ Simple and easy to understand ➢ Flexible ➢ Interpretability ➢ Prediction	➢ Assumes linear relationship ➢ Outliers can have a significant impact ➢ Requires independence of errors ➢ Cannot handle categorical variables
2.	Logistic Regression	➢ Simplicity ➢ Interpretable ➢ Efficiency ➢ Robustness ➢ Flexibility	➢ Linearity ➢ Overfitting ➢ Independence ➢ Sensitive to outliers ➢ Limited to binary classification
3.	Decision Trees	➢ Easy to understand and interpret. ➢ Can handle both categorical and numerical data. ➢ Require less data pre-processing. ➢ Can handle non-linear relationships. ➢ Can perform well with noisy data.	➢ Overfitting. ➢ Instability. ➢ Bias. ➢ Difficulty with continuous variables. ➢ Difficulty with class imbalance.
4.	Random Forest	➢ Accuracy. ➢ Robustness. ➢ Outlier handling. ➢ Feature importance. ➢ Scalability.	➢ Complexity ➢ Interpretability. ➢ Training time. ➢ Overfitting. ➢ Imbalanced data.
5.	Support Vector Machine	➢ Effective ➢ Accurate ➢ Versatile ➢ Efficient ➢ Robust	➢ Sensitivity ➢ Complexity ➢ Overfitting ➢ Non-probabilistic ➢ Parameter-tuning
6.	Convolutional Neural Networks	➢ Efficiency ➢ Generalization ➢ Robustness ➢ Localization ➢ Hierarchical	➢ Overfitting ➢ Complexity ➢ Computationally intensive ➢ Interpretability ➢ Data-dependence

Table 1. (Continued)

S. No	Technique	Pros	Cons
7.	Recurrent Neural Networks	➢ Sequential ➢ Flexible ➢ Adaptive ➢ Memory ➢ Prediction	➢ Overfitting ➢ Computation ➢ Gradient ➢ Vanishing ➢ Exploding
8.	Artificial Neural Networks	➢ Versatile ➢ Efficient ➢ Adaptive ➢ Accurate ➢ Scalable	➢ Black box ➢ Overfitting ➢ Data-hungry ➢ Complex ➢ Interpretability
9.	Generative adversarial networks	➢ Creativity ➢ Realism ➢ Diversity ➢ Efficiency ➢ Novelty	➢ Instability ➢ Bias ➢ Evaluation ➢ Reproducibility ➢ Privacy
10.	Deep Belief Networks	➢ Versatile ➢ Efficient ➢ Reliable ➢ Secure ➢ Scalable	➢ Complexity ➢ Costly ➢ Maintenance ➢ Compatibility ➢ Limited

Once the RBMs have been trained, the DBN can be fine-tuned using supervised learning algorithms such as backpropagation. This involves training the network to classify the input data into different categories based on a set of labelled training examples. One of the key advantages of DBNs is their ability to learn hierarchical representations of the input data. By learning multiple layers of features, the network can capture complex relationships between the input data and the output labels. This makes DBNs particularly effective for tasks such as image classification, speech recognition, and natural language processing.

However, training a DBN can be a complex and computationally intensive process. The learning process involves multiple stages of unsupervised learning, followed by a stage of supervised fine-tuning. Additionally, the training process can be sensitive to the initialization of the weights, and there is a risk of overfitting if the network is too complex or if the training data is insufficient. Despite these challenges, DBNs have been shown to achieve state-of-the-art performance on a wide range of tasks and continue to be an active area of research in deep learning. While solving a real-time problem it is very much necessary to select an appropriate technique that would provide a more suitable solution to the problem. Table 1 provides a brief description of the techniques for machine learning with their advantages and disadvantages.

Conclusion

Through the past years and ages, it has been proved that mathematical, statistical, and machine learning techniques along with deep learning in artificial intelligence provide a helping aid in classification, prediction, and clustering methods. In almost all areas of life, anybody can witness the prevalent existence of these techniques that build automatic systems for the benefit of society. It is also true that humans could accommodate these models in their day-to-day lives for a better living. This chapter has been framed to provide fundamental insights into the various techniques available in machine learning and deep learning systems.

References

[1] Kenneth O. Stanley, J. C. (2019). NeuroEvolution: A Survey of Recent Work. *Nat. Mach. Intell.*, 24-35.

[2] Yang, S. J. (2020). A Comprehensive Survey on Transfer Learning. *Proceedings of the IEEE*, 55-76.

[3] Chelsea Finn, P. A. (2017). Meta-Learning: A Survey. *Proceedings of the 34th International Conference on Machine Learning*, 65-70.

[4] Colin Raffel, N. S. (2020). Exploring the Limits of Transfer Learning with a Unified Text-to-Text Transformer. *Journal of Machine Learning Research 21*, 1-67.

[5] Chiyuan Zhang, S. B. (2021). Understanding Deep Learning Requires Rethinking Generalization. *Communications of the ACM*, 105-115.

[6] Kaiming He, X. Z. (2016). Deep Residual Learning for Image Recognition. *EEE Conference on Computer Vision and Pattern Recognition*, 770-778.

[7] Ashish Vaswani, N. S. (2017). Attention Is All You Need. *Advances in neural information processing systems*, 0-30.

[8] Ian J. Goodfellow, J. P.-A.-F. (2020). Generative Adversarial Networks. *Communications of the ACM*, 135-144.

[9] Alec Radford, L. M. (2015). Unsupervised Representation Learning with Deep Convolutional Generative Adversarial Networks. *arXiv preprint arXiv*, 1-16.

[10] Volodymyr Mnih, K. K. (2013). Playing Atari with Deep Reinforcement Learning. *arXiv preprint arXiv*, 1-9.

[11] Dzmitry Bahdanau, K. C. (2014). Neural Machine Translation by Jointly Learning to Align and Translate. *arXiv preprint arXiv*, 1-15.

Chapter 3

A Comparative Analysis of Machine Learning Algorithms on Intrusion Detection Systems

Vijayan R.[*]**, PhD**
Mareeswari V.[†]**, PhD**
Rathi R.[‡]**, PhD**
Ephzibah EP[§]**, PhD**
and Harshitha KSR[‖]**, MTech (SE)**
School of Computer Science Engineering and Information Systems (SCORE), Vellore Institute of Technology (VIT), Vellore, India

Abstract

Internet usage is quite high, and it is also incredibly important in these times. The Internet has been used for domain transactions, file transfers, and a variety of other operations. In addition to these responsibilities, private data has been sent via the internet through various websites as needed. In the middle of transfers and transactions, these websites, online apps, and the internet must be on the watch for assaults. In technical words, it refers to them as packets, and large packets are transferred across an internet network in a second. Furthermore, the likelihood of delivering malicious packets is great. A mechanism is necessary at crucial spots to identify these attacks. So, as part of this study, the proposed system uses machine learning techniques to detect any potentially harmful network activities. These packets might include data

[*] Corresponding Author's Email: rvijayan@vit.ac.in.
[†] Corresponding Author's Email: vmareeswari@vit.ac.in.
[‡] Corresponding Author's Email: rathi.r@vit.ac.in.
[§] Corresponding Author's Email: ep.ephzibah@vit.ac.in.
[‖] Corresponding Author's Email: harshitha3464@gmail.com.

In: Building Intelligent Systems Using Machine Learning and Deep Learning
Editors: A. Kumar Sahoo, C. Pradhan, B. Shankar Prasad Mishra et al.
ISBN: 979-8-89113-342-6

that is encrypted or not. The essential concept here is that the system detects any interruption in the network, excluding the decryption of packets. For the implementation, Wireshark, Weka tools, the Anaconda framework, Jupiter, and the Python language have been used in this proposed work. Here, we applied four different algorithms, like Naïve Bayes, SVM, KNN, and Random Forest. The accuracy of each algorithm is found, which will prove which algorithm is better for the detection of intrusion.

Keywords: machine learning, intrusion detection system, network security, comparison of machine learning algorithms, random forest, SVM, KNN, Naïve Byes

Introduction

The use of the internet and networks is highly prevalent these days. In some manner, it will be seen everywhere in people's lives. Though the operation of those devices is simple, the background procedure is crucial. Keeping track of everything is the most challenging aspect. Because so much sensitive information has been exchanged and maintained, all of this must be designed securely to prevent hacker assaults.

People interact with one another through machine-to-machine communication. To date, it has been expanded by the Internet of Things (IoT), so people can interact with objects at anytime and anywhere. Nothing gets done nowadays without a network. Cables, telephone lines, satellites, radio, and a variety of other technologies will be used to connect the different network systems. Moreover, secure communication relies on a virtual private network (VPN), which employs wireless personal area networks (WPAN) for private connections such as smartphones, smart TVs, and speakers. Internally, to transmit a file, picture, or any other type of data, it flows through multiple levels on a network, passing via equipment in the center such as routers, switches, and hubs, among others. For this, some form of protocol will be employed for communication where we have to follow those rules. Also, the Hypertext Transfer Protocol (HTTP) has been protected by adding a layer of HTTPS. Furthermore, Transfer Layer Security (TLS) or Secure Socket Layer (SSL) is used to transport data securely.

During this protocol, data is decrypted at the receiver's end after packets are encrypted using TLS or SSL and delivered over the network. So that it may keep these identities hidden. Even when it submits data in a file format, the file is broken into a series of packets and processed using the above-mentioned protocol. Supported protocols are followed by the network. Because a network transmits a large number of packets, the chances of sending malicious packets are also high. To identify such intrusions inside the network without decrypting and inspecting for accuracy, machine learning methods may be used, which can identify any intrusion inside the network excluding decryption of the packet. This IDS (Intrusion Detection System) detects security issues on a network and commonly detects and removes malicious behavior. As a result of this, it frequently improves confidentiality and integrity [1].

Literature Review on Machine Learning in Intrusion Detection System

The author stated that detecting unauthorized activity at the network layer is one of the main security concerns of cloud computing. It suggests a specification for cloud-based network intrusion detection systems (NIDS). Snort and the signature apriori algorithm comprise this NIDS module. It also suggests that NIDS be placed in the cloud. It creates new rules based on the packets it has captured. To boost Snort's performance, these new rules are added to the configuration file. Its goal is to identify recognized attacks and variants of recognized attacks in the cloud by following network traffic while maintaining a low false positive rate and low computing cost. It shows the experimental setup and addresses the design targets that the proposed architecture is intended to achieve. However, the enhanced NIDS by supervised machine learning is hard because it is expensive to train and evaluate the process of classification to label the benign and malignant nodes. Hence, these authors cross-evaluate the existing labels at a low cost with their reliable cross-evaluation-based NIDS using ML [2].

Device administrators may utilize a NIDS to find security vulnerabilities in their company network, according to the author. Designing a flexible and efficient NIDS for unintentional and unforeseen assaults, however, presents various difficulties. It recommends a deep learning-based method for the development of such a powerful and scalable NIDS. It makes use of self-taught learning (STL), using the benchmark dataset for network interference known as NSL-KDD. It outlines the deep learning method's success and compares it to a few earlier types of research. The values of the parameter's accuracy, precision, memory, and f-measure are compared [3].

It is now feasible to link sensors directly to guns that are not under human control, thanks to cyberspace operations, improved cyberspace infrastructure, and machine learning techniques. With the support of technology, computer-generated data will be transformed into their distributed, connected combat zones. To effectively recognize, calculate, and return to a hostile environment, NIDS must operate at machine speed. Generative models such as generative adversarial networks (GAN) and variational auto-encoders fitted using tagged cyber data from a genuine military business network. To produce synthetic computerized information that is realistic, these generative models are employed. After that, training is performed by combining a genuine and a fake set of data. The training of various machine learning models for network intrusion detection then takes place by combining actual and simulated information. The statistical similarity of pure synthetic data to real data is demonstrated. Classified with solely synthetic data underperformed, but there was no statistically significant difference between their performance and that of a qualified classification with both real and synthetic data. Classifiers must be trained using a minimum of 15% actual content to prevent a decline in intrusion detection performance (Chale& Bastian, 2022).

Internet of Things (IoT) applications are being used more often because of the rapid expansion of wireless connectivity and the digital revolution. Every day, more people are using the internet, which increases network traffic and data volume. Due to networking practices, open broadcast communication, etc., the IoT environment's energy-constrained sensor node resources are susceptible to assaults. The network has been readily breached by intruders, who then launch a variety of assaults that reduce service quality and performance as a whole. To choose the best features, a feature selection technique from deep learning is described in this study effort. To categorize the deep characteristics and find threats in the IoT network, the decision tree method is used as a classifier. The standard NSL-KDD dataset has been utilized for testing, and the suggested model's performance has been compared to that of the traditional models using metrics like f1-score, precision, accuracy, and recall demonstrating its superiority. The suggested hybrid model outperforms the traditional intrusion detection systems, with a maximum accuracy of 99.49% [5].

A review of the three categories of deep learning, ensemble learning, and classical machine learning is done to build the most popular algorithm model in the network intrusion detection sector. This study chose the KDD CUP99 and NSL-KDD datasets to experiment with relative tests on decision trees, support vector machines (SVM), random forests, Naive Bayes, XGBoost, convolutional neural networks (CNN), and recurrent neural networks (RNN). For various data sets, these algorithms' detection accuracy, F1, AUC, and other measures are contrasted. The outcomes of the experiments demonstrate that the ensemble learning method has a typically superior impact. Although the Naive Bayes algorithm performs poorly at identifying previously learned data, it has clear advantages when dealing with novel sorts of assaults, and training time is faster. [6]

IoT appliance security has been addressed in several ways, although further development is preferred. Machine learning has proven to be capable of seeing patterns when previous approaches have failed. Deep learning is one cutting-edge technique to improve IoT security [7]. This offers a seamless solution for detection using anomalies. In this research, anomaly-based intrusion detection systems (IDS) based on CNN are presented. This methodology sorts the possibility of the Internet of Things by presenting competencies to effectively analyze the entire IoT transportation. The suggested model demonstrates the capacity to recognize some possible incursions and unusual flow patterns. The model's accuracy existed at 99.51% during training and 92.85% during testing utilizing the NID dataset and BoT-IoT datasets [8].

This research [9] examined recent developments in the field of intrusion detection and took a thorough look back at contemporary NID solutions. The researchers conducted a SWOT (Strengths, Weaknesses, Opportunities, Threats) analysis of modern NIDS in a variety of technological heights, comprising big data processing, huge capacity of network transactions, machine learning, deep learning to train machines by themselves, readiness for zero-day attacks, distributed processing, profitable solutions, and capacity for self-governing processes.

Accessibility is assumed to be a crucial feature among other Quality of Service (QoS) considerations when evaluating the excellence of any web and cloud computing services. The distributed denial of service (DDoS) assault is seen as a danger to all current and future web-based systems [10]. As potential defenses against these types of assaults, intelligent solutions based on data mining techniques are on the horizon. The well-known data mining technique Rule Induction (RI) is viewed as a potential strategy for creating an intelligent DDoS detection system. The "improved RI method" (IRI) presented in this article decreases the examining region for generating classification rules by eradicating any tedious candidate rule items as the classification model is being constructed. The important use of IRI is that it results in a set of rules that are succinct, clear, and simple to apply. Also, IRI's classifiers are smaller, which is a factor that weighs strongly in the creation of any classification system. Afterward, the suggested technique is utilized for identifying DDoS assaults (IRIDOS). The robustness of IRIDOS was validated by empirical analyses utilizing the UNSW-NB15 dataset, which was received from the University of New South Wales [11].

To boost detection rates while maintaining dependability, [12] suggests a novel hybrid approach in this study that fuses machine learning with deep learning. By integrating XGBoost for feature selection and Synthetic Minority Oversampling Technique (SMOTE) for data balance, our suggested strategy assures effective pre-processing. To determine which machine learning and deep learning algorithms are the most effective to use in the pipeline, they compared our established approach to a number of them. Additionally, using a group of standard performance analysis constraints, they selected the network intrusion model that was the most successful. For two datasets, KDDCUP'99 and CIC-MalMem-2022, their technique gives great results with an accuracy of 99.99% for KDDCUP'99 and 100% for CIC-MalMem-2022, without concern of overfitting or Type-1 and Type-2.

Proposed System

The goal of the proposed methodology is to identify the intrusion in a network, excluding the decryption of packets, and improve the sender's confidentiality and the receiver's reliability. The packets are evaluated by using several properties as categorization variables. The system is validated with various data to differentiate between harmful encrypted and unencrypted packets and legitimate encrypted and unencrypted packets. Some unnecessary or incorrect data for some factors may be quickly discovered and an intrusion alert issued. Thus, classifying data based on packet properties rather than content allows for easier and faster intrusion detection while simultaneously preserving secrecy and security. This model classifies the packet as normal or not without decrypting the contents. When compared to the current system, the processing time will be reduced to detect whether the packet is malignant or not.

Proposed System Architecture

Instead of cloning datasets provided on the internet, this proposed work generates datasets using Wireshark. It is a network analyzer tool. Through this, capture the different types of data and categorize them into normal or malicious packets. These packets contain information such as frame size, time to live, source and destination port, protocol, coloring name, coloring string, and many others. At last, convert these data into CSV for practice. So that it can train and test data through various machine-learning algorithms.

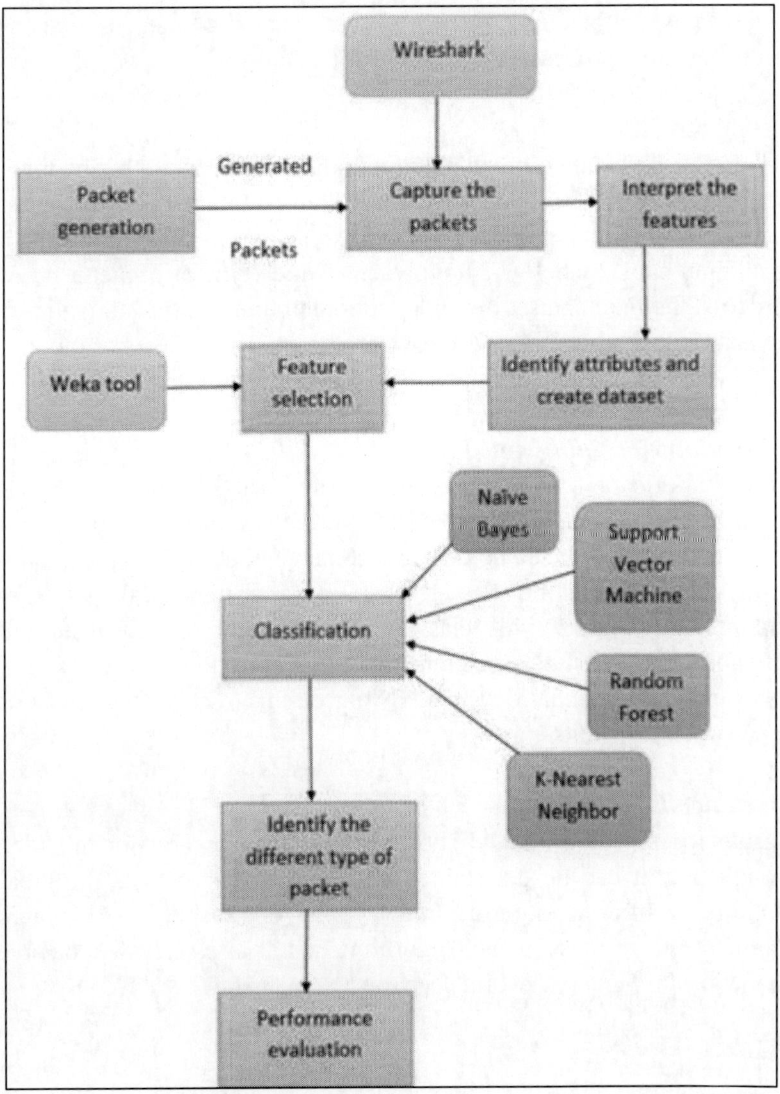

Figure 1. Proposed System Architecture.

Packet Generation

In this module, select the limited features using the Weka tool by loading this dataset into the tool. After feature selection, convert all text data into numeric data and note down those values with corresponding numeric values. At last, add a column named label, which represents which type of packet it is. After this process, the final dataset is employed in the training and testing phases. As in the dataset, it has limited rows due to processing time. As it has more data, it needs more processors to execute algorithms.

Feature Extraction

In this module, select the limited features using the Weka tool by loading this dataset into the tool. After feature selection, converts all text data into numeric data and note down those values with corresponding numeric values. At last, add a column named label which represents which type of packet it is. After this process, the final dataset is employed inthetraining and testing phase. As in the dataset, it has limited rows due to processing time. As it has more data, it needs more processors to execute algorithms.

Classification - Training and Testing

The term classification refers to the process of classifying data using patterns found in the training dataset. It will divide the dataset into two pieces, namely the train and test sections, 80 percent and 20 percent, respectively. As a result, it supplies this information as well as extra parameters particular to each algorithm. Like this, it will classify my data and obtain results. For classification purposes, the machine learning algorithms used are Naïve Bayes, Random Forest, SVM, and KNN algorithms to classify the generated data and conclude results.

Performance Evaluation

The results for each algorithm will be taken after the classification module. As a consequence, it can be determined which method produces the greatest results in terms of network intrusion detection. As a result, it will be able to determine the correctness of each algorithm, and as a result, it will be able to use that algorithm in a real-world scenario.

Results and Discussion

As for the proposed system architecture, first it will collect the data using Wireshark, and after that, it will be preprocessed, and the feature selection is also done in the Weka tool. It will apply four different algorithms to the data set, and after that, through accuracy, it will select which algorithms are best suited for performance evaluation.

The first step is to create a variety of types of packets, including HTTP, HTTPS, and tools. These packets contain different types of data, including text, audio, video, images, and document attachments. Moreover, malicious packets are produced to classify various packet kinds. These data packets are sent through a network from a source address to a destination address. In the second step, Wireshark is used to capture the particulars of these packets. The captured Wireshark data shows the packets' features and factors. Next, the various factors found in the packets are inferred, and particular features with very minor roles in the sorting of varieties of packets are distant, leaving a dataset with the remaining features. The fourth step of attribute selection is performed to select the important features that determine packet classification on the dataset. It is accomplished through the use of the Weka tool. However, the dataset was created with several other features also included in Table 1.

Table 1. Dataset Attributes

Frame size	File data
Epoch time'	Total length
Time delta from the preceding captured packet	Identification
Time delta from the preceding displayed packet	Time to live
Time since the first frame's reference	Window size value
Frame no.	Calculated window size
Protocols in frame	Window scaling factor
Coloring rule name	Time since the first frame in this TCP stream
Coloring rule string	Time since the preceding frame in this TCP stream
Seq	Payload for TCP
Ack	TCP segment data
Len	Label

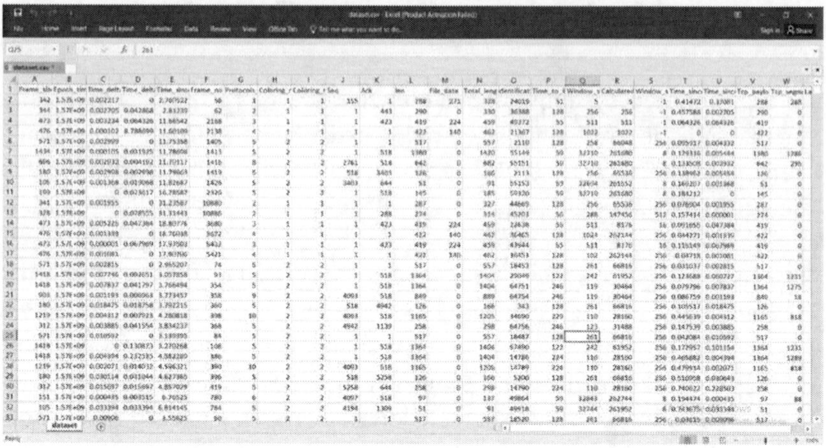

Figure 2. Structure of dataset.

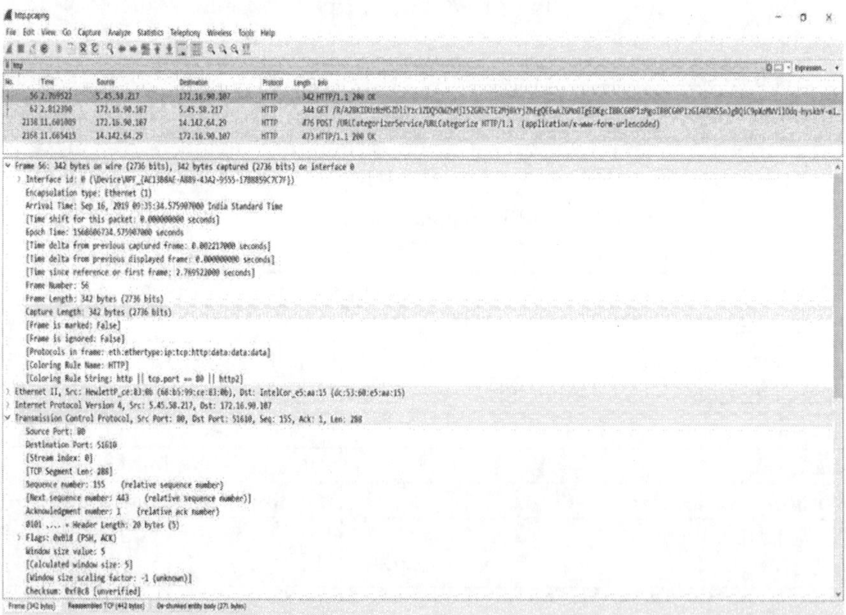

Figure 3. The parameters of Wireshark.

Figure 2 shows the structure of the data set. It displays the attributes present in the data set and the types of attributes in the dataset. In the final step, the various machine learning algorithms, such as Naive Bayes, SVM, Random Forest, and K Nearest Neighbors, are then applied to the created dataset to test the accuracy of classification in distinguishing varieties of packets. The data resource is split into 80% and 20% training and testing sets, respectively. The algorithms' performance is then assessed using their accuracy value.

Figure 3 shows all the parameters available in the Wireshark tool when it is collecting the data while the data is transferring from sender to receiver. From this, it can collect all the details of the transferred data. Figure 4 shows that while the data is transferred from sender to receiver, it will collect the data in this format, and these are all the attributes it is gathering for the dataset. Figure 5 shows how the data is processed in the Weka tool. In this, the collected data is analyzed on a statistical basis, and it will calculate the parameters that affect the output of the data using the best search technique. It will show what the parameters are and what is important so that it can minimize the data and also make the output more efficient.

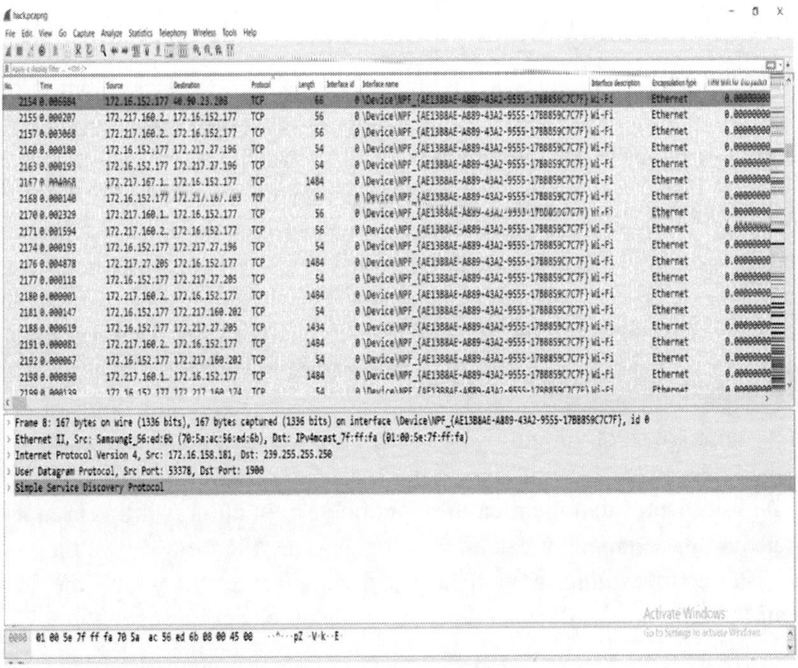

Figure 4. Display of data collection in Wireshark.

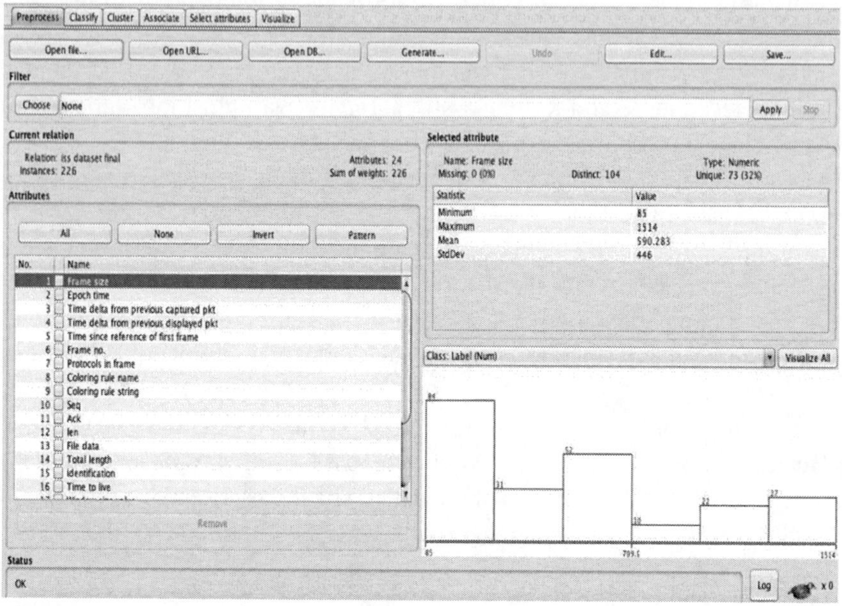

Figure 5. Preprocessing of data in Weka.

Weka is used for preprocessing, and Naive is used for classification on a basic discrete numerical dataset. It makes a probabilistic prediction based on the inputs. It is grounded in the Bayes theorem, which states that P (H/X) = [P(X/H). P(H)]/P(X), where X represents the example set, H denotes the hypothesis that X belongs to class C, and P(X/H) represents the posterior probability of H. Naive Bayes prediction needs zero in each conditional probability since it is heavily influenced by zero probability error. The Laplacian adjustment is used to avoid this. It is the most efficient way to categorize categorical data. NB is a straightforward categorization method. Given these characteristics, it asks whether this measurement belongs in class A or B and responds by multiplying the proportion of all prior measurements with the same features from class A by the percentage of all measures from class A. It indicates that the measurement belongs in class A if this number is greater than the equivalent calculation for class B. Figure 6 shows the result of the Naïve Bayes algorithm. It produces 80.97% accuracy, and the cross-validation score is 77.88% at 0.55067 seconds of execution time.

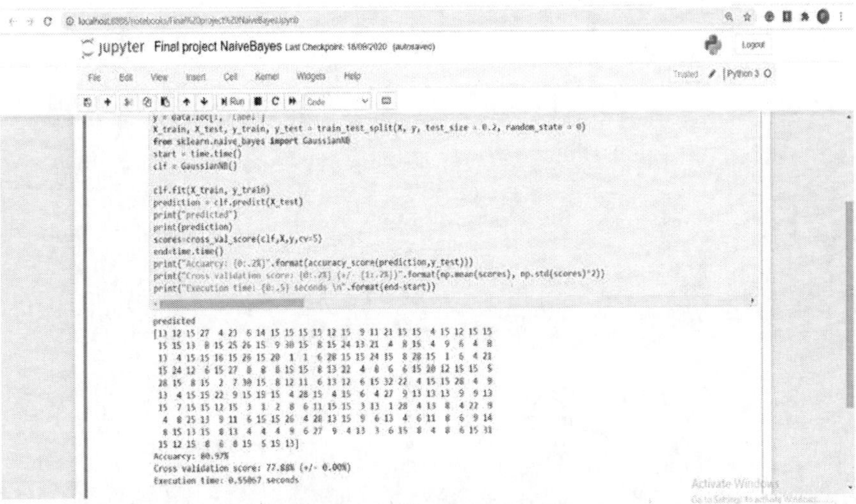

Figure 6. Output of Naïve Bayes algorithm.

As its formal definition suggests, a support vector machine (SVM) is a discriminative classifier with a separating hyperplane. In other words, supervised learning produces an ideal hyperplane that categorizes fresh samples given labeled training data. This hyperplane is a line in two-dimensional space that divides a plane into two halves, with each class on each side. Figure 7 shows the output of the SVM algorithm, and it achieves 98.23% accuracy.

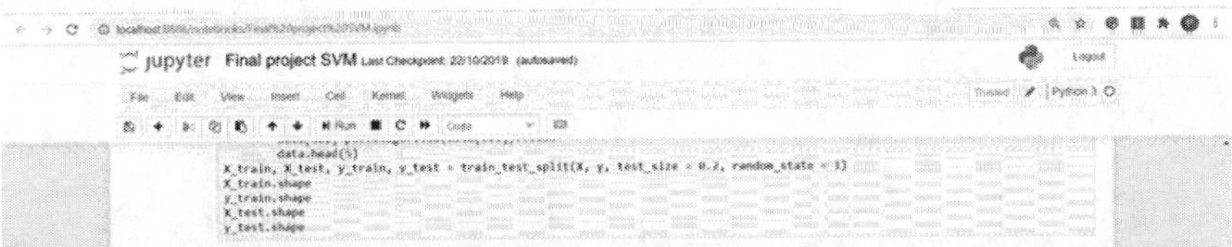

Figure 7. Output of SVM algorithm.

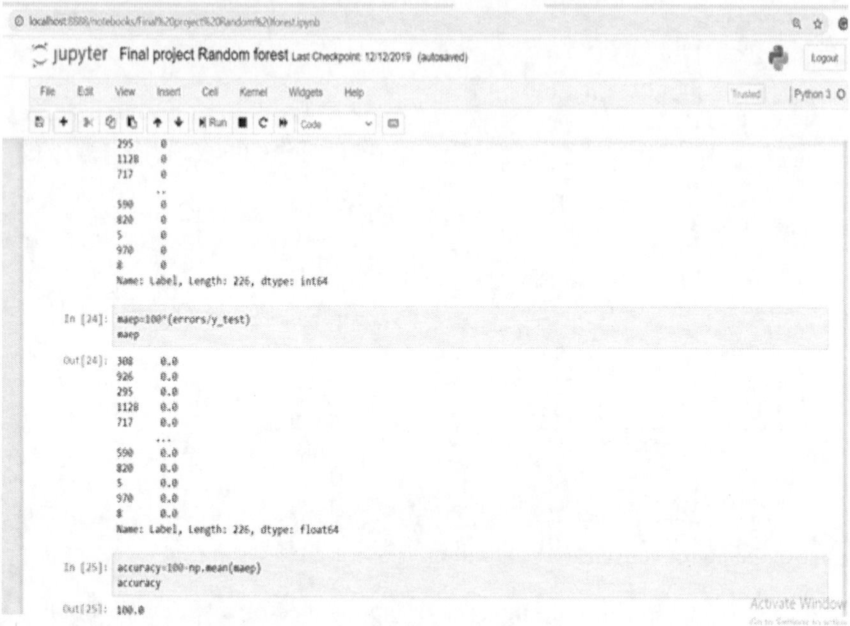

Figure 8. Result of Random Forest algorithm.

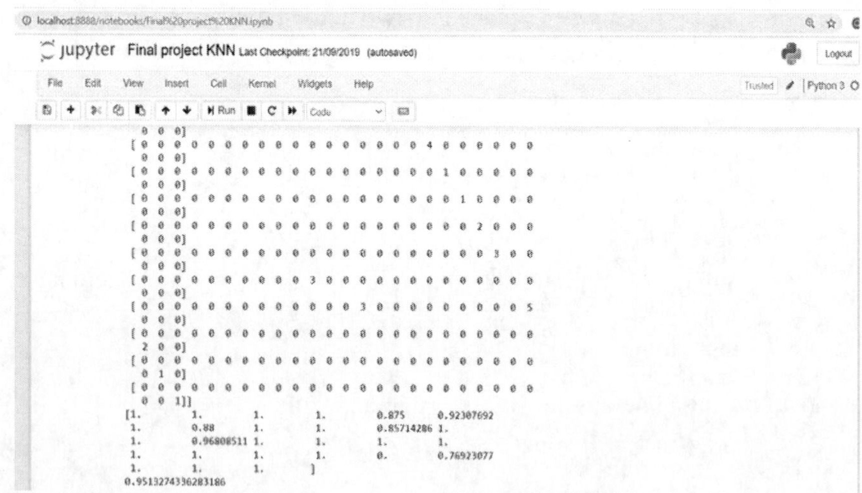

Figure 9. Output of KNN algorithm.

An ensemble of machine learning techniques such as random forest produces a large number of uncorrelated decision trees by averaging a random set of predictor variables. Since building a decision tree classifier does not entail any previous knowledge of the field, it can be used for exploratory knowledge discovery. It is capable of dealing with multi-dimensional files. Decision trees have their own set of complications, such as overfitting and, in some cases, exceptionally poor precision. As a result, a random forest is used to solve the decision tree's limitations. It entails creating multiple decision trees and then using the bagging strategy, which entails resampling the data to locate each tree's result and aggregating, to sum up, the results of all trees. Figure 8 shows the result of 100% accuracy by the Random Forest algorithm.

K-Nearest Neighbors is a fundamental yet critical categorization algorithm in machine learning. Among the applications found in the supervised learning domains are data mining, pattern recognition, and intrusion detection systems. It is commonly used in regular contexts since it is non-parametric and creates no principal norms about data distribution, unlike such methods as GMM, which assume a Gaussian distribution of the given data. It uses prior data, usually referred to as training data, to classify coordinates according to an attribute. Figure 9 shows the output of the KNN algorithm, which achieves 98.13% accuracy.

Conclusion

Intrusion detection systems, which can identify security issues on a network, frequently detect and delete any malicious packet injection. More network visibility is offered, and the contents are not decrypted, giving the sender and receiver additional confidentiality. Hence, the proposed work utilized the ML algorithm for NIDS. When 40% of the data are tested, the Naive Bayes code is run on the Python Jupiter notebook supported by libraries and tested to find the dataset's accuracy as 80.97% and validation score as 77.88%, respectively. When proceeding with 80% of training and 20% of testing data, the SVM machine learning technique is applied to the collected packet dataset and yields 98.23% accuracy. Similarly, the Random Forest technique is employed with 10-fold cross-validation on an 80–20% split-up of the dataset. The random forest is completely accurate in the evaluation of metrics such as the confusion matrix, mean absolute error (MAE), mean squared error (MSE), and root mean squared error (RMSE) and accuracy. K Nearest Neighbors is a clustering method that groups data, in this case, packets, according to their similarities applied to 80–20% of the dataset. Two additional assessment measures are determined in the form of a confusion matrix and an f2 score at the end of 95.13 percent accuracy. Using the Random Forest method for network intrusion detection yields the most accurate results when compared to other algorithms. Further, the alert mechanisms are frequently initiated by recognizing the intrusions using a selective ML algorithm, and backed by the type of intrusion, high-end security is frequently developed, securing the information being transmitted across a network.

References

[1] Y. Zhu, L. Cui, Z. Ding, L. Li, Y. Liu, and Z. Hao, "Black box attack and network intrusion detection using machine learning for malicious traffic," *Comput. Secur.*, vol. 123, p. 102922, 2022.

[2] M. Apruzzese, Giovanni And Pajola, Luca And Conti, "The Cross-Evaluation Of Machine Learning-Based Network Intrusion Detection Systems," *IEEE Trans. Netw. Serv. Manag.*, Vol. 19, No. 4, pp. 5152–5169, 2022.

[3] S. J. Moore, F. Cruciani, C. D. Nugent, S. Zhang, I. Cleland, and S. Sani, "Deep Learning for Network Intrusion: A Hierarchical Approach To Reduce False Alarms," *Intell. Syst. with Appl.*, p. 200215, 2023.

[4] M. Chale and N. D. Bastian, "Generating realistic cyber data for training and evaluating machine learning classifiers for network intrusion detection systems," *Expert Syst. Appl.*, vol. 207, p. 117936, 2022.

[5] J. Simon, N. Kapileswar, P. K. Polasi, and M. A. Elaveini, "Hybrid intrusion detection system for wireless IoT networks using deep learning algorithm," *Comput. Electr. Eng.*, vol. 102, p. 108190, 2022.

[6] C. Zhang, D. Jia, L. Wang, W. Wang, F. Liu, and A. Yang, "Comparative research on network intrusion detection methods based on machine learning," *Comput. Secur.*, vol. 121, p. 102861, 2022.

[7] B. Sharma, L. Sharma, C. Lal, and S. Roy, "Anomaly based network intrusion detection for IoT attacks using deep learning technique," *Comput. Electr. Eng.*, vol. 107, p. 108626, 2023.

[8] T. Saba, A. Rehman, T. Sadad, H. Kolivand, and S. A. Bahaj, "Anomaly-based intrusion detection system for IoT networks through deep learning model," *Comput. Electr. Eng.*, vol. 99, p. 107810, 2022.

[9] J. Verma, A. Bhandari, and G. Singh, "iNIDS: SWOT Analysis and TOWS Inferences of State-of-the-Art NIDS solutions for the development of Intelligent Network Intrusion Detection System," *Comput. Commun.*, vol. 195, pp. 227–247, 2022.

[10] A. Ahmad Najar and S. Manohar Naik, "Applying Supervised Machine Learning Techniques to Detect DDoS Attacks," in *2022 2nd Asian Conference on Innovation in Technology (ASIANCON)*, 2022, pp. 1–7.

[11] R. M. A. Mohammad, M. K. Alsmadi, I. Almarashdeh, and M. Alzaqebah, "An improved rule induction based denial of service attacks classification model," *Comput. Secur.*, vol. 99, p. 102008, 2020.

[12] M. A. Talukder, Khondokar Fida Hasan, Manowarul Islam, Ashraf Uddin, Arnisha Akhter, Mohammand Abu Yousuf, Fares Alharbi, Mohammad Ali Moni. "A dependable hybrid machine learning model for network intrusion detection," *J. Inf. Secur. Appl.*, vol. 72, p. 103405, 2023.

Chapter 4

A Novel Approach for Requirement-Based Test Case Prioritization Using Machine Learning Techniques

Aishwaryarani Behera[1], MTech
Arup Abhinna Acharya[1], PhD
Sanjukta Mohanty[2,*], MTech
and Namita Panda[1], PhD
[1]School of Computer Engineering, KIIT Deemed to be University, Bhubaneswar, India
[2]Computer Science and Engineering, Odisha University of Technology and Research, Bhubaneswar, India

Abstract

Most often the entire application functionality needed to be tested out, in case there is a bug fix or change request demand from the clients or end users. Obviously considerable amount of effort and time is required to test out the entire application sanity. In such cases prioritization technique helps to overcome the limitations of regression testing employed for application sanity. Test case prioritization usually means categorically ranking some test cases higher than others. To lower the price of regression test suites and increase the effectiveness of regression testing, requirement-based test case prioritization (RTCP) is adopted by most of the research practioners to prioritize the test cases. A thorough comparative analysis of RTCP methods have been performed and found that selecting the significant factors in RTCP is a challenging task for fulfilling the objective like reducing execution time and the rate of defect detection being increased. To overcome the issues in existing studies, we have considered an additional most useful parameter 'weight' for assigning weightage to business requirement which enhances prioritized scheduling of test cases in RTCP. The

* Corresponding author's Email: mailtorani.sanjukta@gmail.com.

In: Building Intelligent Systems Using Machine Learning and Deep Learning
Editors: A. Kumar Sahoo, C. Pradhan, B. Shankar Prasad Mishra et al.
ISBN: 979-8-89113-342-6

purpose of this chapter is to rank the requirement-based test cases as higher priority by selecting the relevant features. For this, the machine learning classifier k-Nearest Neighbor, Decision Tree, Random Forest, Bagging, Support Vector Machine algorithms are being used to evaluate the features for the test case prioritization. The experimental result demonstrates that SVC classifier achieves the best performance among the other classifiers. Thus, early prediction of the requirement based prioritized test cases helps to reduce the cost and time required for regression testing. The experimental result convincingly demonstrates that the proposed prioritization strategy drastically increases the fault discovery rate due to weight factor.

Keywords: test case prioritization, requirement-based test case prioritization, machine learning techniques

Introduction

In the field of software development, we always strive for developing high quality applications to minimize cost overheads. Hence software testing plays an essential role in ensuring the application quality to the highest standard [1]. Out of many software testing practices, regression testing stands apart in terms of acknowledging application stability and functionality. Regression testing is defined as the software testing practice done to ensure the application's expected behavior for any source code modifications or upgrades [2]. At the same time, while ensuring the quality we need to keep an eye on the overall cost of software testing inflicted in terms of resources and time. Thus, a certain strategy needs to be adopted so that the overall software testing cost is brought down without compromising the quality the of software. A test case prioritization (TCP) strategy is used to solve this issue which gives us the liberty to test the highest priority scenarios first. Traditional methods used in the existing research studies like: code-based technique require a thorough study of source code. This is a very time intensive procedure for TCP [3]. At the same time, model-based prioritizing the test cases is not able to provide a satisfactory result in finding the fault [4]. Also, the test selection criteria are not so good enough to order the test cases [5]. Hence requirement-based TCP considered as a crucial component of regression testing, plays an important role in ordering the test cases for minimizing the execution time, expense, and effort [6]. In RTCP, the test cases are sorted according to some specific criteria. To diminish on execution time, effort, and expense during software testing, it is determined to execute the most important test cases first. We found that manual classification with regards to requirement-based prioritization perhaps not be the most efficient method based on requirements. As a result, machine learning techniques are employed to address the drawbacks of the conventional TCP [7]. In order to save time, money, and effort, machine learning approaches predict the prioritize the test cases by evaluating some relevant features. Machine learning technique can simplify the work required by testers by offering a streamlined method for managing test cases [8]. In this chapter, we have designed a method for automatically providing priorities of high-rank, medium-sized, and low-set to the test cases. Whenever the high-rank priority test cases run first it lowers the price. Here we employed some machine learning classifiers such as Support Vector Classifier (SVC), Decision Tree (DT), Random Forest (RF), Logistic Regression (LR), K-Nearest Neighbor (KNN), Naïve Bayes (NB) along with boosting and bagging estimator. SVM provides the best result among all along with the ensemble model. Then to optimize the machine learning model we have considered two test case prioritization datasets ("car-lease" and the "MIS-test case") having 6 and 8 number of features and 1314 and 2000 number of samples respectively. Both the datasets are used to evaluate the machine learning classifiers. From the experimental result, we obtained that the performance of the model increases when the significant factor 'weight' is added in the dataset-II. As there is no weight feature in the "carlease" dataset-I, the result is less than 50%. When we dramatically apply the weight feature in dataset-II," MIS system with priority" the outcome outputs to more than 75% accuracy. Our experimental result demonstrated that the machine learning based approach performs better than the traditional test case prioritization-based methods. Also, we have contrasted the existing research papers with our suggested strategy and found that our method outperforms the other.

Contribution of this chapter is explained as follows:

- Designed a requirement based TCP technique with machine learning approach to optimize the model by utilising more than one datasets for obtaining the priority of the tese cases.
- Analyse the dataset throughly and extracted an informative feature, for which the performance of the model drastically improved.
- Existing research studiesof requirement based TCP methods are compared to verify the pros and cons of different TCP approaches.

The remaining paper are organized as follows. In section 2, basic information is provided. Section 3, explained the related work. Section 4, presents the findings and what we really learned through the review study. Section 5, contains the proposed model. The implementation effort is presented in section 6. Section 7 represents the scope of future and Section 8 the conclusion.

Background Details

The concepts linked to software testing, regression testing, test case prioritization, requirement-based test case prioritization, and machine learning methods for test case prioritization are all thoroughly explained in this section.

Software Testing

It is a broad range of tasks carried out with the goal of identifying software flaws." It is a step in the software development process that assesses a software item's functionality, performance, and security in relation to a set of system requirements" [9]. Examples of such software items include systems, subsystems, and features program's functionality is validated and verified through the process of software testing. According to several studies, software testing plays the vital role amongst all phases of software process and requires large investment of time, effort and money. Software testing should consume between 40 and 70 percent of the time and money spent on software development including the test case reduction and prioritizing techniques [10].

Regression Testing

It is a major step in the software testing field since it guarantees the developers that the modified application won't produce any new faults. It is challenging to complete entire test cases because of resource and cost [11]. Regression testing cannot be done in a timely manner due to the fast release cycles for updated software [12]. Regression testing is another activity that is carried out frequently, particularly in large applications, therefore it consumes lots of resources and costs money to maintain [6]. So many methods are available to evaluate the modified program within time and budget limitations. Regression approaches fall into three groups like 1. When retesting all techniques and testing the modified system, take into account all previous test cases. As a result, it requires abundance of time 2. Test case selection, this technique chooses a few test cases, according to a set of criteria. 3. Test case prioritization techniques arrange test cases according to prioritized calculations [13].

Test Case Prioritization

The primary goal of this method to execute higher priority test cases earlier so that to improve the rate of early failure identification [14]. Parallelizing the debugging and testing processes reduces costs. Prioritizing test cases has the advantage of allowing continuous testing while always completing the most important test case first [15]. There are many groups of prioritizing the test cases technique. Prioritizing test cases methodology based on machine learning, history, risk, requirements, models, and coverage.

Requirement Based Prioritization

The techniques for ranking test cases based on requirement documents are known as requirement-based prioritization approaches. The techniques have utilized a variety of weighting factors, like customer allotted priority, need fixed complexity, and volatility.

Requirement supported Factor value, $RFVi$ is computed as

$$RFVi = \sum_{j=1}^{n} Factor\frac{valuej}{n} \quad (1)$$

j = factor
n = no. of requirements
for finding test case weight $RFVi$ is employed.

$$TCW_t=[\textstyle\sum_{x=1}^{i} RFV_X / \sum_{y=1}^{n} RFV_Y] * 1/n \quad (2)$$

where TCW_t = test case weight
x, y = factors
n = number of requirements

Machine Learning Approaches

A computer can learn on its own without being explicitly programmed using a learning approach called machine learning. This technique is a use of intelligence that allows the system the capacity to learn autonomously, carry out its duties competently, and advance [16]. From the knowledge, the goal of learning is to create a model that takes in information and outputs what is needed. According to the type of information they want, it can be broadly divided into three types. Supervised Machine Learning: In supervised learning a labeled or training data set is used to make predictions. The training data set includes both input and output data and labels make up the output vector. The model or the classifier is trained with the labeled data and if the training accuracy is acceptable than tested with new dataset or unknown data to generate the classes labels. Two important techniques come under the supervised machine learning is classification and regression technique [17].

Classification

It falls under discrete category or predict the discrete class labels. Here the inputs are divided into two or more classes. Division of inputs into two classes constitute binary classification and more than two classification forms categorical classification. The application of classification model includes fraud URL detection, spam mail filtering, sentiment analysis, and score card prediction of any examination (Pass or fail) etc. In our problem domain we have used more than two classes that is low, high, medium. Figure4 depicts the typical flow procedure for categorization approach.

In this chapter we have adopted multiple classification of supervised machine learning technique for test case prioritization. Because our aim is classifying the test cases that is low, medium and high. Here we have used various classification techniques like SVC, KNN, NB, Logistic regression, Decision tree and random Forest. Also, we have used ensembled machine learning technique like bagging and boosting to classify the test cases.

2.5 Cross Validation

For evaluation we have employed k-fold cross validation method of machine learning technique [18]. The dataset is splited into k sections and the k value is considered as 10. Every fold is used for validation once during the training's k iterations.

Related Work

In this unit, we have explored the most common existing TCP methods, designed by research partitioner to prioritized the test cases such as Code based technique, Model based technique, Requirement based technique, History based approach and Machine Learning based approach etc., we compared and analyzed thoroughly with each method and provides their pros and cons also. In [1], the author has introduced test case prioritizing strategy (TCP-NNC) based on neural network categorization. In this approach the neural network is trained on the association between requirements, test and discover fault. For measurement purposes, they have employed recall, precision, and accuracy. Also used the optimizer called Adam and SGD (Stochastic Gradient Descent) found that their approach outperforms among all the random approaches. The authors of [18] have proposed an approach based on ensemble method to combine different kinds of model into a single one. They have validated their approaches by using sixteen datasets. The result showed that out of sixteen datasets their approaches outperform in twelve datasets. In [2], the author has developed an innovative method for prioritizing test cases. They employed fuzzy logic for prioritizing purpose. They tested the accuracy of their method by comparing it to bagging, 348 decision trees, and the KSTAR classifier. They have found clearly their approach shows 93% accuracy in comparison to other methodology. In [19] the author has proposed an evolutionary algorithm to reorder the test cases and also for optimizing the cost and fault detection. In [20], the author has put out a paradigm that automatically sets test cases in order of importance, with high priority tests being conducted first and low priority tests being executed later. in this approach they have used k-means and k-medoids technique. the result showed 79.17% accuracy in comparison to other techniques .to validate the approach the authors used a business priority dataset. In [21], the author has provided a supervised machine learning strategy for determining the order of test cases in a continuous integration environment (CI). They used Random Forest and LSTM in deep learning technique. They evaluated their approach by COLEMAN and RETECS dataset which are already used by the authors. They validated the dataset using NAPFD, APFD metric. The result found that 72% accuracy. An innovative technique has proposed in [22] for TCP called TCP-Net. The proposed model is validated by three industrial datasets. They used APFD metric for evaluation. The result found accuracy 97%,98%, and96% respectively in different dataset. In [3], the author has designed an unsupervised machine learning approach for test case prioritization. In this paper they analyzed various clustering technique to achieve the performance. They employed approaches including K-mean clustering. They evaluated their approach by using software repository data set. They validated their performance by using APFD method. In [13], the author has used the newly developed particle swam optimization approach to order the hybrid string metric test cases. They developed the particle swam optimization algorithm and used four non-hybrid string metrics in the trials. The model is validated by Siemens dataset. Their result showed that proposed hybrid string technique achieved good APFD value. The result showed 97.37% APFD value. The authors of [14] has created an ant colony approach for ranking and choosing test cases. The suggested strategy makes advantage of Quality Function Deployment in software (SQFD). The proposed approach validated by simulation with different number of tests. A prioritization technique has been presented in [23] where a novel hybrid regression test case method for fault prediction was considered. This combines BN-established approach with code coverage-based clustering techniques for better prioritization. They developed basically two vital steps for ranking the test cases. First, all test cases are categorized into categories using clustering techniques. Second, the cluster test cases are ranked with the aim of likelihood of failure. The result showed that their approach is promising. In [24], the author has introduced a coverage-based prioritizing the test cases for fault prediction. In this instance, they employed two models to determine the fault detection capability. They suggested a novel strategy for prioritizing test cases in software evolution. They found that their approach outperforms among all the model. In [25], the author has proposed a light weight novel code-based prioritization method which gave us a maximum code coverage. The suggested method is quite efficient in terms of price and efficiency. The proposed approach is validated by 15 statements and 15 test cases. In [15], the author has introduced a novel requirement based prioritizing the test cases. the prioritization builds on the basics of requirement identified and risk factors. The proposed approach is validated by a case study. The authors in [5] has built a priority system for test cases based on requirements. The tester, the customer, and the developer can all determine the priority of the requirements. Then after they execute sever fault first. They used a genetic algorithm. the proposed model is validated by a live project. In [25], the author has discovered a novel test case ranking method based on history. Compared to other approaches, the method demonstrated the highest effectiveness and ability to discover faults. The proposed model is validated by an industrial system called CPMISS having java code with 440,000 lines. To evaluate the performance, they used the APFD metric.

Discussion

The different prioritization techniques of the existing studies along with their pros and cons have been explored in the literature review and the summary is explained in table 1. The disadvantage of the traditional approach is that it is very challenging to rank the test cases without source code. Our research indicates that black box testing is a distinct discipline. Black box testing includes both requirement-based testing and history-based testing. The test cases can be prioritized using this way without the need of source code. In next part, we'll go into greater detail about how machine learning is utilized to prioritize requirement testing.

Table 1. Summary table of different approaches for test case prioritization

Authors	Features set	Methodology	Limitations	Result
Tiutin etal. (2022), [22]	Requirement changed covered, requirement dep covered, cost, fault discovered	TCP-NNC, SGD, Adam	It is not validated for large scale software system.	Accuracy-92.78% Precision-88.57% Recall-95.87%
Purohit et al.,(2017), [2]	Prioritization matrix, project features, industrial dataset.	Fuzzy logic	Difficult to finding out appropriate features.	Accuracy-80%(data misclassifycation) Accuracy-93.33% (data classified)
Khalid et al., (2019), [20]	B_Req, R_Priority, Complexity	K-means, k-medoids	Very limited dataset features	Accuracy = 77.59%
Roza et al., (2022), [21]	Data threshold, individual Threshold, pair threshold	NNE-TCP machine learning approach, Random Forest	The dataset is relatively small.	Accuracy = 0.72
Abdelkarim et al., (2022), [22]	Source file related feature, test case related feature.	Deep Neural Network (DNN), TCP-Net.	Less incremental learning approach is explored.	Accuracy:0.97, 0.98, 0.96
Khatibsyarbini et al., (2017),[18]	Programming language, Fault matrix.	Weight hybrid string distance, particle swam optimization (PSO)	The model is not validated with character-based string metrics.	Accuracy:92.22

Proposed Architecture

To rank the test cases according to the order of priority, a machine learning model is designed that accepts training data as input, evaluates the features and outputs ranked prioritized test cases such as low, medium, high. The schematic diagram for proposed methodology of TCP is depicted in Figure 1.

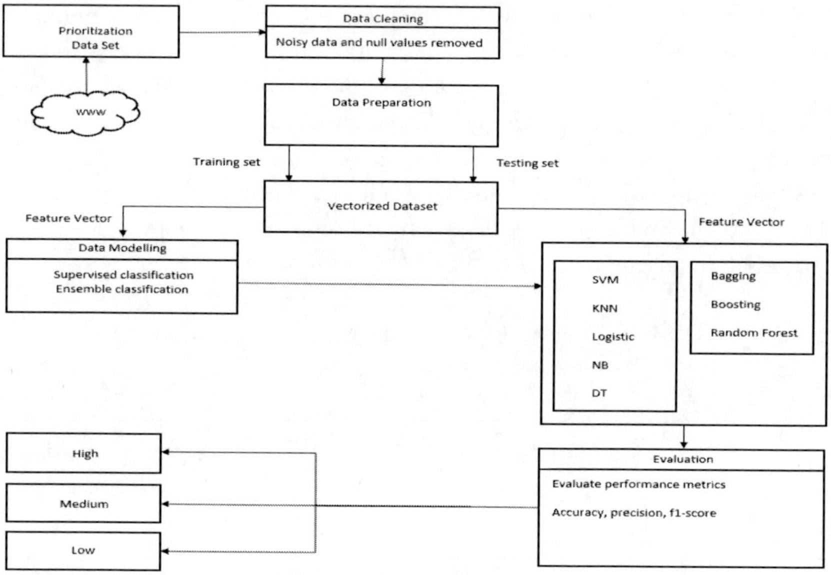

Figure 1. Proposed schematic model for prioritizing the test cases.

Datasets

As always selection of dataset has a significant impact on the classification outcomes. Hence, we have considered two different datasets in the proposed approach, a dataset of an "MIS System with priority "and the dataset "car-lease" are used which are publicly available in Kaggle community [27]. The dataset-I contains 1314 instances and 8 number of features and the datset-II contains 6 features and 2000 records which are presented in table 2 and table 3The snapshot of the data set is presented in Figure 2 and Figure 3.

Table 2. Features characteristics with weight factor

Sl.No	Features	Description
1	B_Req	Business based on Requirement
2	R_Priority	Priority of particular business requirement and explain it in .txt file.
3	Weight	Assigned a weightage against "R_Priority (Requirement Priority)"
4	FP	Function Point of each testing task, which in our case test cases against each requirement under covers a particular FP.
5	Complexity	criticality of a particular Function Point.
6	Time	Estimated max time assigned to each Function Point.
7	Cost	Cost = (complexity multiplied by time) *average amount.
8	Priority	It is the assigned test cases priority against each function point by the testing team.

In [8]:
```
import pandas as pd
df = pd.read_csv("/content/testcase.csv")
df.head()
```

Out[8]:

	B_Req	R_Priority	Weights	FP	Complexity	Time	Cost	Priority
0	1	C	3	T-mis-2708,T-mis- 2151,T-mis- 560,T-mis- 164,T...	3	8.0	168.0	Medium
1	2	C	3	T-mis-1755	3	4.0	84.0	High
2	3	W	3	T-mis-3227	3	1.5	31.5	Medium
3	4	S	2	T-mis-2440,T-mis- 2659,T-mis- 1510	1	4.0	28.0	Medium
4	5	C	3	T-mis-2912,T-mis- 2042,T-mis- 1020	5	4.0	140.0	Medium

Figure 2. Snapshot of the dataset.

Table 3. Features characteristics without weight factor

Sl. No.	Features	Description
1	B_Req	Requirements for business purpose
2	R_Priority	priority of particular business requirement.
3	FP	Function point of each testing task
4	Complexity	Complexity of a particular function point or related module.
5	time	Estimated max time assigned to each function point of particular testing task.
6	Cost	Calculated cost for each function point using complexity and time with function point estimation technique to calculate cost.

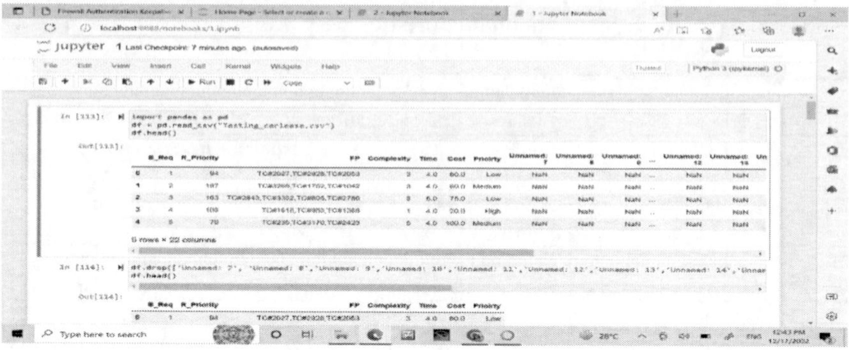

Figure 3. Snapshot of the dataset.

Feature Preprocessing

In this phase, some of the data points in the dataset were missing so mean of the variables were computed for replacing the missing value than the mean max normalization procedure is adopted to normalize data value and make ready for designing a machine learning model for TCP.

Data Preparation

The data for the classification models has been prepared after the appropriate features have been chosen. The unstructured data are formatted after the noisy data have been cleaned by deleting any NULL values that may have been present in the dataset's attribute values. Vector numbers are created. The dataset is then split in half in the proportion of 70:30. 70% is utilized to train the classifiers where as 30% is for testing purpose. In this unit we have used k-fold cross validation for getting best result.

Data Modeling with Machine Learning Classifier

The machine learning models that we took into consideration for test case prioritization are effectively described in the section 2. Several machine learning approaches are utilized to prioritize the test cases, including SVM, logistic regression, random forest, decision tree, NB, bagging, and boosting algorithm. The test cases were prioritized using a large number of supervised classifiers in this chapter, and the results were compared to those obtained using currently available machine learning techniques. The data set is first appropriately prepared before any technique is used, and then the learning ML algorithm is used to train the projected model. Here, we've covered a few classifier strategies, including VM, NB, RF, and ensemble classifiers with bagging and boosting for ranking the test examples. In section 2, many machine learning classifiers are described.

Performance Evaluation Measures

The effectiveness of the trained model must be evaluated using evaluation metrics. We used the classification metrics like accuracy, Precision, Recall and F1-score etc., to assess our trained model. The ratio of the number of accurate forecasts to all of the predictions made can be used to calculate accuracy (number of correctly and incorrectly classified).

$$Accuracy = \frac{number\ of\ correct\ classified\ instances}{total\ number\ of\ instances} \tag{4}$$

$$Precision \frac{True\ Positive(TP)}{True\ Positive(TP)+False\ Positive(FP)} \tag{5}$$

$$Recall \frac{True\ Positive(TP)}{True\ Positive(TP)+False\ (FN)} \tag{6}$$

The F-measure accounts for both measurements and is the harmonic-mean of precision and recall.

$$F\ measure = \frac{2*TP}{2*TP+FP+FN} \tag{7}$$

Research Questions

For our evaluation, we came upon with following questions which we try to figure out in this paper. RQ1: What impact does weight factor feature impose on various algorithms effectiveness? RQ2: Is there a specific Machine Learning algorithm that works effective lying test case prioritization?

Experimental Result

This section finds out the classification results in accordance to low, medium and high ranked test case. So, to achieve this different machine learning classifiers like K-NN, Logistic Regression, Decision Tree, SVC, Gaussian NB, Adaboost, Bagging, Random Forest with the help of python packages like matplotlib, pandas, and NumPy the proposed approach is implemented which allow for the creation of visually appealing and understandable presentations of the code flow. The performance of different classifiers both in traditional train-test split and cross validation methods are explained. The classifiers performance is described with respect to precision, recall, F1-score and accuracy are depicted in Table 4 and 5.

Table 4. Performance of different classifiers with respect to accuracy

Classifiers	Category	Precision	Recall	F1-score	Accuracy	Cross validation
SVC	Low	0.80	0.93	0.86	0.75	77.59
	Medium	0.71	0.81	0.76		
	High	0.00	0.00	0.00		
Logistic Regression	Low	0.82	0.78	0.80	0.71	73.02
	Medium	0.64	0.86	0.73		
	High	0.00	0.00	0.00		
KNN	Low	0.79	0.91	0.85	0.74	72.91
	Medium	0.71	0.81	0.75		
	High	1.00	0.04	0.07		
Decision Tree	Low	0.73	0.71	0.72	0.61	61.92
	Medium	0.59	0.64	0.61		
	High	0.27	0.21	0.24		
Gaussian NB	Low	0.81	0.90	0.86	0.74	75.63
	Medium	0.69	0.82	0.75		
	High	0.00	0.00	0.00		
Random Forest	Low	0.75	0.77	0.76	0.63	67.35
	Medium	0.62	0.66	0.64		
	High	0.23	0.15	0.18		

From the table 4 and table 5 it is evident that the machine learning classifier Support Vector Classifier classifies the test cases as high, medium and low efficiently having the performance 75% in terms of accuracy.

Table 5. Performance of ensemble classifiers with respect to accuracy

Ensemble classifiers	Category	Precision (%)	Recall (%)	F1-Score (%)	Accuracy (%)	Cross Validation (%)
Ada Boost	High	0.20	0.02	0.04	0.75	77.37
	Low	0.80	0.96	0.88		
	Medium	0.73	0.79	0.76		
Bagging	High	0.26	0.15	0.19	0.66	69.75
	Low	0.76	0.81	0.79		
	Medium	0.64	0.69	0.66		

Comparison Between Two Data Sets with or without Weight Factor

In order to respond to research question 1, we compared two data sets, car lease and MIS, in this section. By adding a weight component, the accuracy significantly improves. We used the four classifiers logistic regression, KNN, SVC, and random forest on these two datasets. The outcome revealed that accuracy in the car-lease dataset without weight factor is 37%, as shown in table 6. Similar to this, we discovered that by including the weight component, accuracy rises to 75%, as shown in table 7. This leads us to the conclusion that choosing the right feature can change accuracy from poor accuracy to high accuracy.

Comparison with Existing ML Techniques

The accuracy is shown in Table 7. Further its accuracy is checked and compared with other classification technique such as k-means and k-medoid classifier, Random Forest and LSTM in deep learning technique-net approach to prove the efficiency of TCP using SVC technique. Using K-means and K-medoids accuracy is 70%, using deep learning classifier accuracy is 72%, Using TCP-Net accuracy is 67%. Undoubtedly, accuracy through test case prioritization using support vector classification is 75%. Applying cross validation method its accuracy increases to 77.59% that is the best approach for classification

Table 6. Performance of different classifiers without weight factor

Classifiers	Accuracy
KNN	35%
RF	34%
DT	35%
Bagging	37%

Table 7. Performance of different classifiers with weight factor

Classifiers	Accuracy
KNN	74%
RF	63%
DT	61%
Bagging	67%
SVC	75%

Table 8. Proposed performance with other techniques

Sl.no	Proposed techniques	Accuracy
1	k-means and k-medoids	70%
2	Deep Learning Technique	72%
3	TCP- Net	67%
4	TCP-SVC	77.59%

After comparing proposed approach with the existing studies, it was found that our approach is the best method among all approach which is represented in Table 7, table 8 and Figure 4.

Results for RQ2

We use all of the methods and their ensemble on both two datasets to examine research question 2. We see that SVC (support vector classifier) has a superior performance than other ML methods used in the data set.

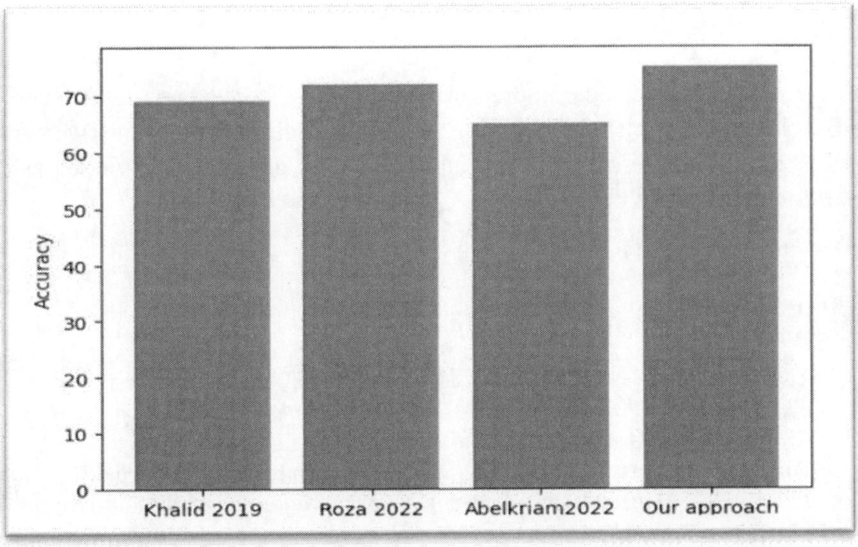

Figure 4. Comparison of proposed approach with existing model.

Conclusion

In the event of our detailed investigation for test case prioritization, we realized that it is difficult to prioritize the test cases without source code access. To mitigate this problem, a novel approach called requirement-based test case prioritization is offered. According to the requirement-based strategy test cases were prioritized using machine learning techniques, with requirement factors as the input. The proposed method is verified with the dataset MIS System with car lease dataset. To assess the performance in terms of accuracy, we have employed seven machine learning classifiers including bagging, random forest, decision tree and KNN, Support Vector Classifier (SVC), NB and Logistic Regression have been used. From our experiments we concluded that SVC algorithm outperformed all in terms of test case prioritization.

Future Scope

In future we can consider more relevant features for achieving the best performance of the machine learning model. And at the same time, we can think about the usage of optimization algorithm to get better prioritized test cases for speedy fault detection.

References

[1] Tiutin, C. M., Vescan A. Test case prioritization based on neural networks classification. *In Proceedings of the 2nd ACM International Workshop on AI and Software Testing/Analysis* (2022) pp. 9-16.

[2] Purohit, G. N. Classification model for test case prioritization techniques. *In 2017 International Conference on Computing, Communication and Automation (ICCCA)* (2017) pp. 919-924. IEEE.

[3] Chaudhary, S., Jatain A. Performance evaluation of clustering techniques in test case prioritization. *In 2020 International Conference on Computational Performance Evaluation (ComPE)* (2020) pp. 699-703. IEEE.

[4] Mohd-Shafie, M. L., Wan-Kadir W. M. N., Khatibsyarbini M., Isa M. A. Model-based test case prioritization using selective and even-spread count-based methods with scrutinized ordering criterion. *PloS one* (2020) 15(2), e0229312.

[5] Sujata, M. K., Kumar D. V. Requirements based test case prioritization using genetic algorithm. *International Journal of computer science and technology* (2010) 1(2) :189-191.

[6] Dahiya, O., Solanki K. An efficient requirement-based test case prioritization technique using optimized TFC-SVM approach. *International Journal of Engineering Trends and Technology* (2021) 69(1): 5-16.

[7] Muthusamy, T. Measuring the Effectiveness of Test Case Prioritization Techniques Based on Weight Factors. *In CS & IT Conference Proceedings* (2014) 4(10).

[8] Rahmani, A., Ahmad S., Jalil I. E. A., Herawan A. P. A systematic literature review on regression test case prioritization. *International Journal of Advanced Computer Science and Applications* (2021) 12(9).

[9] Roongruangsuwan, S., Daengdej J. A test case prioritization method with practical weight factors. *J. Software Eng* (2010) 4, 193-214.

[10] Mohd-Shafie, M. L., Wan-Kadir W. M. N., Khatibsyarbini M., Isa M. A. Model-based test case prioritization using selective and even-spread count-based methods with scrutinized ordering criterion. *PloS one* (2020) 15(2), e0229312.

[11] Meçe, E. K., Paci H., Binjaku K. The application of machine learning in test case prioritization-a review. *European Journal of Electrical Engineering and Computer Science* (2020) 4(1).

[12] Beena, R., Sarala S. Code coverage -based test case selection and prioritization. *International Journal of SEKE 2022 : The 34th International Conference on Software Engineering and Knowledge Engineering* (2022) pp.9-18.

[13] Khatibsyarbini, M., Isa M. A., ABANG JAWAWI, D. N. A hybrid weight-based and string distances using particle swarm optimization for prioritizing test cases. *Journal of Theoretical & Applied Information Technology (2017)*, 95(12):2723-2732.

[14] Silva, D., Rabelo R, Campanha M., Neto P. S., Oliveira P. A., Britto, R. A hybrid approach for test case prioritization and selection. *In 2016 IEEE Congress on Evolutionary Computation (CEC) (2016) pp. 4508-4515.*

[15] Srivastva, P. R., Kumar, K., Raghurama, G. Test case prioritization based on requirements and risk factors. *ACM SIGSOFT Software Engineering Notes* (2008) 33(4), 1-5.

[16] Khatibsyarbini, M., Isa M. A., Jawawi, D. N., Shafie, M. L. M., Wan-Kadir, W. M. N., Hamed, H. N. A., Suffian M. D. M. Trend Application of Machine Learning in Test Case Prioritization: A Review on Techniques. *IEEE Access*, 9(2021) 166262-166282.

[17] Mohanty, S., Acharya, A. A., Sahu, L. Improving Suspicious URL Detection through Ensemble Machine Learning Techniques. *In Society 5.0 and the Future of Emerging Computational Technologies* (2022) (pp. 229-248).

[18] Lachmann, R., Schulze, S., Nieke, M., Seidl C., Schaefer, I. System-level test case prioritization using machine learning. *In 2016 15th IEEE International Conference on Machine Learning and Applications (ICMLA)* (2016) (pp. 361-368).

[19] Vescan, A., Şerban, C., Chisăliţă-Cretu, C., Dioşan, L. Requirement dependencies-based formal approach for test case prioritization in regression testing. *In 2017 13th IEEE International Conference on Intelligent Computer Communication and Processing (ICCP)* (2017) pp. 181-188. IEEE.

[20] Khalid, Z., Qamar, U. Weight and cluster-based test case prioritization technique. *In 2019 IEEE 10th Annual Information Technology, Electronics and Mobile Communication Conference (IEMCON)* (2019) pp. 1013-1022. IEEE.

[21] Da Roza, E. A., Lima, J. A. P., Silva, R. C., Vergilio, S. R. Machine Learning Regression Techniques for Test Case Prioritization in Continuous Integration Environment. *In 2022 IEEE International Conference on Software Analysis, Evolution and Reengineering (SANER)* (2022) pp. 196-206.

[22] Abdelkarim, M., ElAdawi, R. TCP-Net: Test Case Prioritization using End-to-End Deep Neural Networks. *In 2022 IEEE International Conference on Software Testing, Verification and Validation Workshops (ICSTW)* (2022) (pp. 122-129).

[23] Zhao, X., Wang, Z., Fan, X., Wang, Z. A. clustering-Bayesian network-based approach for test case prioritization. *In 2015 IEEE 39th Annual Computer Software and Applications Conference* (2015) Vol. 3; pp. 542-547.

[24] Lou, Y., Hao, D., Zhang, L. Mutation-based test-case prioritization in software evolution. *In 2015 IEEE 26th International Symposium on Software Reliability Engineering (ISSRE)* (2015) pp. 46-57.

[25] Lachmann, R. Machine learning-driven test case prioritization approaches for black-box software testing. *In The European test and telemetry conference, Nuremberg, Germany* (2018).

[26] Wang, X., Zeng, H. History-based dynamic test case prioritization for requirement properties in regression testing. *In Proceedings of the International Workshop on Continuous Software Evolution and Delivery* (2016) pp. 41-47.

Chapter 5

The Detection and Prevention of Phishing Threats in OSN Using Machine Learning Techniques

Smrutisrita Samal[1,*], BTech
Sanjukta Mohanty[1,†], MTech
and Arup Abhinna Acharya[2], PhD (ABD)
[1]Department of Computer Science and Engineering, OUTR, Odisha, India
[2]School of Computer Engineering, KIIT Deemed to be University, Odisha, India

Abstract

The widespread usage of the web increases the number of social media and online social networks (OSNs) users rapidly. Most of the users of OSNs are unaware of security issues such as privacy violations, identity theft, sexual harassment, etc. Recent studies have shown that OSNs users willingly provide personal information about themselves, including phone number, birth details, educational background, mail id, relationship status, and even present location. The mistreating of this personal information has the potential to hurt consumers both online and offline. When children are the users, these risks increase in severity and easily they become the victim of it. Among the different OSNs cyber threats, phishing is the leading threat which deceives the internet users to reveal their secret information and affects the online users' overall well-being and the safety of children in particular. In this chapter, we provide a comprehensive analysis of the various OSNs security and privacy threats and their detection and prevention along with predicted the

[*] Corresponding Author's Email: samalsmrutisrita@gmail.com.
[†] Corresponding Author's Email: mailtorani.sanjukta@gmail.com.

In: Building Intelligent Systems Using Machine Learning and Deep Learning
Editors: A. Kumar Sahoo, C. Pradhan, B. Shankar Prasad Mishra et al.
ISBN: 979-8-89113-342-6

phishing threats by implementing the approaches of machine learning. Also, a brief summary of current resolutionwhich can better defend the users' of OSN privacy, safety, and protection is discussed. The experimental result demonstrates that after implementing the feature selection methods (FSM) like Information Gain (IG), Chi-square and Anova test on the phishing dataset, the significant features so created able to evaluate the machine learning classifiers such as k-Nearest Neighbor (KNN), Logistic Regression (LR), Decision Tree (DT) and Naïve Bayes (NB) efficiently and obtained the performance in terms of accuracy as 99.7% in KNN classifiers for detecting the phishing threat.

Keywords: machine learning, phishing, threats, online social networks

Introduction

Nowadays, OSNs have helped people through virtual meeting environments in their daily lives to improve communication globally. These networks support users in expanding their global connections and making new friends. Sharing ideas and information is another crucial aspect of OSNs. With the aid of the OSNs, users can exchange photographs, videos, interests, applications, recent activities, and much more [1]. OSN usage has dramatically increased during the past few years. The basic purpose of social networking websites is that users spend the majority of their time updating their stuffing, interacting with existing users, and browsing other users' accounts to locate specific data. Attacks on OSN users are more likely when OSN is more widely used. Most of the OSNs users disclose their personal information, which invites the attacker to engage in specific malicious behavior [2].

As the users store a substantial quantity of personal data on OSNs, it becomes an enviable target for intruders. Utilizing the OSNs, adversaries can gather user confidential information. Furthermore, because of the high user activity, attackers are invited as confidential information is regularly exchanged on those networks. Users are required to submit personal information to OSNs sites, including name, birth details, gender, interest, permanent address, educational background, birthplace, bank information, and some other sensitive information about themselves. The more data a person broadcasts, the more data an adversary will acquire. Some of the more important information like bank account information and passwords about the user can be indirectly revealed by the users even though they did not post this information on the network. This knowledge might be used by adversaries to carry out a significant network crime [3]. To solve these issues, we have adopted a machine learning technique to predict the phishing links efficiently. So, the contributions made by this study are more precisely as follows: We begin by outlining the OSN threats that are directed at all social network users, with a special emphasis on kids and teens. Second, we demonstrate a machine learning method for phishing attack detection. Our experimental result demonstrated that after using the appropriate feature selection procedure, able to obtain the significant features which when evaluated by the different machine learning estimators gives the best performance of 99.7% accuracy in detecting the phishing threats. Finally, we suggest easy-to-implement suggestions for OSN users to follow in order to increase their protection. The principal contribution of this research could be summarized as follows:

- We provide various OSNs security and privacy threats and their detection and prevention methods.
- Also, predicted the phishing threats in OSNs using machine learning techniques. We implemented the FSM like IG, Chi-square and Anova test on the phishing dataset and used machine learning classifiers efficiently.
- This research also gives a brief summary of current solutions that can better protect the OSN users' privacy.

The remaining part of the research is described as follows. We provide basic information for OSN security, OSN threats, and brief overview of phishing attack in section 2. Sections 3 explain the related works on different attacks. In Section 4, we discuss how phishing attacks popular all over the globe. And how to detect phishing attack and proposed methodology described by us in section 6. Section 7, mostly describes about the solution to prevent phishing attack. In Section 8, we provide some best practices to safeguard your system, account, and information for user knowledge. In section 9, conclusion and some future aspects based on the current threats are discuseed.

Preliminaries

OSN is now the fastest technology with the most slashing Smartphone features. OSN consumers have been constantly rising on a global scale day by day which is evident from the recent statista survey reportrepresented in Figure 1, where the number of OSN users who are actively using various OSNs worldwide.

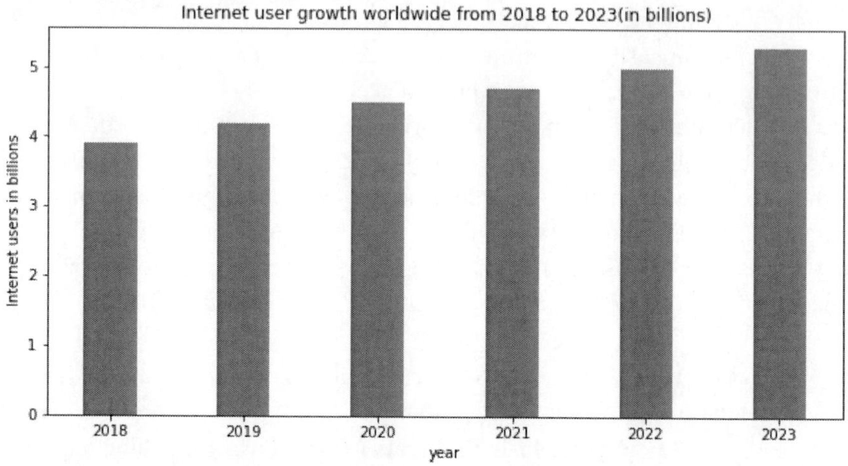

Figure 1. Analysis of Internet user growth from 2018 to 2023.

OSN is a fantastic platform for disseminating information about goods, companies, and services. If a follower enjoys a specific item you sell, they might share those pages with their contacts, which will foster stronger relationships with and loyalty from your customers. The developer interacts directly with the clients through the process of gaining client insights, asking them about the features they would like and gathering input on new concepts. By setting goals and posting regularly, users of any product can come to expect more from developers. Therefore, it's crucial to create an agenda for those goods and keep followers updated on it.

Adversaries have intensely targeted a huge number of users with various attack types, including malware, phishing, clickjacking, false profiles, spamming, and more [4, 5]. Compared to other social networking sites, Facebook faces more threats because of its larger user base and more flexible operation restrictions [6]. Similarly, the attacker's next objectives are Twitter and Instagram. According to the study [2, 7, 8], a huge percentage of users browse websites with porn and erotic content. The best method for the attacker to access that system via that site is through it. The parental control over that website is implemented to protect the system and information.

OSN Threats

The rising usage of OSNs forces the users to expose themselves to threats to their security and privacy. These threats are categorized into 4 broad groups which are explained in Figure 2. The first consists of classical threats such as threats of privacy and security. The second comprises modern threats, that are mostly unique to the environment of OSNs, and which uses the OSN infrastructure to endanger user privacy and security and the third one contains special social threats, where today's attacker specially attacks children. And the fourth category is combination threats, which is the merger of classical and modern threats.

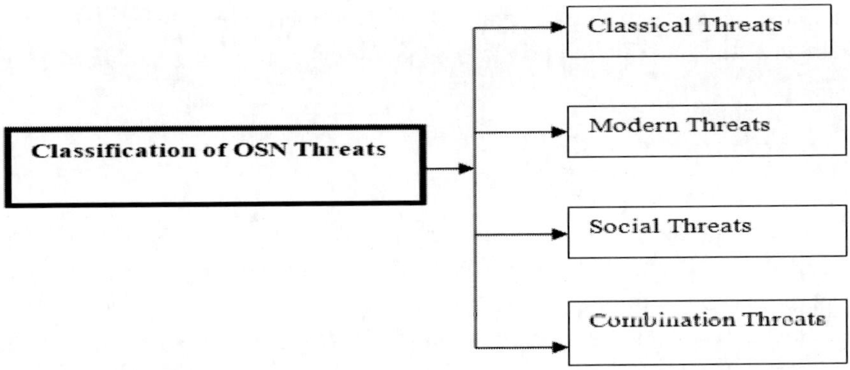

Figure 2. Classification of OSN Threats.

Classical Threats

The OSN's structure and functionality allow for the quick spread of classical threats among users in the network. By obtaining the user's personal information, classical threats frequently impact the user's profile and credentials. When a person mistakenly acts on that malignant link or code, it can spread among users. This threat has obtained the user's login information, allowing it to send messages on the user's behalf and alter personal content. Since the internet started to be used extensively, classical threats have been an issue. They continue to be a problem and are frequently known as spam, cross-site scripting (XSS) assaults, or phishing and malware. Despite the fact that these threats have previously been addressed, OSNs' structure and nature have made them more viral and able to spread rapidly among network users.

Modern Threats

These threats are very specific to the environments of OSNs. The personal information of users as well as the personal information of their contacts is typically the target of these threats. For instance, a hacker attempting to access the school's name of a Facebook user's which is only visible to the user's friends can establish a forgedsketch with the necessary information and send the targeted user a friend request. The user's information will be made available to the attacker if he or she accepts the friend invitation. Another option is for the attacker to gather information from the user's friends and use an inference attack to deduce the identity of the school's name from the information gathered from the user's friends. The following provides examples of current threats and situations where they have seriously endangered the security and privacy of OSN users.

Social Threats

The threats used by intruders to hassle and trail the people who are using OSNs are called social threats. Young users, primarily teenagers, are the primary target of this sort of threat. Young children and adolescents both encountered. The attackers typically harass a target on social media through mail and instant messaging. Through their pictures, OSN users repeatedly reveal location-based information. By using content-based retrieval techniques, an adversary can collect this information and use it later to carry out risky social engineering attacks.

Combination Threats

Attackers of today have the ability to combine both classical and modern threats to launch a more complex assault. For instance, a hacker could use a phishing attack to obtain the Facebook password of a target user, then post a message on the target user's timeline that contains a clickjacking attack [5], tricking the user's Facebook friends into clicking the message and downloading a hidden virus onto their own computers. Be aware that the recovery procedures for threats from the past and the present are different. It is typically possible to recover from a classical assault, such as a virus, by simply reinstalling the operating system, updating the passwords, and canceling the impacted credit cards. But resetting personal information takes too long and is occasionally impossible, more effort must be made in order to pull through from a modern OSN attack like we could alter our email address, but changing our home location would be much more difficult.

Phishing Attack

Phishing is a type of social engineering attack that is regularly engaged to whip the information of people, such as credit card details and login ID. It occurs when an intruder misleads a target to open an email, instant message, or text message by misrepresenting themselves as a trustworthy source. By using web pages that look visually similar to an authentic site, phishers frequently take advantage of users' confidence in a site's appearance. Users might reveal their passwords, for instance, if a criminal requested them to update via an HTTP link. This phishing detection survey was started because the phishing issue is so widespread [9].

Phishing attacks are primarily caused by deceptive emails, a lack of user awareness, a lack of secure desktop tools, vulnerabilities in applications and browsers, a lack of strong authentication on websites of banks and financial institutions, among other factors. These factors lead to financial loss for the original institutions as well as internet fraud, identity theft, erosion of public trust in the internet, and other problems. As a result, early detection and prevention of this attack are necessary because it is currently the leading attack in the world. The overall phishing cycle is explained in Figure 3 where the occurrence of phishing is represented. Phishing damages e-commerce and online finance, among other sectors. There are several methods available to protect users from phishing attacks such as heuristic approach, rule-based approach and machine learning based approach. Among all the methods used to identify phishing websites, supervised ML algorithms are the effective methods used for classification.

Machine Learning (ML): A machine can learn on its own without being explicitly programmed using a learning method called machine learning. It is an application of Artificial Intelligence that has the ability to learn automatically, to perform their job skillfully and improve from the experience [10]. The objective of learning is to generate a model that receives the input and produces the required output. It can be broadly classified into three categories according to the kind of data they require.

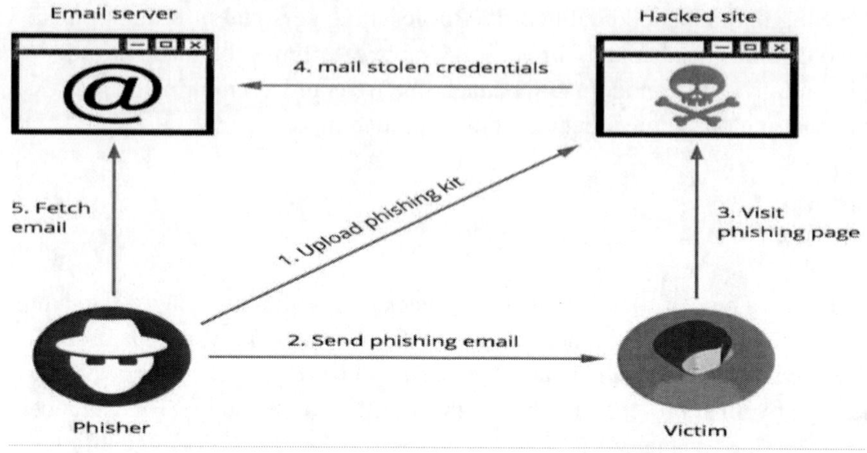

Figure 3. Phishing Lifecycle.

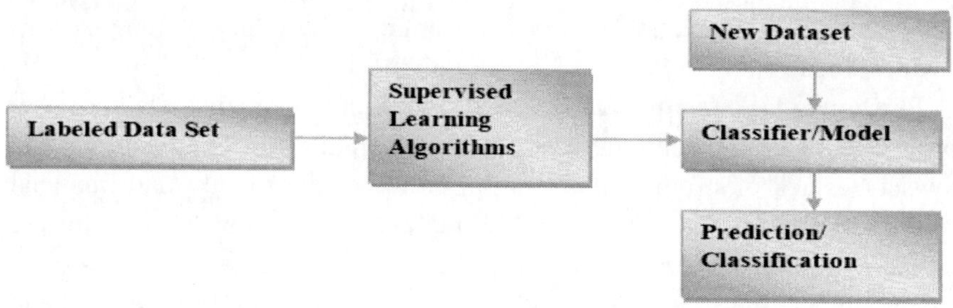

Figure 4. Working principle of Supervised learning algorithms.

Supervised Learning: In supervised learning, predictions are made using a labeled or training dataset. The input and output data from the training sample are combined to create a training example. Each training sample present in the training data has a label or tag in the output vector [11]. The model or the classifier is trained with the labeled data and if the training accuracy is acceptable then tested with new dataset or unknown data to generate the class labels which is represented in Figure 4. Two important techniques that come under supervised machine learning are regression and classification.

In the context of threat detection of OSNs, we have used the supervised machine learning classifiers like KNN (K-Nearest Neighbor), LR (Logistic Regression), DT (Decision Tree), NB (Naïve Bayes) that uses a known dataset (training set) to classify the link as phishing or non-phishing.

Literature Reviews

Several researchers have conducted a related survey on OSNs in the past as shown below. Researchers and academicians from various fields discuss various threats to users and their work on social network platforms, as well as their solutions.

In [12], the researchers have explained about a variety of applications and functionalities of OSNs. Additionally, they focused on a number of factors that put into the growth of the model, including a business viewpoint, difficulties, and risks related to the social network platform. The different OSN-related threats and solutions have been discussed in [1] where the authors presented different security solutions based on academicians and researchers, along with potential future research areas. Also, the various computational methods for incongruity identification basing upon the user behavior and shared data is elaborated on and analyzed in [13]. Static and dynamic anomalies are separated into named and unlabeled categories. The authors recommended for the detection of anomalies derived from network structures and noted in feature space. The authors of [14] explained an overview of different problems relating to privacy and safety in OSN. They discussed different classification of attacks along with some current mitigation techniques for social network platforms. In [15], the authors discussed different methods for maintaining privacy. A number of factors were used to compare their survey to others. The authors presented a few overheads and their benefits in accordance with the privacy management policies. By examining recent and existing technical contributions, the authors described different fake detection frameworks in OSNs [16]. In [17], different identification methods of XSS attacks are elaborated. The authors also discuss a number of advantages and disadvantages of XSS attacks on social network platforms, as well as a number of existing gaps. In [18, 19] described the classification of OSN threats and solutions and some defense mechanisms too. In [20], the authors have described a general solution of the attack detection problem using machine learning tools.

However, not all of the threats and research solutions associated with the social network platform have been covered by the various surveys illustrated by various authors. Our survey identified several recent OSN threats, including those that impact user performance and accounts. After analyzing, we identified phishing as the riskiest attack and detect phishing attacks in OSNs. We also go over some practical advice that can be used by users to safeguard their accounts, networks, and private data.

Discussion

The various types of attacks covered in section 3 are indicative of the well-known threats existing on the OSN platform and are depicted in Table 1.

Table 1. Comparison of most popular attacks across the globe

Measure	Social bots	Phishing	Spamming	Malware
Difficulty in attack	Hard	Easy	Easy	Hard
Threat to User	Medium	High	Low	High
Defence by Server	Yes	No	Yes	Yes
Defence by User	No	Yes	No	Yes

After analyzing different major popular attacks in Table 1, we found that phishing is the leading attack around the globe and the remaining three attacks are defended by the server but phishing could not.

- According to the IBM report, phishing was one of the top attack vectors in cybercrime at 16%.
- According to the FBI report, in 2021 nearly 83% of companies experienced phishing attacks and an extortion of over 33 million records is expected to occur by 2023.
- Phishing sites are 75% higher in presence compare to malware sites,

So, it's important to detect and know the safety measures of phishing attacks in OSNs.

Proposed Methodology

This section comes up with a comprehensive discourse of our suggested procedure to single out the phishing website. As classifying phishing threats depends on the relevant features, dataset and data pre-processing technique, therefore, we have discussed five stages and are represented in Figure 5.

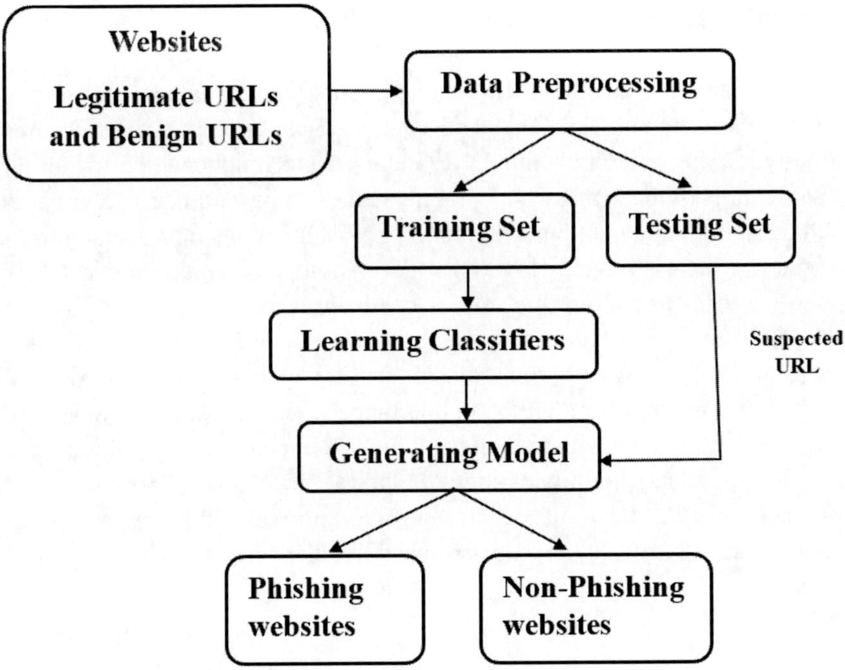

Figure 5. Proposed Framework.

Dataset

For differentiating the suggested system, we have attempted to find a globally accepted dataset and picking of datasets has an important impact over standard of classification. For building admissible or stabilized datasets, two classes of URLs are needed: legitimate and phishing URL. The dataset is collected from internet sources like kaggle database which is composed of both phishing and non-phishing websites, and it has 10,000 records and 50 numbers of features. The dataset comprises of 5000 phishing links and 5000 non-phishing links. It has had the lexical based features or Structural based features, page content features. Hence, we have collected a considerable dataset with high efficiency, and it outperformed the results. A snapshot of the dataset is shown in Figure 6.

Feature Extraction and Scaling

Numerous approaches are utilized in extracting the relevant features for identifying the phishing link. In this chapter, we have brought out the features randomly relating to the phishing URL and used a technique which will bring all the features in the same scale. Feature scaling is needed because variable which is having large magnitude in this case phishing will suppress the impact of variable which is having less magnitude. So, to prevent this mismatch to happen we want to capture the impact of all the variables and the distance between the feature columns are computed to scale the feature on the same scale so that all the values of the variables will fall within the range 0 to 1 and -1 to 1 and all the numbers will be in that range when we compute some kind of distance or run some anomaly algorithm. Two types of feature scaling are available in data preprocessing methods like standardization and normalization. We have used the min-max normalization technique of machine learning to scale the data and make free the dataset from outliers and null values.

Feature Selection

The feature selection or attribute selection plays a major role in predicting the phishing threats in OSNs. When the raw data is generated and that data is brought to the training phase, it gives very low efficiency because the data has number of features and may not be relevant to obtain the objective of classifying phishing threats. Therefore, an efficient feature selection methodology is required to design an accurate model to achieve the objective and gives the best performance in terms of accuracy. In this research, the mutual information gain and chi-square test of filter method is adopted because it does not use the machine learning classifier for evaluating the relevance of feature rather these methods utilized some statistical procedure to find the informative features hence, incurs less training time and works well even for large number of dataset, in contrary to it's complement method wrapper based feature selection technique where machine learning classifiers are used to find the significant features which is a more time consuming process. The informative features which are filtered out in mutual information gain are represented in Figure 7.

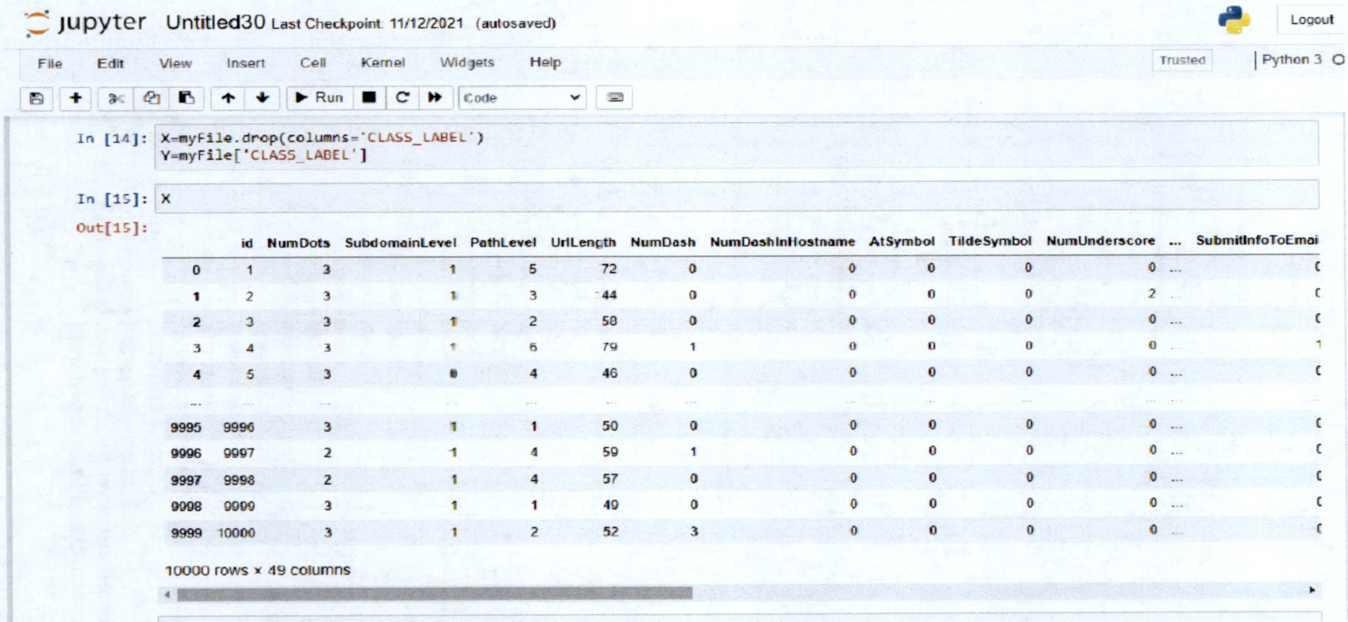

Figure 6. A snapshot of phishing dataset.

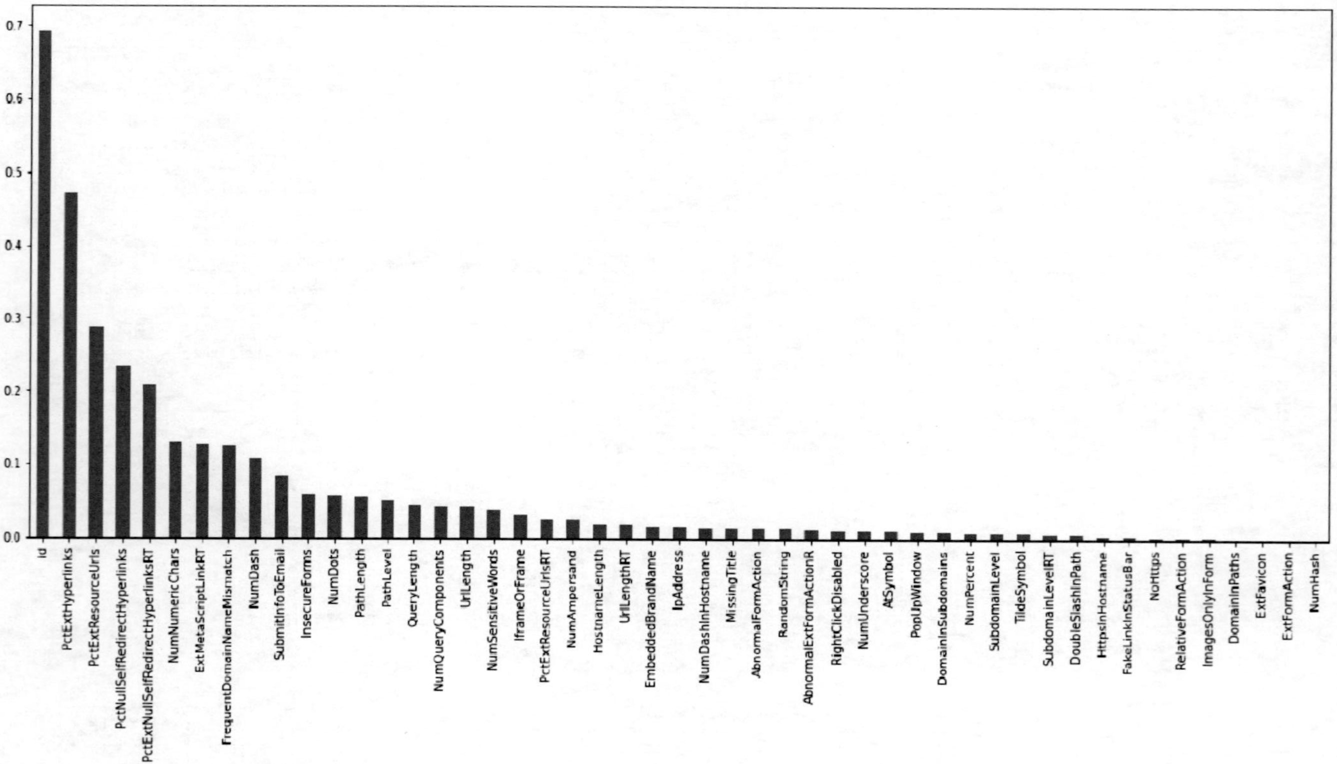

Figure 7. Image of relevant features frequency graph.

Model Building and Training

We conducted a model selection approach by evaluating the relevant phishing features so obtained from feature selection process in section III. The dataset is divided into a ratio of 80:20 where 80% of the dataset is used for training/validation and the remaining 20% (the holdout half) is utilized for testing. In order to maintain the same ratio of classes in both the training and testing data, each train/test split is carried out in a stratified way so that the model can work in a generalized way.

Evaluation

We first took the dataset from the website, tried the suggested procedure, and then compared it to other detection procedures to see if the website was a phishing website or not. This is a form of methodical, disciplined research to confirm the validity of the procedure. 10,000 samples overall are included in the dataset, 5000 of which are from phishing websites and 5000 from genuine websites. The abundance and complexity of the samples in datasets not only increase the reliability of comparisons between various methods, but also guarantee that the suggested model can fulfil detection requirements in the actual network environment. In our chapter the proposed procedures we first pre-processed the data by checking the null values. After that we done the train-test split for evaluating the performance of the different algorithms. By the usage of static analysis approach, the classification of URL is done by some effective and discriminative features. We have used different evaluating approaches for the performance of the classification model.

Experimental Results

Numerous tests have been conducted by implementing machine learning classification algorithms such as logistic regression (LR), K-Nearest Neighbour (KNN), Decision Tree (DT), Gaussian Naive Bayes (NB). Each of the tests were ciphered and done with python accompanied by its packages such as matplotlib, pandas, numpy, seaborn, Scikit-learn and many more alluring and comprehensible presentation of the flow of the code can be build. Then we differentiate the performance of the four machine learning classifiers.

The relevant features are selected by using filter methods which are explained as:

Filter Methods: Compared to wrapper approaches, filter techniques are quicker and more computationally efficient even in high-dimensional data [21, 22]. Hence, we have adopted the filter method for extracting significant features for detecting phishing threats. The different types of features selection techniques of filter methods are Information gain (IG), Chi-square test, Anova test and correlation-based feature selection techniques etc. In this chapter, the IG, Chi-square test, Anova test of filter methods are used for selecting the phishing features in OSNs.

Information Gain

It determines the entropy loss caused by transforming a dataset. By assessing each variable of information gain in reference to the goal variable, it can be used for feature selection.

Chi-Square Test

A dataset's categorical characteristics are analyzed using the Chi-square. By calculating the chi-square between each feature and the desired outcome, we can choose the optimal number of features [23]. For evaluating the informative features formula 1 is used in Chi-square test.

$$x^2 = \sum \frac{(O_i - E_i)}{E_i} \quad (1)$$

where x^2 represents the chi-square result
O_i indicates the observed value and
E_i says the expected value

Anova Test

A statistical technique called analysis of variance is used to determine whether the means of two or more groups vary significantly from one another.

These feature selection methods are employed on the dataset to find the relevant features and the machine learning classifiers like KNN, DT, LR and NB are evaluated using the significant features obtained from the filter methods. From the table 2, it is evident that the classifiers KNN and DT provides best performance of 99.7% in terms of accuracy by the features obtained from IG method of filter feature selection technique to detect the phishing and non-phishing URL.

Table 2. Performance of classifiers after using feature selection techniques

Classifiers / Methods	KNN	LR	DT	NB
Information Gain	99.7%	96.3%	99.7%	92.9%
Chi-square	62.35%	69.55%	69.55%	62.35%
Anova	99.7%	97.4%	99.7%	96.25%

Solutions to Phishing Attack

Phishing Protector: A Firefox add-on called Phishing Protector alert users of online social networking sites when suspicious activity is discovered.

Recommendation

OSN users are exposed to a wide range of common security and privacy threats, as this research has shown. Fortunately, there are numerous software options and strategies available right now that can help OSN users to efficiently protect themselves against threats. We advise OSN users to adopt the following seven recommendations in their OSN accounts if they want to better protect themselves on these platforms:

Act like puzzled – In the modern environment, OSN is the greatest source for information sharing and business communication. An OSN is used by people to discuss recent news, events, and activities. Sometimes, attackers circulate malicious contents in the network also. So, do not trust solely the information provided on the website. Use various sources to correctly verify the message before clicking on that news or event. Sometimes, malicious software is automatically downloaded into your system when a user clicks on that action.

Don't Accept Friend Requests from Strangers - As is well known, fake profiles are common and rottenly hazardous. As a result, we advise users to ignore friend requests they receive from people they don't know. We advise OSN users to occasionally review their friend list and remove friends they don't know.

Security and privacy settings – To secure their website and user behavior, each OSN site has its own security and privacy settings. Make sure the security options are correct before using the website. You might receive installation instructions from some social networking sites. Some services enable you to share various types of content while restricting your security settings for specific activities like sharing pictures with others.

Set strong passwords – Always try to use strong and secure passwords. Use a different password if your date of birth or its sequential digits are the same as your password. The password should, if at all possible, be a mixture of alphabets, special characters, numerals and symbols. Always attempt to use a password management tool or include a password hint to securely store the passwords in order to help you remember them. Avoid using simple passwords that are easy to predict, such as your name, birthday, or other personal information. The information that is made publicly accessible on the network is frequently used by attackers to guess the password.

Secure your password – You shouldn't share your password with anyone. Before inputting your password check the website carefully. In some instances, an attacker makes a duplicate copy of that website and disseminates it using a phishing scam. A fake profile assault or cloning attack is other names for it. Before performing any type of action or entering your information, make sure the website's original source is verified. It's wise to regularly change your passwords and log in to the initial server from a clean computer.

Always tread carefully – Some online profiles of individuals don't match their aesthetic. On social networking sites, the individuals you follow might just be other users or staff. Some attackers create an account that looks exactly like their friend's to gather information about the individual or office details. Verify the profile information and shared friends with anyone whose friend request you intend to approve.

Don't share irrelevant Information - We suggest OSN users go over the information they've entered and delete unnecessary details about themselves, their family, and their friends. To avoid implication attacks, it is also advised that users, if at all possible, conceal their friend list.

Conclusion

The "big picture" of the current significant attacks and phishing attack detection are presented in this research. The offerings made by this study are more precisely as follows: We begin by outlining the OSN threats that are directed at all social network users, with a special emphasis on kids and teens. Second, we demonstrate a machine learning method for phishing attack detection. Our experimental result demonstrated that after using the appropriate feature selection procedure, able to obtain the significant features which when evaluated by the different machine learning estimators gives the best performance of 99.7% accuracy in detecting the phishing threats. Finally, we suggest easy-to-implement suggestions for OSN users to follow in order to increase their protection and privacy when using social networks.

Future Aspects

OSN safety and privacy is an up-and-coming research platform because information sharing on it is so well-liked by users. Security experts consistently develop more effective ways to counter OSN threats and uncover new threats that have an impact on user behavior. However, OSN still has some issues that need to be found and fixed. Phishing attacks are currently the greatest problem in the OSN network. Particularly many social media users are currently being attacked by fake profiles. We require a correct and improved framework that acknowledges the fake account in the network in order to recognize a fake profile in the network. Posting advertisements from various third-party solutions that contain some harmful websites is another problem. The user will be redirected to various sites when they participate. Finding the malicious text on that link and blocking the third-party advertising on that link are both difficult tasks in OSNs. Furthermore, no solution explains the OSN system's performance following the implementation of security measures. The fake website attack is an additional attack in the present situation. Also, there are a lot of assaults. But since phishing attacks are the biggest problem, we only identified them in our paper. In the future, we'll work to identify every significant attack that OSN users have experienced in daily life.

References

[1] Fire, M., Goldschmidt, R., Elovici, Y. Online social networks: threats and solutions. *IEEE CommunicationsSurveys & Tutorials* (2014) *16*(4), 2019-2036.

[2] Kefi, H., Perez, C. *Dark Side of Online Social Networks: Technical, Managerial, and Behavioral Perspectives*; (2018).

[3] Boshmaf, Y., Muslukhov, I., Beznosov, K., Ripeanu, M. The social bot network: when bots socialize for fame and money.In *Proceedings of the 27th annual computer security applications conference* (2011) pp: 93-102.

[4] James, N. https://www.getastra.com/blog/security-audit/cyber-crime-statistics/ (2023).

[5] Shamsi, J. A., Hameed, S., Rahman, W., Zuberi, F., Altaf, K., Amjad, A. Clicksafe: Providing security against clickjacking attacks. *IEEE 15th International Symposium on High-Assurance Systems Engineering* (2014) pp:206-210.

[6] Diego, C. Facebook PhishingProtector. [Online]. Available: https://addons.mozilla.org/en- US/firefox/addon/facebook-phishingprotector/.

[7] Taylor, P. https://www.statista.com/statistics/ (2023).

[8] Unuchek, R. SECURELIST. *Kaspersky Lab.* (2017) *28*.

[9] Mahajan, R., Siddavatam, I. Website detection using machine learning algorithms. *International Journal of Computer Applications* (2018) *181*(23):45-47.

[10] Sahu, L., Mohanty, S., Mohapatra, S. K., Acharya, A. A. Malignant Web Sites Recognition Utilizing Distinctive Machine Learning Techniques. In *Computer Networks, Big Data and IoT* (2021) pp:497-506.

[11] Mohammed, M., Khan, M. B., Bashier E. B. M. *Machine learning: algorithms and applications*; (2016) CRC Press.

[12] Heidemann, J., Klier, M., Probst, F. Online social networks: A survey of a global phenomenon. *Computer Networks* (2012) *56*(18):3866-3878.

[13] Savage, D., Zhang, X., Yu, X., Chou, P., Wang, Q. Anomaly detection in online social networks. *Social networks* (2014) *39*:62-70.

[14] Kayes, I., Iamnitchi, A. A survey on privacy and security in online social networks. *Information Sciences* (2015) *arXiv preprint arXiv:1504.03342*.

[15] De Salve, A., Mori, P., Ricci, L. A survey on privacy in decentralized online social networks. *Computer Science Review* (2018) 27:154-176.

[16] Ramalingam, D., Chinnaiah, V. Fake profile detection techniques in large-scale online social networks: A comprehensive review. *Computers & Electrical Engineering* (2018) *65*:165-177.

[17] Sarmah, U., Bhattacharyya, D. K., Kalita, J. K. A survey of detection methods for XSS attacks. *Journal of Network and Computer Applications* (2018) *118*:113-143.

[18] Gupta, B. B., Sangaiah, A. K., Nedjah, N., Yamaguchi, S., Zhang, Z., Sheng, M. Recent research in computational intelligence paradigms into security and privacy for online social networks (OSNs). *Future Generation Computer Systems* (2018) 86:851-854.

[19] Sahoo, S. R., Gupta, B. B. Classification of various attacks and their defense mechanism in online social networks: a survey. *Enterprise Information Systems* (2019) *13*(6):832-864.

[20] Berghout, T., Benbouzid, M., Muyeen, S. M. Machine learning for cybersecurity in smart grids: A comprehensive review-based study on methods, solutions, and prospects. *International Journal of Critical Infrastructure Protection* (2022) 10054715.

[21] Chiew, K. L., Tan, C. L., Wong, K, Yong, K. S., Tiong, W. K. A new hybrid ensemble featureselectionframework for machine learning-based phishing detection system. *Information Sciences*(2019) 484:153-166.

[22] Mohanty, S., Achary, A, A., Sahu L. Improving Suspicious URL Detection through Ensemble Machine Learning Techniques. In *Society 5.0 and the Future of Emerging Computational Technologies* (2022) pp:229-248. CRC Press.

[23] Mohanty, S., Sahoo, M., & Acharya, A, A. Predicting Phishing URL Using Filter based Univariate Feature Selection Technique. In *2022 Second International Conference on Computer Science, Engineering and Applications (ICCSEA),* IEEE, (2022) pp. 1-5.

Chapter 6

A Novel Approach to Detecting Apple Disease Using CNN

Chittaranjan Pradhan
Mritunjay Kumar
Divyansi Mishra
and Biswaroop Nath
School of Computer Engineering, Kalinga Institute of Industrial Technology, Odisha, India

Abstract

The loss caused by apple disease is a primary concern in countries that produce apples in high numbers. This study presents a solution to tackle the problem by developing a model that employs both deep learning and transfer learning methodologies. The model was trained on a dataset of about 10000 images categorized into four classes, namely healthy, black rot, cedar apple rust, and apple scab. The research presented in this paper involves testing different combinations of activation functions and optimizers to identify the most effective one for our customized model. Furthermore, the dataset was also assessed using transfer learning models such as ResNet50 and DenseNet121. The custom model produced the highest accuracy rate of 98.49% when utilizing the Adam optimizer and ReLU activation function. As for the transfer learning models, DenseNet121 attained the precision of 95.4%, while ResNet50 yielded the highest accuracy rate of 99.5%.

Keywords: apple disease, convolutional neural network, deep learning

In: Building Intelligent Systems Using Machine Learning and Deep Learning
Editors: A. Kumar Sahoo, C. Pradhan, B. Shankar Prasad Mishra et al.
ISBN: 979-8-89113-342-6

Introduction

Food safety is mainly dependent on agriculture, which also holds a considerable share of the global economy. Nevertheless, environmental deterioration has caused a rise in the incidence of plant diseases in recent years. This has resulted in substantial losses for the global agricultural industry. However, manually inspecting trees for disease diagnosis is a challenging, expensive, and time-consuming process. Apples are currently one of China's crucial crops and fruits from an economic standpoint, with the largest cultivation area and production worldwide [1]. Nevertheless, diseases affecting apple leaves can cause substantial economic losses, as well as reductions in both the quantity and quality of fruit produced by the industry [2]. As a result, there is a high need for reliable methods of apple leaf disease identification.

In recent years, there have been advancements in using traditional machine learning methods to detect apple leaf disease. Researchers have investigated the use of standard machine learning algorithms, including random forest, k-nearest neighbor, and Support Vector Machine (SVM), to diagnose plant diseases automatically and enhance accuracy and efficiency [3, 4]. However, these techniques have limitations as they rely on human experience for feature selection and are vulnerable to artificial feature selection. A novel area of study in agricultural information technology has emerged, referred to as the deep convolutional neural network approach, to overcome these constraints. This approach offers various advantages, including direct input of images into the model and shared weights that enhance performance while minimizing memory usage. Convolutional neural networks have demonstrated potential in recognizing patterns and are considered among the leading techniques for identifying disease images at an early stage. In the field of crop disease detection, Convolutional Neural Networks (CNNs) are widely researched and applied, as they have been found to improve recognition accuracy and eliminate the need for image preprocessing, motivated by the favorable outcomes of CNN in image-based recognition [5, 6].

The study outlines a novel method for diagnosing apple leaf diseases using a CNN-based approach and transfer learning. The upcoming sections will delve into previous studies carried out by experts who have developed solutions to address the issue outlined in the preceding paragraphs. Additionally, we will examine our model's flow chart, tabulated outcomes, and compare our findings with other comparable studies.

Deep Learning

Over the last several years, there has been a significant increase in the application of machine learning (ML) across multiple fields including text analysis, spam identification, video suggestions, image categorization, and retrieval of multimedia concepts. Deep learning (DL), also known as "representation learning" (RL), is a commonly employed machine learning (ML) technique for these objectives [6, 7].

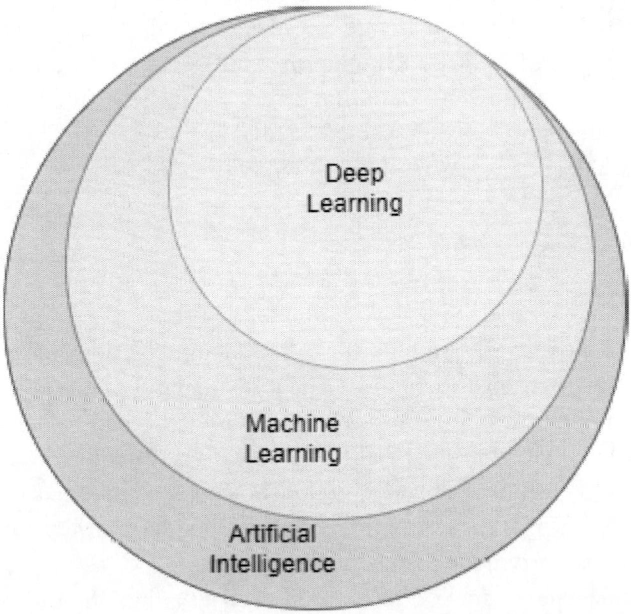

Figure 1. An Overview of Artificial Intelligence, Machine Learning and Deep Learning [8]

Deep learning (DL) is a branch of machine learning (ML) that imitates the way human brains process information (as shown in Fig 1). Unlike traditional rule-based programming, DL uses large sets of data to create models that can classify or identify patterns in new inputs. These models are built using artificial neural networks (ANNs) consisting of multiple layers of algorithms that extract and interpret different features of the input data.

Convolutional Neural Network (CNN) Model

Convolutional Neural Network (CNN) refers to a particular category of neural network, which is frequently utilized in the analysis of visual images. CNNs are especially helpful for applications like picture segmentation, object detection, and classification. The basic element of CNN architecture is the convolutional layer. This layer is responsible for performing a mathematical operation called "convolution," which involves multiplying and adding up the elements of a small matrix (filter) with the input image. This process is repeated throughout the input image to create a feature map. Convolutional Neural Networks (CNNs) usually employ multiple convolutional layers as their primary layer, followed by pooling layers that decrease the feature map's dimensions, and then fully connected layers that execute classification or regression tasks.

Optimizers

Deep learning models rely on algorithms to make predictions based on new, unseen data and attempt to generalize patterns using a given algorithm. To map inputs to outputs, an optimization algorithm is needed to determine the parameter values (weights) that minimize error. The effectiveness of a deep learning model is heavily impacted by the choice of the optimization method or optimizer [9]. The choice of optimization method or optimizer also affects the speed at which the model can be trained.

An optimizer is a function or method used to adjust the properties of a neural network, such as weights and learning rates, intending to reduce total loss and increase precision. Choosing the correct weights for a deep-learning model can be difficult due to the sheer number of parameters involved. As a result, selecting an optimization algorithm that is tailored to the specific task at hand is of utmost importance.

Few optimizers are used.

a) SGD (Stochastic Gradient Descent)

Stochastic Gradient Descent is an iterative method used to optimize an objective function that has enough smoothness properties (such as being differentiable or sub differentiable). It is regarded as a stochastic approximation of gradient descent optimization because it substitutes the real gradient, which is calculated from the entire dataset, with a prediction of it that is generated from a randomly selected subset of the data.

b) RMSprop (Root Mean Square Propagation)

RMSProp is an optimization algorithm used in deep learning to adjust the learning rate of each parameter according to their gradient magnitudes. It utilizes a running average of the recent gradients to divide the learning rate of weight. RMSProp is a preferred choice in deep learning, especially for image recognition tasks performed by convolutional neural networks (CNNs). It offers faster convergence and better optimization performance than other optimization algorithms.

c) ADAM (Adaptive Moment Estimation)

The enhanced version of stochastic gradient descent is the Adam optimizer. It employs a different approach to adjust learning rates compared to RMSProp. It utilizes the average of the second moments of gradients instead of the average first moment used in RMSProp. This approach calculates the exponential moving average of gradients and square gradients, with the decay rates of these moving averages being controlled by the parameters β1 and β2. Adam optimizer is a widely used optimization algorithm in deep learning, as it provides better convergence and optimization performance than other optimization techniques.

We use some of the optimizers along with different activation functions. The results are shown in section 5.

Activation Functions

Artificial neural networks use activation functions to transform the net inputs into output signals, which are then passed on as input to the next layer in the network. The activation functions are also known as the threshold function or transfer function, which is a mapping from a scalar input to a scalar output that has a crucial function in the neural network. The output of the activation function is known as unit activations, which serve as the basic components of a neural network.

Few activation functions to know about:

a) Sigmoid

Given that it is non-linear, it is the activation function that is most frequently utilized. The sigmoid function changes values from 0 to 1.

Mathematically it can be expressed as:

f(x) = 1/e-x

The graph is shown in Figure 2 below:

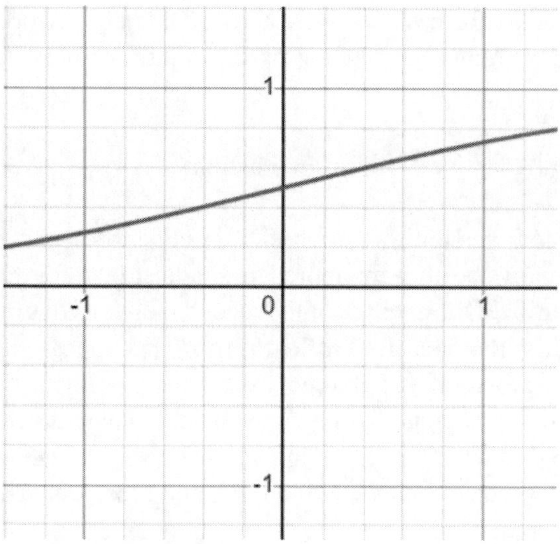

Figure 2. Visualization of Sigmoid Function.

b) ReLU

Rectified linear unit, commonly known as ReLU, is a type of non-linear activation function that is often utilized in neural networks.

Mathematically it can be expressed as:

f(x) = max (0, x)

The graph is shown in Figure (3) below:

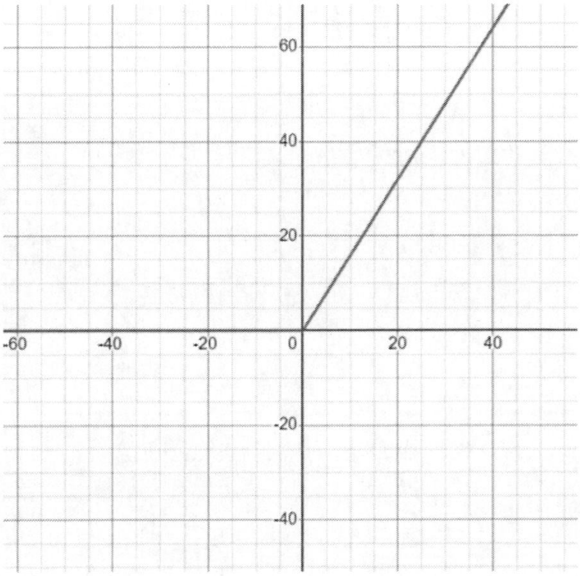

Figure 3. Visualization ReLU Function.

c) LeakyReLU

Leaky ReLU is a variant of the ReLU activation function that is adjusted by introducing a small slope for negative input values, rather than simply setting them to zero. This modification allows for the propagation of a small gradient signal even for negative inputs, which can help improve the training of deep neural networks.

Mathematically it can be expressed as:

$f(x) = 0.01x, x < 0$

$f(x) = x, x >= 0$

The graph is shown in Figure 4 below,

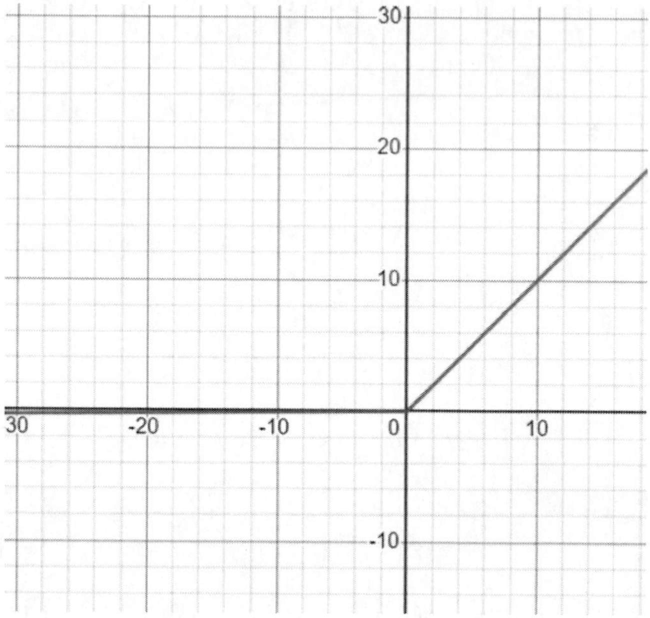

Figure 4. Visualization of LeakyReLU Function.

Transfer Learning

In machine learning, transfer learning is a method that employs an already established model as a basis for a similar undertaking. The insights gained by the model while resolving one issue are applied to another similar problem.

Transfer learning involves utilizing a pre-existing model that has been trained on a related task or a large dataset, rather than creating a new model from scratch, to optimize performance for a new task. The pre-trained model used in transfer learning is usually a deep neural network that has acquired the ability to identify useful features and patterns through training on an extensive dataset, such as ImageNet, for image classification. Our research incorporates two commonly used pre-trained models.

1. ResNet 50

ResNet-50 is a convolutional neural network composed of 50 layers, including 48 convolutional layers, one MaxPool layer, and one average pool layer.

Residual neural networks belong to a category of artificial neural networks that build networks through the combination of residual blocks [10]. The architecture of ResNet 50 has been shown below in Figure 5.

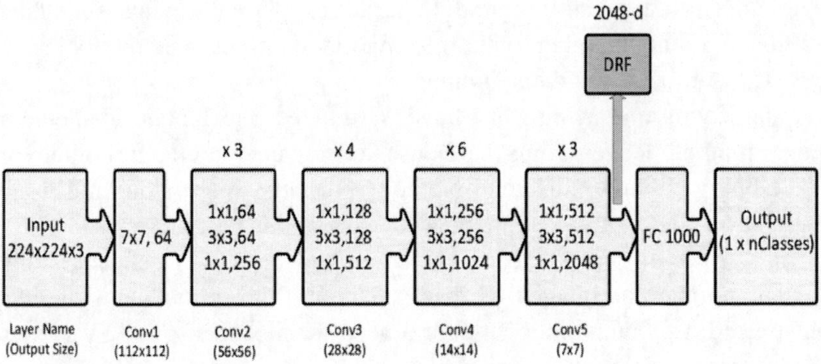

Figure 5. Various layers of Resnet 150 architecture

2. DenseNet 121

DenseNet-121 is a convolutional neural network that includes 120 convolutional layers and four average pooling layers. It is a member of a group of networks called DenseNets, which link each layer to every other layer in a feed-forward manner [11]. The architecture of DenseNet 121 has been shown below in Figure 6.

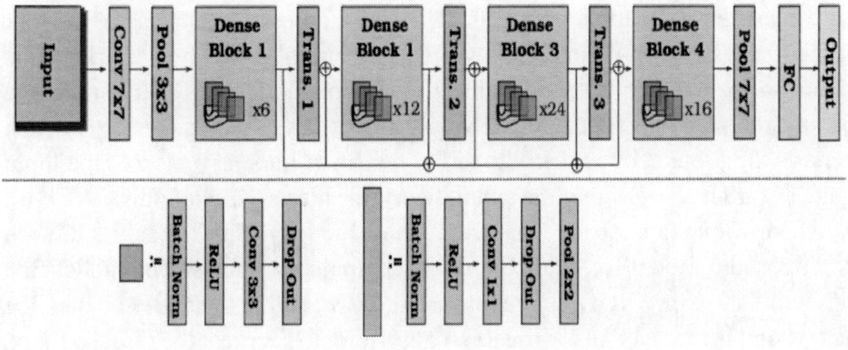

Figure 6. Various layers of Densenet121 architecture.

Literature Review

The latest research articles and publications were examined to incorporate a more up-to-date and effective strategy for the classification issue at hand while maximizing the deep learning model's accuracy. The following is a list of a handfuls of them, together with information on their methodologies, the dataset they utilized, and their findings:

Yong Zhong and Ming Zhao have introduced a technique for detecting diseases in apple leaves using the DenseNet-121 deep convolution network. They employed three different methods, namely regression, multi-label classification, and focus loss function, to achieve this task [12].

Bin Liu et al., have created a technique that involves generating a sufficient number of images of diseased apple leaves and constructing a sophisticated deep convolutional neural network model inspired by AlexNet to detect diseases in apple leaves [13].

Jie Di, and Qing Li came up with a deep learning model named DF-Tiny-YOLO that can quickly and efficiently detect diseases in apple leaves. They reduced the model's computation parameters and increased detection speed by implementing Resize and Re-organization (Reorg) techniques and compressed the convolution kernel to enable feature stacking for feature fusion [14].

According to Sharad Hasan, Sarwar Jahan, and Md. Imdadul Islam, a system based on machine learning and computer vision can be divided into three parts: first, identifying and separating the diseased area; second, extracting relevant characteristics; and third, categorizing the extracted features [15].

Hee-Jin Yu, and Chang-Hwan Son have proposed a novel approach for detecting diseases in apple leaves using a deep Convolutional Neural Network (CNN) that is region-of-interest-aware. Their method involves training two sub networks, namely an encoder-decoder network and a VGG network, in the relevant region of interest. They have also incorporated a fusion layer, which overlays the predicted feature map of the region of interest on top of the input image before feeding it into the sub network for identifying leaf diseases [16].

Zhang Chuanlei, Zhang Shanwen, Yang Jucheng, Shi Yancui, and Chen Jia proposed a model for detecting diseased spots in images. The model first transforms the input RGB image into HSI, YUV, and gray models. Then, the background is removed using the RGA algorithm to segment the diseased spot. Finally, the most valuable features are extracted using a combination of genetic algorithm (GA) and correlation-based feature selection (CFS) [17].

Subham Divakar et al., utilized a technique that entailed applying the SMOTE approach to address dataset imbalances. They then employed the Ensemble algorithm, which incorporates both the F1 score and accuracy to assess performance. Their primary aim was to minimize the number of inaccurate predictions [18].

Again, Dattatraya Vhatkar Shivling et al., used a Beta regression model as a standard equation for the severity of diseases in apples and used a separate model for prediction of the diseases [19].

Kahkashan Perveen et al., suggested a model called DBNet, which is a convolutional neural network with two branches, designed to reduce the impact of environmental factors or lesions on apple leaves that could affect disease diagnosis. The DBNet comprises a multiscale joint and an attention joint, both of which work together as part of the model's branches [20].

Mercelin Francis and C. Deisy utilized a prediction model consisting of four convolutional layers followed by pooling layers, and two fully connected dense layers with a sigmoid function. They incorporated a dropout of 0.2 to avoid overfitting in the model [21].

Proposed Model

Figure 7 shows the image of our model. Each box represents a layer and each layer processes the input and produces an output that is fed into the next layer in a neural network. The Conv2D layer uses a convolution kernel to convolve with the input layer, generating a tensor of outputs.

This output is passed through MaxPooling2D which acts as an input for this layer. The MaxPooling2D layer down samples the input along its spatial dimensions by taking the maximum value for each input channel over a window determined by the pool size. The window is shifted by one step at a time along each dimension. This happens alternately unless the data reaches the Flatten and Dense layer. The Flatten layer transforms the input into a flattened format, without changing the batch size. In contrast, the dense layer in keras contains interconnected neurons, where each neuron receives input from every neuron in the previous layer. This interconnected structure allows for more complex learning and feature representation.

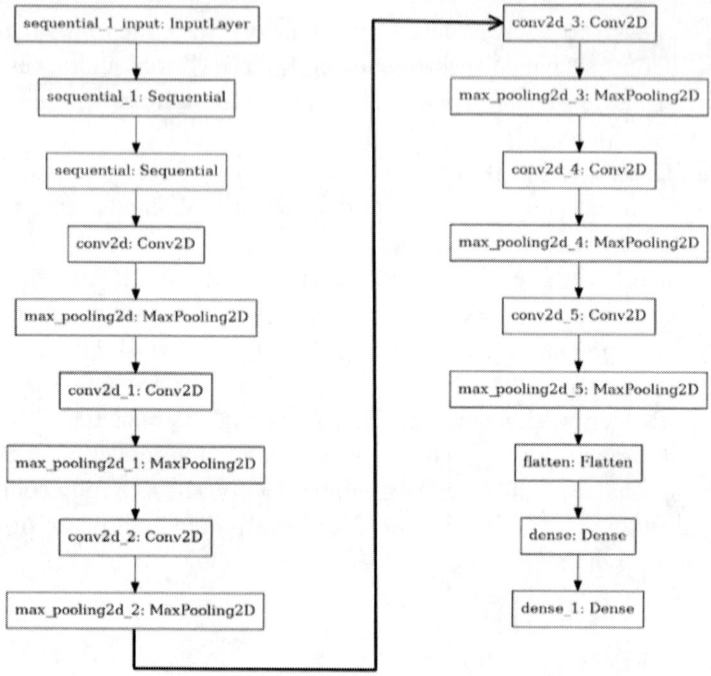

Figure 7. Visualization of different layers of our proposed CNN model/

Observations

Before moving on to the observations let us understand how to use Learning Curves to diagnose machine learning models' performance. When we build a model, there are likely to be 3 cases which are:

a) Under fitting: A case where a model performs poorly on both training as well as testing data.
b) Over fitting: A case where a model performs extremely well on training data but fails to give results on testing data.
c) Good fit: A case where model performance is good on both training and testing data.

Ideally, we desire a good-fit model.

To evaluate the model, we utilized two distinct sets of data. Initially, we partitioned the entire dataset into three parts for training, testing, and validation. The divisions were made in a ratio of 70-15-15 and 80-10-10, respectively.

Table 1. Summary of performance metrics for Adam optimizer

Epochs	Data Division (70-15-15)		Data Division (80-10-10)		Activation Function
	Test Loss	Test Accuracy	Test Loss	Test Accuracy	
50	0.0558	0.9849	0.0806	0.9721	ReLU
50	1.3894	0.25	1.3888	0.2567	Sigmoid
50	0.2031	0.9560	0.0527	0.9824	LeakyReLU

From table 1 we can observe that when adam is used with 'ReLU' or 'LeakyReLU' it gives good results compared to the sigmoid.

Table 2. Summary of performance metrics for RMSprop optimizer in our model

Epochs	Data Division (70-15-15)		Data Division (80-10-10)		Activation Function
	Test Loss	Test Accuracy	Test Loss	Test Accuracy	
50	0.2232	0.9760	0.4778	0.9351	ReLU
50	1.3848	0.2596	1.3848	0.2598	Sigmoid
50	0.2377	0.9670	0.3920	0.9639	LeakyReLU

From table 2 we can see that the best result was obtained for the 70-15-15 split when ReLU was used as activation function along with RMSprop optimizer.

Table 3. Results of loss and accuracy for SGD optimizer

Epochs	Data Division (70-15-15)		Data Division (80-10-10)		Activation Function
	Test Loss	Test Accuracy	Test Loss	Test Accuracy	
50	0.0304	0.9876	0.1034	0.9618	ReLU

In our attempt to implement SGD, we experimented with ReLU activation function, but unfortunately, the results were not satisfactory as we can see in

Table 3. Likewise, when we employed Sigmoid and LeakyReLU activation functions, we encountered a similar outcome. Although the model was trained successfully up to 40 epochs, beyond that point, the accuracy significantly declined, reaching zero accuracy by the 50th epoch. As a consequence, we decided not to include it in our analysis.

Table 4. Results of loss and accuracy for ResNet50 and DenseNet121

Model	Data split	Test Accuracy	Loss	Val Accuracy	Epochs
ResNet50	70-15-15	0.973	0.096	0.971	35
ResNet50	80-10-10	0.995	0.013	0.99	35
DenseNet121	70-15-15	0.929	0.256	0.898	15
DenseNet121	80-10-10	0.954	0.144	0.927	27

Table 4 showcases the results obtained from the transfer learning models ResNet50 and DenseNet121 before applying any image distortions. After introducing random noise to images, the outcomes were collected and organized, as displayed in Table 5. This table presents the results obtained from the transfer learning models ResNet50 and DenseNet121 following the application of image distortions.

Table 5. Results of loss and accuracy for 70-15-15 and 80-10-10 splits

Model	Data split	Test Accuracy	Loss	Val Accuracy	Epochs
ResNet50	70-15-15	0.739	2.810	0.971	35
ResNet50	80-10-10	0.860	0.948	0.99	35
DenseNet121	70-15-15	0.545	5.353	0.898	15
DenseNet121	80-10-10	0.529	7.441	0.927	27

Comparative Analysis

Table 6. Comparison of various model w.r.t. accuracy

Model	Test Accuracy
Proposed Model (CNN)	0.9849
Bin Liu, Yun Zhang's CNN Model [22]	0.9762
Proposed ResNet50	0.995
Proposed DenseNet121	0.954
Yong Zhong Ming Zhao's DenseNet121 Model [12]	0.937
ResNet18[23]	0.972

The ResNet50 model proposed in the study achieved the highest accuracy of 0.995, which was significantly better than the other models considered. Furthermore, the custom CNN model proposed in the study also performed well, achieving an accuracy of 0.9849, which is comparable to transfer learning. This indicates that our custom model is more efficient in terms of training time, as compared to the more complex ResNet50 model. These results and details can be cross-referenced in Table 6. In summary, ResNet50 model exhibited the highest accuracy among the models discussed, while CNN also performed well, although slightly lower. Although more complex models such as ResNet50 and DenseNet121 may yield better accuracy, they may also require longer training times and more intricate model architectures.

Conclusion

The paper introduces a new approach to identifying diseases in apple leaves. The proposed model, which utilized the Adam optimizer and ReLU activation function, demonstrated exceptional performance. Its accuracy on the 70-15-15 dataset split exceeded 98%, surpassing Resnet50's accuracy on the same dataset. Our CNN model was compared with existing work on apple leaf disease identification using deep convolutional neural networks. When applying transfer learning with DenseNet121, we achieved an accuracy of 95.5% on an 80-10-10 split and 92.9% on a 70-15-15 split. Our model performed better on the 80-10-10 split but was similar to the results of a previous study conducted by existing work on apple leaf disease, which achieved a maximum accuracy of 93.71%. To maximize the usefulness of the model for farmers, the authors intend to modify the approach for future use and implement it in a mobile or web-based application.

References

[1] M. Shahbandeh, *Global leading apple-producing countries in 2021/ 2022.*

[2] Siddharth Sharma, Simone Sharma, Anidhya Athaiya; *Activation Functions in Neural Networks.*

[3] Rothe, P. R., & Kshirsagar, R. V. (2015). Cotton leaf disease identification using pattern recognition techniques. In 2015 International Conference on Pervasive Computing (ICPC). 2015 International Conference on Pervasive Computing (ICPC). *IEEE.*

[4] Islam, M., Anh Dinh, Wahid, K., & Bhowmik, P. (2017). Detection of potato diseases using image segmentation and multiclass support vector machine. In 2017 IEEE 30th Canadian Conference on Electrical and Computer Engineering (CCECE). 2017 IEEE 30th Canadian Conference on Electrical and Computer Engineering (CCECE). *IEEE.*

[5] Kawasaki, Y., Uga, H., Kagiwada, S., & Iyatomi, H. (2015). Basic Study of Automated Diagnosis of Viral Plant Diseases Using Convolutional Neural Networks. In *Advances in Visual Computing* (pp. 638–645). Springer International Publishing.

[6] Sarker, I. H. Deep Learning : A Comprehensive Overview on Techniques, Taxonomy, Applications and Research Directions. *SN COMPUT. SCI.* 2, 420 (2021)

[7] Samira Pouyanfar, Saad Sadiq, Yilin Yan, Haiman Tian, Yudong Tao, Maria Presa Reyes, Mei-Ling Shyu, Shu-Ching Chen, S. S. Iyengar; *A Survey on Deep Learning : Algorithms, Techniques, and Applications*, 92 pp 1–36.https://doi.org/10.1145/3234150

[8] Alzubaidi, L., Zhang, J., Humaidi, A. J., Ayad Al-Dujaili, Ye Duan, Omran Al-Shamma, J. Santamaría, Mohammed A. Fadhel, Muthana Al-Amidie & Laith Farhan. Review of deep learning: concepts, CNN architectures, challenges, applications, futures directions. *J. Big Data* 8, 53 (2021).

[9] Sujay Bashetty, Kalyan Raja, Sahiti Adepu, Ajeet Jain; Optimizers in Deep Learning : A Comparative Study and Analysis; *IJRASET* 48050; 2022-12-10; IJRASET; 2321-9653.

[10] Mahmood, A., Ospina, A. G., Bennamoun, M., An, S., Sohel, F., Boussaid, F., Hovey, R., Fisher, R. B., & Kendrick, G. A. (2020). Automatic Hierarchical Classification of Kelps Using Deep Residual Features. In *Sensors* (Vol. 20, Issue 2, p. 447), MDPI.

[11] Radwan, N. (2019). *Leveraging sparse and dense features for reliable state estimation in urban environments.* Albert-Ludwigs-Universität Freiburg.

[12] Yong Zhong, Ming Zhao, Research on deep learning in apple leaf disease recognition, *Computers and Electronics in Agriculture*, Volume 168, 2020, 105146, ISSN 0168-1699.

[13] Bin Liu, Yun Zhang, DongJian He, and Yuxiang Li; Identification of Apple leaf diseases based on Deep Convolutional Neural Network; *Symmetry,*2018, 10(1), 11

[14] Di J, Li Q (2022) A method of detecting apple leaf diseases based on improved convolutional neural network, *PLoS ONE* 17(2).

[15] Sharad Hasan, Sarwar Jahan, Md. Imdadul Islam; Disease detection of apple leaf with combination of color segmentation and modified DWT; *Journal of King Saud University - Computer and Information Sciences;* Volume 34, Issue 9, 2022, Pages 7212-7224, ISSN 1319-1578.

[16] Hee-Jin Yu,https://arxiv.org/search/cs?searchtype=author&query=Son,+CChang-Hwan Son,Apple Leaf Disease Identification through Region-of-Interest-Aware Deep Convolutional Neural Network; *Journal of Imaging Science and Technology*, vol. 64, no. 2, pp. 20507-1-20507-10, Jan. 2020.

[17] Zhang Chunlei, Zhang Shanwen, Yang Jucheng, Shi Yancui, Chen Jia; *Apple leaf disease identification using genetic algorithm and correlation based feature selection method.*; Vol 10 No 2 (2017).

[18] Divakar, S., Bhattacharjee, A., & Priyadarshini, R. (2021). Smote-DL : A Deep Learning Based Plant Disease Detection Method. In 2021 6th International Conference for Convergence in Technology (I2CT). 2021 *6th International Conference for Convergence in Technology* (I2CT). *IEEE.*

[19] Shivling, D. V., Sharma, S. K., Ghanshyam, C., Dogra, S., Mokheria, P., Kaur, R., & Arora, D. (2015). Low cost sensor based embedded system for plant protection and pest control. In 2015 International Conference on Soft Computing Techniques and Implementations (ICSCTI). 2015 International Conference on Soft Computing Techniques and Implementations (ICSCTI). *IEEE.*

[20] Rijwan Khan, Kahkashan Perveen, Sanjay Kumar, Sahil Kansal, Mukesh Soni, Najla A. Alshaikh, Shanzeh Batool, Mehrun Nisha Khanam, Bernard Osei (2023), "Multidimensional Attention-Based CNN Model for Identifying Apple Leaf Disease", https://doi.org/10.1155/2023/9504186;10.1155/2023/9504186*Journal of Food Quality, Hindawi.*

[21] Francis, M., & Deisy, C. (2019). Disease Detection and Classification in Agricultural Plants Using Convolutional Neural Networks — A Visual Understanding. In 2019 6th International Conference on Signal Processing and Integrated Networks (SPIN). 2019 6th International Conference on Signal Processing and Integrated Networks (SPIN). *IEEE.*

[22] Liu, B.; Zhang, Y.; He,D.; Li, Y. Identification of Apple Leaf Diseases Based on Deep Convolutional Neural Networks. *Symmetry* 2018, *10*, 11.

[23] Ding, R., Qiao, Y., Yang, X., Jiang, H., Zhang, Y., Huang, Z., Wang, D., & Liu, H. (2022). Improved ResNet-Based Apple Leaf Diseases Identification. In *IFAC-PapersOnLine* (Vol. 55, Issue 32, pp. 78–82). Elsevier BV.

Chapter 7

A Novel Sigmoid Butterfly Optimization Deep Learning Model for Big Data Classification

R. Umanesan[1,*], PhD
R. Kanchana[1], PhD
R. Rathi[2], PhD
and P. Visvanathan[2], ME
[1]Computer Science and Engineering, Vel Tech Rangarajan Dr. Sagunthala R&D Institute of Science and Technology, Chennai, India
[2]School of Information Technology and Engineering, VIT University, Vellore, India

Abstract

Big data has gained popularity among the general population and business organizations in recent years. Deep learning and machine learning models, which have recently become available, can be used to analyze large data more effectively. Many different fields have recently begun working with large datasets that contain numerous sets of characteristics. The goal of feature selection models is to minimize noise, repeating features, and undesirable traits that reduce the effectiveness of categorization. It is hard to filter out effective findings for huge datasets from Conventional feature selection (FS) techniques. As far as big data analytics is concerned, FS is essential to handle huge datasets. Big data comprises many characteristics and necessitates a lot of computation; as a result, feature selection approaches using metaheuristic optimization algorithms can be employed to choose the optimal set of features, improving classification performance. Effective feature selection methods can be created using metaheuristic optimization algorithms. In this approach, Apache Spark environment is used to handle big data. This

* Corresponding Author's Email: drumanesanr@veltech.edu.in.

In: Building Intelligent Systems Using Machine Learning and Deep Learning
Editors: A. Kumar Sahoo, C. Pradhan, B. Shankar Prasad Mishra et al.
ISBN: 979-8-89113-342-6

technique is assigned to design and implementa novel sigmoid butterfly optimization algorithm with a deep learning model. A new Sigmoid Butterfly Optimization Algorithm with Optimal Gated Recurrent Unit (SBOA-OGRU) model is suggested for classification. The SBOA-OGRU strategy involves constructing a feature selection algorithm. OGRU classification model helps to group the big data. Then, Adam planner is used to tune the GRU model's hyperparameters. Additionally, the Apache Spark platform is used for efficient big data analysis. By utilizing various performance measures across several distinct aspects, the proposed model's results are validated. Additionally, a thorough comparison is made with cutting-edge techniques to demonstrate how well the suggested solutions perform. The experiment's findings showed that the suggested models performed noticeably better than the compared approaches.

Keywords: big data, FS, SBOU, OGRU, GRU

Introduction

One of the strongest business intelligence research areas is the analysis of large data and the extraction of value from it. Therefore, researchers are limited to the academic world but are also extensively employed in other domains like commerce, science, and technology [1]. Big data is made from heterogeneous and numerous resources, involving emails, online transactions, social networking sites, video recordings, audio recordings, etc. Each organization/corporation which produces this data needs to analyze and manage it. Big data frameworks have been designed for identifying analytics to use versatile, quick, and reliable computation design, provide effective quality attributes involving accessibility, flexibility, and resource pooling with ease-of-use and on-demand. These steadily rising standards contribute significantly to the improvement of massive industry data analytics frameworks. Any algorithms used to collect huge data make the need for appropriate frameworks for big data analytics evident. Local systems have one Central Processing Unit (CPU). When dataset increases, for boosting speed, multi-core Graphics Processing Units (GPU) have become more popular. Many publicly accessible technologies use a cluster of computers to distribute processing and data storage to manage huge data volumes. Numerous smaller projects were added, such as MapReduce, Hadoop Distributed File System (HDFS), Hive, HBase, Pig, and others. With the concept of classification, most machine learning (ML) issues can be solved. Additionally, in the age of big data, even simple operations like hash mapping and single inner products may take longer because of the quantity of operands used and how they are distributed across the shared file system. Due to huge data, even hash mapping and single inner products operations will take longer time. Most iterative training approachin classificationlead to complicative computations. To enhance accuracy, feature transformation/selection might take place beforehand of the actual classification [2]. Even though this pre-processing phase requires time, the resultant feature set might have much lesser attributes that might more demonstrated the several classes in an easily separable manner. Consecutively, this results in an effective classification method based on overall computational and accuracy time.

To classify huge data in the Apache Spark environment, this study develops a new Sigmoid Butterfly Optimization Algorithm with Optimal Gated Recurrent Unit (SBOA-OGRU) model [3,4]. Optimal feature selection done using the SBOA-OGRU technique. OGRU classification and Adam planner are used to tune the GRU model's hyperparameters. A thorough simulation analysis is conducted to confirm the superiority of the SBOA-OGRU technique, and the experimental findings show this to be the case.

Literature Survey

More machine learning techniques are used to do research on sentiment analysis. The accuracy of this approach is most considered. To overcome this challenge, a productive method for sentiment mining in the context of big data was presented. Carousel greedy is a flexible greedy algorithm approach that combines a bio-inspired metaheuristic algorithm with a versatile greedy approach. Following that, cat swarm optimization is performed as classification, and the effectiveness of the method is analyzed considering the outcomes of experiments [5].

During 2018, feature selection technique was introduced by the binary butterfly optimization approach (bBOA). This is based on butterfly food finding procedure. Also, another mechanism namely evolution population dynamics (EPD) is used. For optimization checking K closest neighbor classier is used. Since the number of characteristics chosen are minimum, Wilcoxon's rank sum test supportsOEbBOA's ability to maximize classification accuracy [6].

This work investigated how to successfully classify the violence content in online movies using deep neural networks with monarch butterfly optimization (DNNMBO). VSD2014 YouTube videos datasetare used for analysis. The outcomes are contrasted with those of related modified methods like DNNPSO and the original DNN. DNNMBO categorization rate for violence produced the result of 94% [7].

Data mining techniques allow us to analyze diseases at their earliest stages, by finding the best features. The best features are chosen from the datasets using a cutting-edge optimization method. The preprocessing stage removes the missing values from the input datasets. Modified Monarch Butterfly Optimization (MMBO) algorithm selects the best attributes. Dataset used is divided into healthy and non-healthy using Deep Neural Network (DNN) classifier. On multiple datasets, the proposed method and classifier are evaluating some parameters. Those parameters are sensitivity, specificity, and accuracy. Accuracy and execution time of MMBO-DNN was found to be good when compared with other methods [8].

ABCs (Artificial Bee Colonies) feature selection technique provides pertinent information from transaction level credit card datasets. This data is made ready to carry out this work to provide better accuracy. Distinct datas are collected and used for processing. In this the Modified Butterfly Optimization Algorithm (MBOA) based feature selection has been used. Convolutional and recurrent neural networks are combined in this instance to enhance the efficacy of transaction identification. This suggested deep learning model outperforms other currently available models in terms of dependability and recognition rate [9].

The proposed butterfly Optimization algorithm and particle swarm optimization (BOAPSO) is assessed on a 25-dataset using three metrics to gauge its effectiveness: classification accuracy, features chosen, and computational time. ThePSO, BOA, and GWO produced results for COVID-19 dataset are 91.07%, 87.2%, 87.8%, and 87.3%, respectively [10].

An improved butterfly optimization algorithm (IBOA) was proposed in this research. This IBOA algorithm enhances its search dynamically. To know the effectiveness of IBOA, 13 benchmark functions are widely used for testing. For analysis, IBOA-MLP calculates the measures such as sensitivity, specificity, accuracy, F1-score, and Friedman test. This method is successful for training and testing of the feed-forward artificial neural networks [11].

Transfer learning techniques using butterfly species were discussed. In this work, neural network models for butterfly species identification based on transfer learning are discussed. The datasets are taken from the 10,035 photos of 75 different butterfly species on the Kaggle website. When the dataset is increased, the accuracy of the data modelis also increased. Categorization of butterfly species is done into various groups using transfer learning-based approaches likeVGG16, VGG19, MobileNet, Xception, ResNet50, and InceptionV3. Parameters such as precision, recall, F-Measure, and accuracyare assessedfor each suggested model. Compared to other CNN networks, InceptionV3 CNN design offers an accuracy of 94.66% [12].

The butterfly optimization algorithm (BOA) is good enough to optimize issues, thereby providing global optimal solutions. To find such novel solutions it is necessary to enhance the ANNs weights and biases. Once convergence speed is increased, decrease in local optima is achieved. The mentioned classification approach is implemented with cutting-edge methods. This method has proven its better findings, hence earned its name and fame [13]. The existing approaches concerning methodologies are presented in table 1.

Table 1. Existing methodologies

S.No	Author	Methodology
1	Khalid AitHadi et al., 2019 [5]	Carousel greedy algorithm, cat swarm optimization classification
2	Zhang, B et al.,2020 [6]	Binary butterfly optimization approach (bBOA). Optimization and extension of binary butterfly optimization techniques (OEbBOA) for classification
3	Ali, A et al., 2019 [7]	Deep neural networks with monarch butterfly optimization (DNNMBO).
4	Balakumar, N. and Prabadevi, B, 2019 [8]	Modified Monarch Butterfly Optimization (MMBO) algorithm
5	Geetha, N. and Dheepa, G., 2022 [9]	Modified Butterfly Optimization Algorithm (MBOA)
6	EL-Hasnony, I.M., et al., 2022[10]	Butterfly optimization algorithm to improve the fundamental BOA for global optimization (BOAPSO) algorithm
7	Irmak.,et al.,2022[11]	Improved butterfly optimisation algorithm (IBOA)
8	FathimathulRajeena P. P et al., 2016[12]	Butterfly species identification based on transfer learning approaches. VGG16, VGG19, MobileNet, Xception, ResNet50, and InceptionV3.
9	Jalali et al., 2019[13]	Butterfly optimization algorithm (BOA)

The Proposed SBOA-OGRU Technique

A novel SBOA-OGRU technique is developed in this paper for big data categorization in an Apache Spark context. The SBOA-OGRU technique consists of two stages: FS based on SBOA and categorization based on OGRU. In addition, the Apache Spark platform is used for efficient large data processing. The next sections provide a full explanation of how these modules function.

Apache Spark Tool

The Apache Spark has been distributed computing environment utilizing under the big data condition which is developed most powerful structures. Issues raised by Hadoop structures are solved using the spark structure. With a huge dataset, better performance can be achieved. With limited dataset, chances are more to get lower system performance. Other samples are the cause of an imbalanced loading from the Spark when the size of the image is thought to change between them [14]. The researchers developed two strategies to address this problem: feature extraction with segmentation and feature extraction in order. Figure 1 Apache Spark framework.

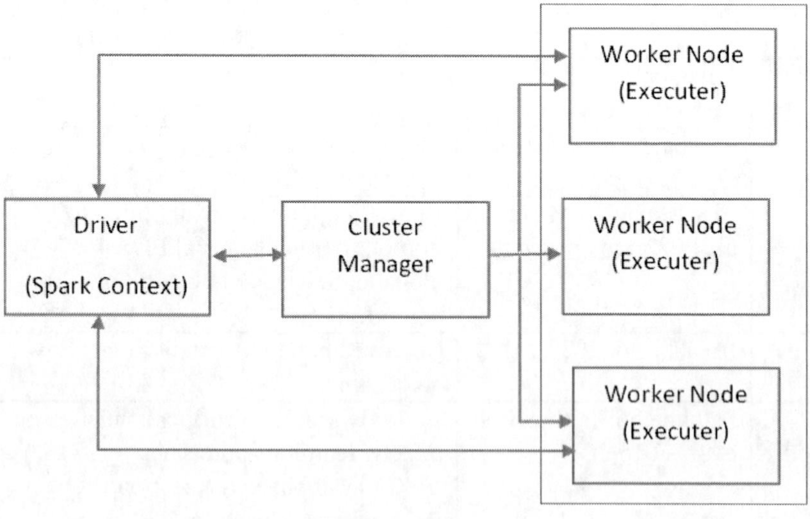

Figure 1. Architecture of Apache Spark.

This method uses a comparable MapReduce stage to perform both the combined prediction and the query. Utilizing large data platforms and related embedding libraries, such as MLlib (Machine Learning libraries), is made possible by adopting the Spark structure.

Algorithmic Design of SBOA-FS Technique

BOA imitates the butterfly searching performance. If the butterfly transfers from one place to another place in the search spaces, their fitness is altering similarly. The scent that is created by butterflies is felt by distinct butterflies present from the region and collection of social learning models was designed. From the search space, the optimum butterfly is selected using the butterfly sense fragrance. In the global search stage of BOA, it generates a stride near optimum butterfly. During the second state, if the butterfly could not capable of detecting the scent of any other butterfly from the search spaces, it can generate arbitrary stride. This isthe local search stage. The fragrance of BOA, has been expressed in Equation (1):

The butterfly is a place vector which is upgraded in the optimized procedure utilizing in Equation (2):

$$x_i^{(t+1)} = x_i^t + F_i^{(t+1)} \tag{2}$$

There are 2 essential steps in BOA technique: global search step as well as local search step. These steps are expressed in Equations (3) and (4) as:

$$F_i^{(t+1)} = (r^2 \times g^* - x_i^t) \times pf_i \tag{3}$$

$$F_i^{(t+1)} = \left(r^2 \times x_j^t - x_k^t\right) \times pf_i \tag{4}$$

where x_j^t and x_k^t are jth and kth butterflies in the solution spaces. When x_j^t and x_k^t goes to the similar populations and r represents the uniform arbitrary probabilities 0 and 1 afterward Equation (4) develops the local random walk. The switch probability p has been utilized for switching amongst general global to local searches.

For solving the Feature Selection (FS) issue, a novel version of BOA, SBOA, is projected that utilized a sigmoid (S-shaped) function making the butterfly for moving in binary search spaces. This sigmoid function is provided in Equation (5):

$$S\left(F_i^k(t)\right) = \frac{1}{1+e^{-F_i^k(t)}} \tag{5}$$

where $F_i^k(t)$ refers the continuous-valued fragrance of ith butterflies from the kth dimensional at iterations t.

Afterward, the stochastic threshold has been implemented as stated in Equation (6) for reaching the binary solution against sigmoid functions. The S-shape function map the infinite input efficiently to finite outcome.

$$X_i^k(t+1) = \begin{cases} 0, if\ rand < S\left(F_i^k(t)\right) \\ 1, otherwise \end{cases} \tag{6}$$

where $X_i^k(t)$ and $F_i^k(t)$ signifies the place and fragrance of ith butterfly at iterations t from kth dimensional.

According to the binary nature of FS issue, the search agents were limited to binary [0, 1] values only. Hence all solutions of SBOA are considered as single dimension vectors. The length of the vectors considered are independent of the number of features. All the cells of vector are comprised of one or zero. Value one illustrates that the equivalent feature was selected but the value zero demonstrates that the feature could not choose.

Hence, the FS is regarded as multi-objective optimized issue. In SBOA, optimum solutions contain a minimal number of features with maximum classifier accuracy. Therefore, the Fitness Function (FF) of this technique is expressed in Equation (7):

$$Fitness = \alpha\gamma_R(D) + \beta\frac{|R|}{|N|} \tag{7}$$

where $\gamma_R(D)$denotes classification error rate. $|R|$denotes the feature subsets selected.$|N|$denotes the entire original dataset.α defines quality andβ defines subset length given as $\alpha \in [0,1]$ and $\beta = (1-\alpha)$.

This FF has been utilized from every optimized technique for evaluating the solution with generating balance amongst classifier accuracy and the number of elected features.

Data Classification Using OGRU Model

Once the features were selected, the next step is the data classification process where the data instances are allotted to distinct class labels using OGRU model. RNNs are appropriate for non-linear time-series modeling. The RNN has input layer x, hidden layer h, and resultant layer y. Equations (8) & (9) define the resultant and hidden layers' computation.

$$y_t = g(s_t * w_{hy}) \tag{8}$$

$$s_t = f(x_t * w_{sx} + s_{t-1} * w_{ss}) \tag{9}$$

The RNN technique is familiar inhandling with gradient vanishing issues. Gradients have been computed in the resulting layer to initial layer of RNNs throughout the training process. The gradient of the initial several layers is developed small with numerous multiplications when the gradients are smaller than one. Conversely, the gradient has been developed extremely huge when the gradient is superior to one. So, it sometimes reasons the gradient for developing nearly 0 or extreme huge if it gains the primary layer of RNN. Accordingly, the weight of the initial layer is not attained during the training procedure. So, easy RNNs could not be appropriate to any difficult issues [15].

This chapter addresses the vanishing gradient problem by presenting a GRU-based method for handling multivariate time-series imagery data [16]. As per GRU structure, according to preceding output h_{t-1} and present input x_t, the reset gate has been utilized for determining that part of data must be reset as computed in Equation (10), but an upgraded gate has been utilized for upgrading the outcome of GRU h_t, as computed in Equation (11). The candidate hidden layer has been computed based on Equation (12). The present outcome is attained based on Equation (13). The gates such as z_t and r_t, and parameters like W_z, W_r and W of GRU has been upgraded during the trained procedure.

$$z_t = \sigma(W_z \cdot [h_{t-1}, x_t]) \tag{10}$$

$$r_t = \sigma(W_r \cdot [h_{t-1}, x_t]) \tag{11}$$

$$h_t' = \tan h(W \cdot [r_t * h_{t-1}, x_t]) \tag{12}$$

$$h_t = (1 - z_t) * h_{t-1} + z_t * h'_t \tag{13}$$

To perform optimal hyperparameters adjustment for optimally adjusting the hyperparameters involved in the GRU model, the Adam optimizer is applied to it.

The exponential average of past gradient m_k used in the Adam algorithm is given in equation (14). Also, equation (15) shows the past squared gradient v_k.

$$m_k = \beta_1 m_{k-1} + (1 - \beta_1) g_k, \tag{14}$$

$$\mathrm{v_k} = \beta_2 v_{k-1} + (1 - \beta_2) g_k^2, \tag{15}$$

whereas g_k represent the gradient, $\beta_1 \& \beta_2$ denotes the decay rate, that is closer to 1. The first moment i.e., mean estimate is represented as m_k. The second moment i.e., uncentered variance estimate is denoted as v_k. This bias is counteracted with The bias-corrected 1st and 2nd moment estimate are counteracted to create a bias which are presented in equation (16) and (17) as

$$\widehat{m} = \frac{m_k}{1-\beta_1^k}, \tag{16}$$

$$\hat{v}_k = \frac{v_k}{1-\beta_2^k}. \tag{17}$$

Therefore, Adam update rule is given in equation (18):

$$w^{(k+1)} = w^{(k)} - \alpha \cdot \frac{\widehat{m}}{\sqrt{\hat{v},k} + \delta}, \tag{18}$$

Here δ represents the smoothing term utilized for avoiding division by zero. The evaluation process of Adam approach is summarized as in Algorithm 1.

Algorithm 1: Adam algorithm
Data: given the initial value $w^{(0)} = w_0$, the number of samples n, the step size α, and the tolerance ε. Set $k = 0$. Step 1: compute the augmented objective function. Step 2: evaluate the stochastic gradient. Step 3: set the arbitrary index j.

Step 4: calculate the decaying average of past and past squared gradients.
Step 5: compute the bias corrected first moment estimates.
Step 6: upgrade the vector $w^{(k)}$. When $\|w^{(k+1)} - w^{(k)}\| < \varepsilon$, then end the iteration. Or else, set $k = k + 1$, and repeat from Step 1.
Remark:The default value for the decay rate is $\beta_1 = 0.9 \& \beta_2 = 0.999$, the tolerance is
$\varepsilon = 10^{-6}$, as well as the learning rate is $\alpha = 0.001$.

Experimental Validation

Epsilon and ECBDL14-ROS datasets are used in SBOA-OGRU technique to provide its performance validation. The former dataset holds 400000 training and 100000 testing instances. Besides, the latter dataset comprises 65003913 training and 2897917 testing instances. The number of features under Epsilon and ECBDL14-ROS datasets are 2000 and 631 respectively. Evaluated performance of SBOA-FS procedure using these datasets is presented in Figure2. This process results in the selection of 1051 features from the 2000 features in the Epsilon dataset. Also 349 features are selected from 631 features of ECBDL14-ROS dataset.

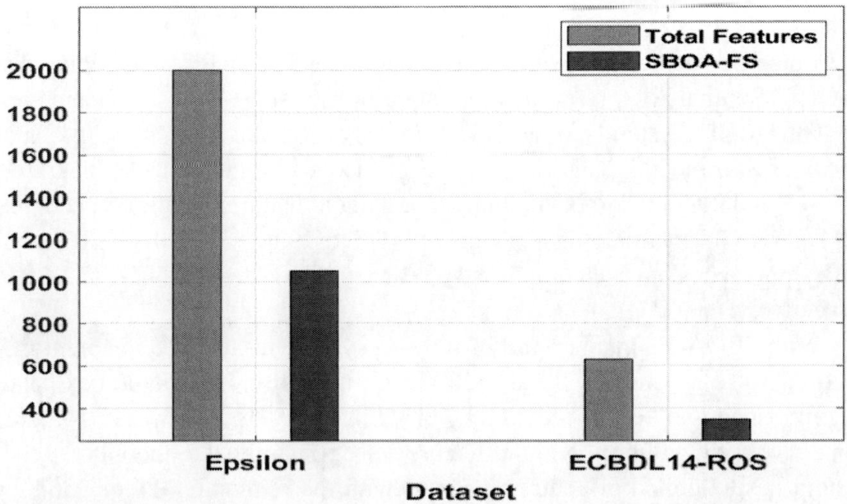

Figure 2. SBOA-FS procedure outcome.

Epsilon Dataset

Maximum AUC analysis is obtained when SBOA-FS procedure under DL-OGRU technique is implemented. The MapReduce for Evolutionary Feature Selection(MR-EFS) and sequential CHC are also implemented to record AUC values. This DL-OGRU technique produces higher AUC of 96.87%. On comparison, SVMC, LRC, and NBC techniques have attained a lower AUCs of 86.34%, 88.91%, and 90.48%. Without feature selection approach, the DL-ORGU model has produced AUC of 76.85%. And SVMC, LRC, and NBC techniques have accomplished a reduced AUC of 59.00%, 62%, and 64% respectively.

The SBOA-FS under DL-OGRU technique proved reduced TRT. With SBOA-FS approach, the DL-ORGU model has resulted in a decreased TRT of 167.71s whereas the SVMC, LRC, and NBC techniques have accomplished an increased TRT of 210.61s, 272.45s, and 187.20s respectively. Without feature selection approach, the DL-ORGU shown minimal TRT of 302.63s, whereas the SVMC, LRC, and NBC techniques have attained a maximum TRT of 400.38s, 430.48s, and 340.42s respectively.

ECBDL14-ROS Dataset

The outcomes depicted that the SBOA-FS under DL-OGRU technique has reached maximal AUC over the other algorithms. With SBOA-FS technique, the DL-ORGU system has achieved an enhanced AUC of 95.97%. And SVMC, LRC, and NBC algorithms have reached a minimum AUC of 85.72%, 89.34%, and 91.57% correspondingly. For without feature selectionprocedure, the DL-ORGU methodology has given AUC of79.09%. SVMC, LRC, and NBC approaches have accomplished a reduced AUC of 56%, 58%, and 61% respectively.

With SBOA-FS manner, the DL-ORGU system has resulted in a minimal TRT of 108.50s whereas the SVMC, LRC, and NBC methodologies have accomplished an enhanced TRT of 776.49s, 715.32s, and 143.76s respectively. In addition, without feature selection approach, the DL-ORGU system has exhibited effectual outcomes with the minimal TRT of 356.89s whereas the SVMC, LRC, and NBC algorithms have gained an increased TRT of 978.37s, 1012.47s, and 369.98s correspondingly.

It is abundantly evident from the findings and discussion that the proposed model outperforms other similar approaches. As a result, the suggested method is suitable for big data classification in a real-time setting. The accuracy of this proposed model is evaluated against the previous works, and the results are shown in table 2.

Table 2. Proposed models comparison with existing

S.No	Author	Methodology	Obtained accuracy
1.	Ali, A et al., 2019 [7]	Deep neural networks with monarch butterfly optimization (DNNMBO).	94%
2.	EL-Hasnony, I.M., et al.,2022 [10]	Butterfly optimization algorithm to improve the fundamental BOA for global optimization (BOAPSO) algorithm	87.8%
3.	Dr.R.Umanesan et al., 2023(Proposed model)		
	Epsilon dataset	Without feature selectionunder DL-ORGU	76.85%
		SBOA-FS under DL-OGRU	96.87%
	ECBDL14-ROS dataset	Without feature selectionunder DL-ORGU	79.09%
		SBOA-FS under DL-OGRU	95.97%

Conclusion

In this chapter, big data classification is done using the novel SBOA-OGRU in Apache Spark environment. This novelty work is being carried out using FS and OGRU classification approaches. Using SBOA technique, optimal feature selection process is done. In this classification approach, ORGU model is used to distinct class labels. In the GRU model, the Adam optimizer is used to adjust the hyperparameters. To process the big data in an effective way, the Apache Spark platform is applied. A greater number of experiments are conducted to check the supremacy of the SBOA-OGRU technique. Those experiments highlight the dominance of the SBOA-OGRU technique.

References

[1] Abbasi, A, Sarker, S & Chiang, RH 2016, 'Big data research in information systems: Toward an inclusive research agenda', *Journal of the Association for Information Systems, vol. 17*, pp. 1–33.

[2] El-Hasnony, IM, Barakat, SI, Elhoseny, M & Mostafa, RR 2020, 'Improved feature selection model for big data analytics', *IEEE Access*, vol. 8, pp. 66989-67004.

[3] Alexopoulos, A, Drakopoulos, G, Kanavos, A, Mylonas, P &Vonitsanos, G 2020, 'Two-step classification with SVD preprocessing of distributed massive datasets in Apache Spark', *Algorithms,* vol. 13, no. 3, pp. 71-84.

[4] Bi, L, Hu, G, Raza, MM, Kandel, Y, Leandro, L & Mueller, D, 2020, 'A Gated Recurrent Units (GRU)-Based Model for Early Detection of Soybean Sudden Death Syndrome through Time-Series Satellite Imagery', *Remote Sensing,* vol. 12, no. 21, pp. 3621.

[5] Hadi, K., Lasri, R. and El Abderrahmani, A., 2019. An efficient approach for sentiment analysis in a big data environment. *International Journal of Engineering and Advanced Technology (IJEAT)*, *8*(4), pp.263-266.

[6] Zhang, B., Yang, X., Hu, B., Liu, Z. and Li, Z., 2020. OEbBOA: A novel improved binary butterfly optimization approaches with various strategies for feature selection. *IEEE Access*, *8*, pp.67799-67812.

[7] Ali, A., Senan, N., Yanto, I.T.R. and Lashari, S.A., 2019. Classification Performance of Violence Content by Deep Neural Network with Monarch Butterfly Optimization. *International Journal of Advanced Computer Science and Applications*, *10*(12).

[8] Balakumar, N. and Prabadevi, B., Modified Monarch Butterfly Based Feature Selection for Multi Medical Data Classification Using Deep Neural Network. *International Journal of Recent Technology and Engineering (IJRTE)* ISSN: 2277-3878, Volume-7, Issue-6S5, April 2019.

[9] Geetha, N. and Dheepa, G., 2022. A Hybrid Deep Learning And Modified Butterfly Optimization Based Feature Selection For Transaction Credit Card Fraud Detection. *Journal of Positive School Psychology*, *6*(7), pp.5328-5345.

[10] EL-Hasnony, I.M., Elhoseny, M. and Tarek, Z., 2022. A hybrid feature selection model based on butterfly optimization algorithm: COVID-19 as a case study. *Expert Systems*, *39*(3), p.e12786.

[11] Irmak, B., Karakoyun, M. and Gülcü, Ş., 2022. An improved butterfly optimization algorithm for training the feed-forward artificial neural networks. *Soft Computing*, pp.1-19.

[12] Rajeena PP, F., Orban, R., Vadivel, K.S., Subramanian, M., Muthusamy, S., Elminaam, D.S.A., Nabil, A., Abulaigh, L., Ahmadi, M. and Ali, M.A., 2022. A

novel method for the classification of butterfly species using pre-trained CNN models. *Electronics*, *11*(13), p.2016.

[13] Jalali, S.M.J., Ahmadian, S., Kebria, P.M., Khosravi, A., Lim, C.P. and Nahavandi, S., 2019. Evolving artificial neural networks using butterfly optimization algorithm for data classification. In *Neural Information Processing: 26th International Conference, ICONIP 2019, Sydney, NSW, Australia, December 12–15, 2019, Proceedings, Part I 26* (pp. 596-607). Springer International Publishing.

[14] Xu, Y, Liu, H & Long, Z 2020, 'A distributed computing framework for wind speed big data forecasting on Apache Spark', *Sustainable Energy Technologies and Assessments, vol. 37*, p. 100582.

[15] Suthaharan, S 2016, 'Machine learning models and algorithms for big data classification', *Integr. Ser. Inf. Syst.,* vol. 36, pp. 1-12.

[16] Nair, LR & Shetty, SD 2018, 'Applying spark based machine learning model on streaming big data for health status prediction', *Comput. Electr. Eng*., vol. 65, pp. 393–399.

Chapter 8

An Analysis of Optical Character Recognition-Based Machine Translation for Low Resource Languages

P. Mahesha
Trisiladevi C. Nagavi*
Harshitha L. P.
Swathi Alse
and Shifali B. Shetty
Department of Computer Science and Engineering, S. J. College of Engineering, JSS Science and Technology University Mysore, India

Abstract

Natural Language Processing (NLP) is a sub field under artificial intelligence that deals with the communication languages between computers and humans. A major process in NLP is machine translation which is the conversion of input text from one source language to target language without affecting the meaning. The input and output for NLP is natural language text. To implement the system, a new model for machine translation using Optical Character Recognition (OCR) is employed. The system also uses Bidirectional Recurrent Neural Network (BRNN) and dictionary-based approaches for English to Kannada and Marathi language translation. These two low resource languages are spoken in Indian state of Karnataka and Maharashtra respectively. The efficiency of the system is achieved through the improvement of accuracy and learning by comparing with different datasets and inputs.

* Corresponding Author's Email: tnagavi@yahoo.com.

In: Building Intelligent Systems Using Machine Learning and Deep Learning
Editors: A. Kumar Sahoo, C. Pradhan, B. Shankar Prasad Mishra et al.
ISBN: 979-8-89113-342-6

Keywords: optical character recognition, machine translation, natural language processing, low resource languages, bidirectional recurrent neural network

Introduction

The process of translation can be defined as conversion of the text from source language to target while preserving the same meaning. It is a major topic because of the difficulty of understanding language grammar and the context with which each sentence is spoken. The method of translating word to word is even though effective for easy and simple communication purposes, it is not suitable for dialogues which have important information. The societal sectors such as law, medicine, education, business and religion are sensitive even for a small change in the meaning. In these sectors, placing the word contextually is more suitable than the direct translation. A well-trained translator only can convey an intended message to the other person. Humans have the ability to communicate with each other through spoken language. Approximately 7,000 languages are being used worldwide. Hence, language translation systems act like an important bridge between people from different countries and ethnic groups.

Most spoken and high resource language in the world is English. Also, it is frequently mentioned as the language of global business and translation. Further interpreting services remain a vital part of doing business around the world. Everyone responds better to their native language [1, 2, 3]. It is important to speak the language of people's heart not the language they understand. In the present study, two low resource languages such as Kannada and Marathi are considered.

A significant portion of Karnataka consists of people who are most fluent and comfortable conversing in Kannada [1, 2]. Even in Maharashtra which is a significant Indian state more percentage of people speak Marathi. So, whenever there is a need to convince them of something it is best to do so in Kannada or Marathi rather than in a language that they are not very familiar with. To meet these needs, researchers are focusing on machine translation systems. Keeping this importance of language translation in mind we have developed and analyzed a machine translation model that is used to translate English text to corresponding Kannada or Marathi text. Here, the system takes input from images using OCR. Also, the system ensures that the translated text is grammatically correct. The performance is analyzed using BLEU score metric.

Applications

The proposed system has application as listed below:

a. Information written on hoardings and boards in other natural languages can be translated to desired language.
b. Foreign markets display promotions in their respective languages, and they can be translated and analyzed in the desired language.
c. During the visit to other countries and regions, for a better understanding of their regional language we can translate their language.
d. Reservations of tickets, banking etc. are all displayed in standard languages, they can be translated to desired language.
e. Since the contents of the image would be difficult to describe, caption or text generations from images and translating that text.

Review of the Existing Models

The existing models are described as a culmination of nearly half a century of efforts [1-8] poured into the translation of input from source language to target. It is summed up over a timeline as-

- *Hire local translators* who help to translate the language to that of a target language [1].
- *Syntactic analysis and machine translation (1960s-1970s)*. Machine translation during this period focused mainly on ensuring the rules of the languages were stratified and conserved. The work made use of the new perceptron model [2].
- *Linguistic formalism and rule-based machine translations (1980s)* The research work carried out during 1980s was relied on machine translation systems thorough linguistic representation consisting of morphological, syntactic and semantic analysis [3]. The systems designed using rules make use of a combination of language and its

grammar rules plus dictionaries of common words. The special dictionaries are created specifically for industries and disciples. The systems based on rules usually deliver translations which are consistent and accurate with specialist dictionary training.

- *Data-driven machine translation (1990s).* Large data collection and analysis systems contributed significantly to the expansion of machine translation systems. This led to the design and development of low-cost powerful computers. During 1990, machine translations made used mainframes to small personal computers and workstations [4].
- *Statistical machine translation (2000)* - The advent of BLEU-bilingual evaluation under study lead to the shift into machine translation systems based on statistics and example-based machine translation. They have no prior knowledge of language grammar rules. The learning for translation happens through large amount of data for every language pair. The learning can be based on specific industry need [5].
- *Neural Machine Translation (NMT)* – Here neural networks are used where multiple processes simulate the working of the human brain. Currently this is the most popular method used in most research works, and it is yielding high accuracy [6].

The current model is a neural network based and utilizes a network of artificial neural networks.

Machine Translation System Design for Low Resource Languages

The system aims to develop an interface which helps in translating English text to low resource languages such as Kannada and Marathi. The proposed system based on sequence-to-sequence modeling associates encoder and decoder and behaves like recurrent network. The encoder summarizes the input into a context variable, also called the state. This context is then decoded, and the output sequence is generated. Figure 1 depicts the overview of working of the system.

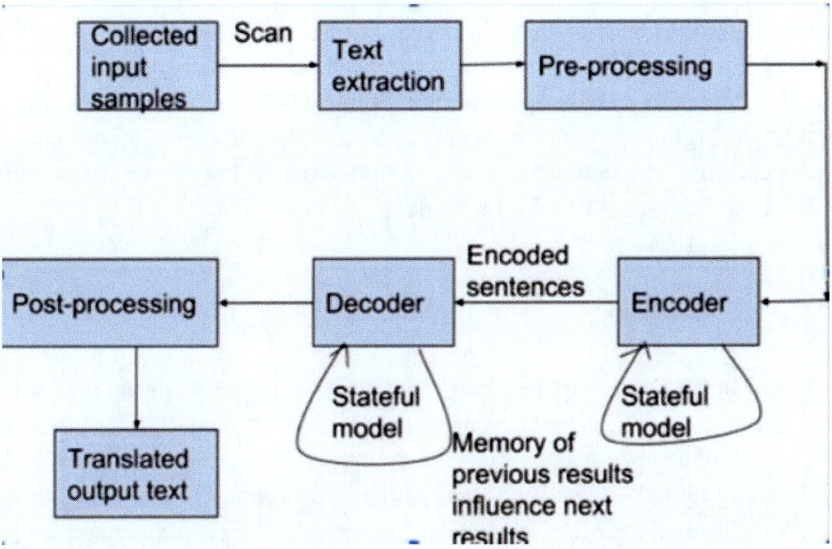

Figure 1. Machine translation system.

Data Set Collection

The datasets are collected from different sources. Table 1 depicts the source along with the dataset details. In the proposed system simple text images are used as test samples.

Table 1. Source language and dataset details

Dataset	Number of lines
Tatoeba	149
Bible (short)	2150
Bible	63590
English-Kannada	26989
English-Marathi (tatoeba)	34270

Text Extraction

The OCR tool is employed for extracting text from images or documents. It is the mechanical or electronic conversion of images of typed, handwritten or printed text into machine- encoded text. Further the extraction may be from a scanned document, a photo of a document or a scene-photo. The text on signs and billboards in a landscape photo or from subtitle text superimposed on an image during a television broadcast are examples of scene-photo. The text extracted from this is stored in a suitable format which can be easily fed as input to the proposed translation model.

Pre-Processing

- In the beginning the data is loaded and examined. During the training phase both English simple sentences and its respective low resource language sentences were fed to the model for learning. During data examination, we keep track of the word count.
- Secondly the data is cleaned like spacing between the words as well as punctuations have to equal.
- Next step is the tokenization of input text. That is the conversion of each word to numerical values. This allows neural network to perform operations on the inputs. In the proposed system every word and punctuation will have a unique id. The tokenizer helps to create a word index which is then used to convert sentence into vector.
- Padding is done in order to have the same length.
- Embedding layers are used to convert each sentence to a vector. The size of the vector depends on the complexity of the vocabulary.

Encoder

- Among several recurrent units of Long Short-Term Memory (LSTM) neural network, each unit accepts a single element of the input sequence and collects information for that element as well as propagates it forward.
- The input sequence is a collection of all words from the sentence. Each word is represented as x(i) where i is the order of that word.
- The hidden states are computed using suitable formula.

It takes n time steps based on the length of sentence to encode the whole input. At each step, it reads the input word and applies transformation to its hidden state. Then the output is passed to the next step. The hidden state indicates the suitable context of the network. The larger hidden state leads to more learning capacity for the model with more computation requirements. Figure 2 provides the visual representation of the encoding process.

Encoder Vector

The encoder vector is the last output state obtained from the encoder calculated with suitable formula. This vector aims to encapsulate the information for all input values for helping the decoder for making proper predictions.

- It acts as the initial state of the decoder part of the model.

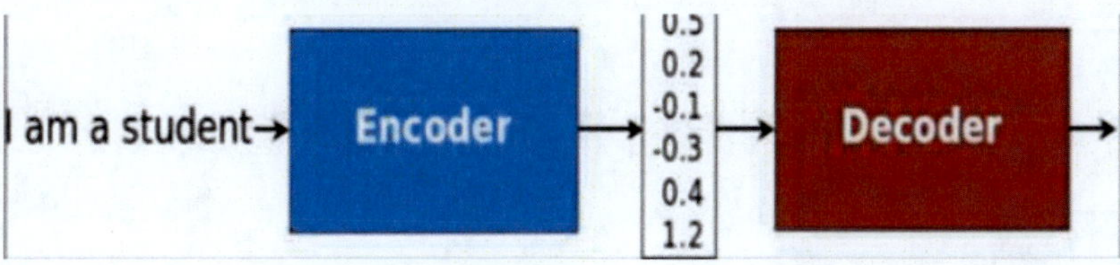

Figure 2. Illustrates how encoder encodes the sentence and sends it to the decoder.

Decoder

- It consists of several recurrent units, each one predicting an output y(t) at a time stamp t. Also, each unit takes hidden state from the previous unit and produces output along with hidden state.
- The output produced is a series of words from the sentence. Hidden states are estimated using suitable formula. The output at time step t is computed using the softmax formula.

Finally, will generate predictions and output the decoded source. Along with that we iterate back the decoded source, target and predicted sequences.

Post-processing

The translated Kannada and Marathi sentences are aligned and are displayed in user desired format.

Output

Finally, the generated output is suitably post-processed to get the desired output.

Development of Machine Translation System for Low Resource Languages

Translation from one language to another using a neural network requires a large collection of language-pair parallel corpus. The language-pair English-Kannada has no adequate datasets, of the order of magnitude required for proper training of the neural network. Available datasets are stunted, and datasets that can be extracted through web-scraping are highly domain-specific, and mostly revolve around obscure phrases. Thus, the dataset used is a parallel English-Marathi corpus, which has tab-separated translated texts. The output is translated to Kannada or Marathi. Figure 3 depicts the system development.

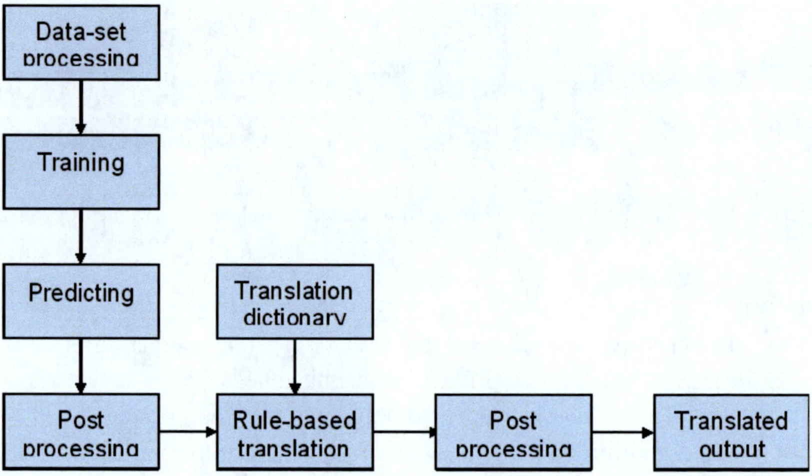

Figure 3. Development of machine translation system for low resource languages.

Dataset Preparation

The dataset to be used for training must first be cleaned to obtain sentences in their normalized forms. Cleaning includes replacing punctuation, splitting words on white space and normalizing words to lowercase.

Data Pre-Processing

Here, the dataset is separated into English and Marathi sentences. Both of these subsets are tokenized. Then these words are converted to lowercase, stripped off numbers and punctuation. Later these tokenized words are joined to form sentences. The individual sentences are grouped into two lists, the train and test dataset in a 1:9 ratio.

Encode Data

Word index is computed from all the words in the data set based on their frequency. Then words in each individual sentence are replaced with corresponding word index. Maximum sentence length is calculated for each language. Each sentence is padded with 0s until they are all the same maximum sentence length.

Training

Encoding Phase

The training sentences which are in English are input to the embedding layer, which creates a vector representation of the same. This is fed to the encoding layer, which selectively learns the word features and sequence through a forget, retain and learn function in each unit which changes the state of the unit. The next sentence is fed to this hidden state. The final hidden state is fed to the decoding layer in the training phase.

Decoding Phase

The final hidden layer is supplied as the initial values for the decoder layer. The training sentences for Kannada and Marathi are fed to this layer.

Sentence Prediction

The English sentence is fed to the decoder. The decoder takes in one word at a time, predicts a corresponding Kannada or Marathi word. The next English word, as well as the previous Kannada or Marathi word, is fed as input again, and the output is modified.

Post-Processing

The translated sentence is tokenized to generate individual words, stored as a list. The words are lemmatized through a rule-based stemmer to generate the root word. The words are joined on.

Rule-Based Translation

a. Marathi-Kannada Dictionary: A Marathi-Kannada translation dictionary which is Part-of-Speech tagged is used.
b. Rule-based translation: The Marathi words are chunked and tagged. They are then analyzed to find corresponding Kannada words. The words are strung together in the right order, by using the syntax rules to generate the final sentence.

Post-Processing

The final sentences words are split to identify individual Kannada words. If the translated word is not found, the Marathi word is eliminated from the final sentence. If multiple translations are available, the first translation, which is more frequently used, is selected. The remaining words are appended as such. The individual Kannada words are joined to form a sentence.

Experimental Results and Analysis

The modules concerned with the machine translation system design are data set generation, collection, text extraction, pre-processing, encoder, decoder, post-processing and output. Initially data is cleansed, and it is separated into training and testing data. While extracting datasets, web-scraping was performed. This data then had to be assembled and further cleaned to obtain the appropriate datasets. This would require the removal of punctuation as well as sentence alignment.

A Kannada-English bible was utilized to generate a parallel corpus. It contained compound sentences which required to be broken into simple sentences for training purposes. The cleaning module performed the translations. The detail of the samples obtained through web scraping is shown in table 2.

The next data-set was generated by translating simple sentences of major data-sets, such as German-English to Kannada-English. This was performed using text blob, an API built upon NLTK and Google translate. The data set details are tabulated in Table 3.

Table 2. Details of samples obtained through web scraping

Details	Number of samples
Total number of sentences generated through web scraping	30,690
Total number of sentences obtained after cleaning	37,536
Number of sentences that did not align	1,484
Number of sentences that were usable	36,052
Percentage of usable sentences	0.96

Table 3. Details of samples obtained through an API built upon NLTK and Google translate

Details	Number of samples
The original number of sentence pairs in the multilingual corpora	19,453
Number of pairs generated by the module	6,371
Total percentage of corpora utilized in sentence generation	32

The last dataset used was an English-Marathi corpus, the number of sentences used are tabulated in Table 4.

Table 4. Details of number samples used from English-Marathi corpus

Details	Number of samples
The original number of sentence pairs in the multilingual corpora	34495
Number of pairs generated by the module	20,000
Total percentage of corpora utilized in sentence generation	57

The translation module was trained on these datasets, as well as the toteoba sentence- pairs. The measure of translation is through the Bilingual Evaluation Understudy score. This score utilizes precision measure while also considering the n-grams. Scores are estimated for each and every translated segment, usually sentences, by matching them with a set of quality reference translations. Those scores are then averaged over the whole corpus to reach an estimate of the translation's overall quality. The highest BLEU score obtained, for a English-Marathi corpus module is 0.40365. Translations obtained by the bible corpus are shown in Table 5.

Table 5. Translations obtained by the bible corpus

Test No	Test sentence	Expected Result	Actual Result	Remarks
1	Let them be confounded and troubled for ever	ಅವರನ್ನು ನಾಚಿಕೆಪಡಿಸಲಿ ಮತ್ತು ತೊಂದರೆಗೊಳಗಾಗಿರುವಂತೆ ಎಂದೆಂದಿಗೂ		No translation
2	He turned their heart to hate his people, to deal subtilly with his servants	ಅವರು ತಿರುಗಿಕೊಂಡರು ತನ್ನ ಜನರನ್ನು ದ್ವೇಷಿಸುವಂತೆ ಅವರ ಹೃದಯವು ತನ್ನ ಸೇವಕರನ್ನು ಸೂಕ್ಷ್ಮವಾಗಿ ಎದುರಿಸಲು	ತನ್ನ ಜನರನ್ನು	Partial Translation
3	The bricks are fallen down, but we will build with hewn stones	ಇಟ್ಟಿಗೆಗಳು ಬಿದ್ದವು, ಆದರೆ ನಾವು ಕತ್ತರಿಸಿದ ಕಲ್ಲುಗಳಿಂದ ನಿರ್ಮಿಸುತ್ತೇವೆ		No translation

Translations obtained by the English-Marathi corpus are shown in Table 6.

Table 6. Translations obtained by the English-Marathi corpus

Test No	Test sentence	Actual Sentence	Predicted Sentence	Remark
1.	I need your help.	ನನಗೆ ನಿನ್ನ ಸಹಾಯ ಬೇಕು	ಸಹಾಯ ಬೇಕು	Partial Translation
2.	I am a teacher.	ನಾನು ಒಬ್ಬ ಶಿಕ್ಷಕ	ಶಿಕ್ಷಕ	Full translation
3.	I need food.	ನನಗೆ ಆಹಾರ ಬೇಕು	ಆಹಾರ ಬೇಕು	Partial translation

Conclusion

Our model converts English sentences to equivalent Kannada or Marathi sentences provided the sentences are not too complex. Every converted sentence is also grammatically correct. The performance of the system can be improved by creating more datasets.

References

[1] Antony P. J., Ajith V. P. and Soman K. P., Feature Extraction based English to Kannada Transliteration, In *Third International Conference on Semantic E-business and Enterprise Computing (SEEC),* Cochin India 2010.

[2] Antony P. J., Ajith V. P. and Soman K. P.: Kernel Method for English to Kannada Transliteration, International Conference on Recent Trends in *Information, Telecommunication and Computing (ITC 2010*), Kerala, India, pp. 336-338, IEEE Xplore.

[3] Dhandra B. V., Mallikarjun Hangarge and Gururaj Mukarambi, Spatial Features for Handwritten Kannada and English Character Recognition, *International Journal of Computer Applications, Special Issue on RTIPPR*, pp. 146-151, 2010.

[4] Sutskever Ilya, Oriol Vinyals and Quoc V. Le, *Sequence to Sequence Learning with Neural Networks, 2014.*

[5] Xu Mia Chen Orhan Firat Ankur Bapna Melvin Johnson Wolfgang Macherey Noam Shazeer Ashish Vaswani Mike Schuster Zhifeng Chen, The Best of Both Worlds: Combining Recent Advances in Neural Machine Translation, In *Proceedings of the 56th Annual Meeting of the Association for Computational Linguistics, Vol. 1: Long Papers, July, 2018*, Melbourne, Australia, Association for Computational Linguistics Publisher, pages – 76-86.

[6] Ignat Oana, Jean Maillard, Vishrav Chaudhary and Francisco Guzmán, OCR Improves Machine Translation for Low-Resource Languages", *Findings of the Association for Computational Linguistics: ACL 2022, pages 1164 – 1174.*

[7] Alireza Akbari, An Overall Perspective of Machine Translation with its Shortcomings, *International Journal of Education & Literacy Studies*, ISSN 2202-9478, vol. 2, No. 1; January 2014, pp. 1-10.

[8] Gu Jiatao, Yong Wang, Kyunghyun Cho, Victor O.K. Li., *Search Engine Guided Neural Machine Translation*, 2017.

Chapter 9

Generative AI for Bio-Signal Analysis and Augmentation

Shiyona Dash[1], Mtech
Ashis Kumar Parida[1], Btech
Kunal Pal[1], PhD
and Mirza Khalid Baig[1,*], PhD
Department of Biotechnology and Medical Engineering, National Institute of Technology, Rourkela, Odisha, India

Abstract

Artificial Intelligence is increasingly used in various healthcare-related applications ranging from diagnostics to therapeutics and prosthetics. A new class of Artificial Intelligence (AI) models, known as Generative AI, has emerged in recent years. Generative AI has been used extensively in image reconstruction and augmentation. This is particularly helpful in healthcare systems to produce substantial synthetic data which could be used for analysis and devising personalised therapeutics. Generative Adversarial Networks have earned notoriety for producing synthetic data which are virtually indistinguishable from real data. This chapter presents a comprehensive overview of existing generative AI models and how they can be used in healthcare applications to perform data augmentation of Electroencephalogram (EEG) data and image regeneration of visual stimulus from EEG signals. Various data collection, data pre-processing and data selection methods have also been summarised. We have also enlisted the challenges, evaluation metrics, and methodologies of various generative models.

* Corresponding Author's Email: baigm@nitrkl.ac.in.

In: Building Intelligent Systems Using Machine Learning and Deep Learning
Editors: A. Kumar Sahoo, C. Pradhan, B. Shankar Prasad Mishra et al.
ISBN: 979-8-89113-342-6

Keywords: generative AI, generative adversarial networks, data augmentation, image regeneration

Introduction

Brain is the seat of control for consciousness, intelligence, cognitive functions, locomotion etc. It has also been one of the most crucial research topics, ranging from cognitive computational neuroscience analysis to intense psycho-philosophical discourse. The brain controls the five senses: smell, touch, taste, vision and sound.

The brain coordinates these functions with twelve pairs of cranial nerves. These nerves are olfactory (nose), optic (eyes vision), oculomotor (eye movement), trochlear (movement in the eye's superior oblique muscle), trigeminal (facial sensations), abducent (or abducens; lateral eyeball movement), facial (facial movements), vestibulocochlear (hearing, balance, spatial sensation and posture), glossopharyngeal (tongue and pharynx), vagus (regulation of internal organs activity such as respiration, vomiting, coughing etc.), accessory (neck and shoulder movement), and hypoglossal (tongue innervation).

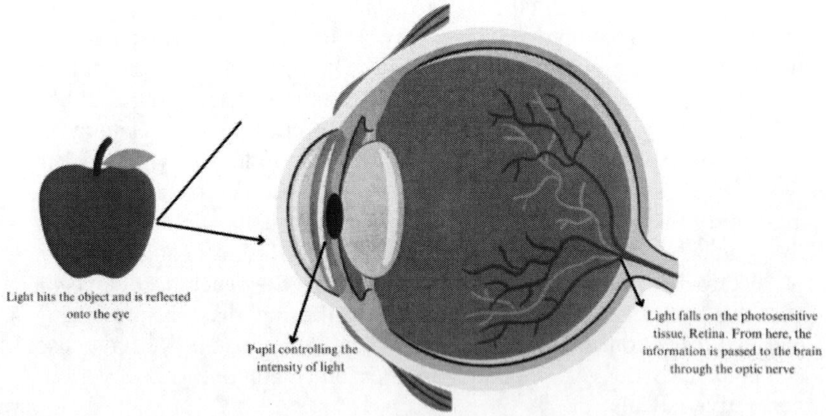

Figure 1. A simple illustration showing the transmission of light rays from an object to the optic nerve.

In the context of the optic nerve's function to aid in vision, it is important to understand the pathway of light reaching the aforementioned nerve. The light incident on the desired object reaches the eyes. Upon reaching the aperture-like structure, the pupil controls the intensity of light that should be incident on the lens. The various muscles attached to the eyes also aid in this intensity control with the aid of trochlear, abducens and oculomotor nerves. After entering the eye, the pattern falls on the light-sensitive tissue called the retina. The retina comprises several photosensitive cells called rods (controls night vision) and cones (controls bright vision). The retina interprets this information into electrical impulses, which, through the optic nerve, is sent to the brain to form the corresponding image leading to 'image perception', as can be seen in Figure 1.

Bio-Signal Recording Modalities

Electroencephalography

The brain can control the working of all the organs of the body with the network of neurons. The communication of neurons happens with the release of neurotransmitters and the passage of electrical impulses. These electrical impulses lead to the presence of 'electrical activity', which can be captured with the aid of an Electroencephalograph (EEG). EEG is a technique by which the neuron's electrical activity in the brain is captured. It is used to observe the working of different cerebral lobes in various conditions. These conditions can range from the normal observatory, disease/disorder diagnosis or experimental setups.

The International 10-20 EEG electrodes placement system is an internationally accepted protocol for placing scalp electrodes for EEG study. The values '10' and '20' signify the distance between adjacent electrodes. It means that 10% or 20% of the total distance from certain landmark points on the head are marked, as seen in Figure 2. The front-back distance is measured from Nasion (the most anterior part of the frontonasal suture) to Inion (occipital protuberance), while the right-left distance is measured between the two preauricular points. The ground electrodes are usually fixed on the zygomatic arch (upper cheekbone below the eye) and mastoid bones (behind the ears). The reference electrode can be chosen as per requirement, usually a CZ electrode or on the ear. A digital reference can also be added by subtracting the average of all channels from individual ones. The EEG recording system focuses on different lobes, such as pre-frontal, frontal, temporal, parietal and occipital. There is an additional central lobe which is not present anatomically, but the readings obtained from those electrodes exhibit the activities of the other lobes.

EEG is a widely implementable modality since it is non-invasive. It provides spatially rich information when high-density electrode systems are used. It is used for diagnostics, experimental studies and research protocols.

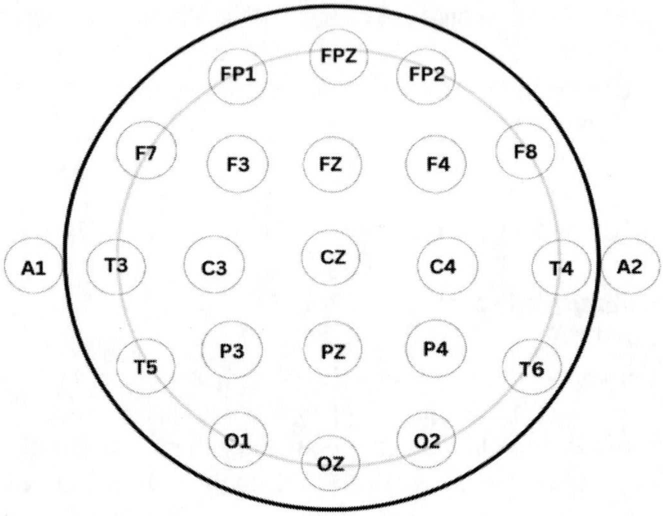

Figure 2. The International 10-20 EEG System Electrodes. The A1 and A2 electrodes are ground electrodes fixed on mastoid positions.

Generative AI Models

In recent decades, Artificial Intelligence (AI) based algorithms have been developed to control prosthetics that can replicate the functionality of organs, should they fail to act normally. The primary requirement for these algorithms to be robust is access to good-quality data. Data is the game-changing attribute of any Machine Learning (ML) or Deep Learning (DL) algorithm. Good quality data capturing the variance of the population is of utmost importance when building a model. However, the majority of the time, the medical data collected is noisy or insufficient to test the efficiency of the model. This is where generative AI models come to play. These models rely upon the underlying data distributions and associated features to generate similar data. The working of a generative model can be broadly described in three steps.

- *Training:* The model is first trained on the available datasets. During this step, the model learns the underlying data distributions and statistical patterns in the original data. This is followed by optimising the model's parameters to minimise the difference between the generated samples and actual data.
- *Sampling:* Post-model training, the new data samples are generated. Typically, generative models take some form of random noise or a starting sequence as input. The learned patterns are then used to generate new outputs.
- *Evaluation:* The generated samples are then evaluated on several criteria to check their degree of similarity (or dissimilarity) to the training data. This step is used to refine the model performance lest there be a scope for improvement.

Instances of various generative AI models have been described below:

- *Autoencoders:* Autoencoders are unsupervised learning-based neural networks that are used to 'compress' and 'decompress' data. These networks learn a compressed or encoded version of the input sequence and reconstruct the original input in a higher dimensional space. The backpropagation method can update model weights to reduce the difference between original and reconstructed data. They are used for data compression, denoising and anomaly detection.
- *Variational Autoencoders (VAEs):* Variational Autoencoders are a combination of autoencoders which also work on probabilistic or Bayesian inference for learning the compressed input data to reconstruct it later. These models typically assume the input data distribution to be Gaussian, with a mean and standard deviation. They typically use a loss function which includes a reconstruction error term (to match the original data with reconstructed data) and a KullbackLeibler (KL) divergence term (to configure learned latent space into a Gaussian distribution). They are used for image and text generation.
- *Recurrent Neural Networks (RNNs):* RNNs can also be generative models. They can be visualised as language models which predict the sequences based on the given input, by learning its probability distribution. The hidden layers in an RNN model capture the context of previous input supplied to predict the next object in a sequence.

The network is thus trained to minimise the difference between the actual predicted distributions of the next object in the training data. These are used for generating text, music, or speech. Long Short-Term Memory (LSTM), Gated Recurrent Unit (GRU), and Bidirectional RNNs models are advanced modifications of RNNs that can be used to overcome the problem of lack of coherence that comes with the former.

- *Transformers:* Transformers were introduced as an improvement over the RNNs. They work on the 'self-attention' mechanism by which the model weighs the importance of different parts of the input sequence to make predictions. They also consist of an encoding block and a decoding block. The encoder produces a sequence of hidden representations, while the decoder uses these to produce the output sequence at the rate of one token at a time. These representations are stored as 'attention scores.' Transformers are used for natural language processing (NLP) tasks such as text classification, translation etc.
- *Generative Adversarial Networks (GANs):* GANs consist of a 'Generator' which produces synthetic data and a 'Discriminator' which ascertains the authenticity of the generated synthetic data.

In this chapter, we will discuss the working of various Generative Adversarial Networks, their structure, and working in the Background. Their applications in image reconstruction and the generation of medico-synthetic data will be discussed in depth along with the various steps involved in the Methodology Section. In the Methodology, we will be discussing time-series GAN and image-reconstruction GANs, both of which will be dealing with EEG data. The existing challenges faced in the development and training of GANs as well as the future scope have been discussed in the later sections of Future Scope and Conclusion.

Background

Generative Adversarial Networks

GANs found their inception by Ian Goodfellow in 2014. GANs were proposed as an improvement over the then-existing generative models (VAEs) by introducing a game theoretic approach. GAN can be visualised as a bi-agent game in adversarial mode, as shown in Figure 3. To produce a synthetic data sample, the 'Generator' network is trained on the latent random variable (noise vector as input). The primary objective of the generator is to produce samples with features similar to those of the original ones. Simultaneously, the discriminator tries to find any difference existing between the actual and 'counterfeit' samples. As training continues, the discriminator tries to classify between both with increasing accuracy, and the generator keeps improving to increase the samples' authenticity.

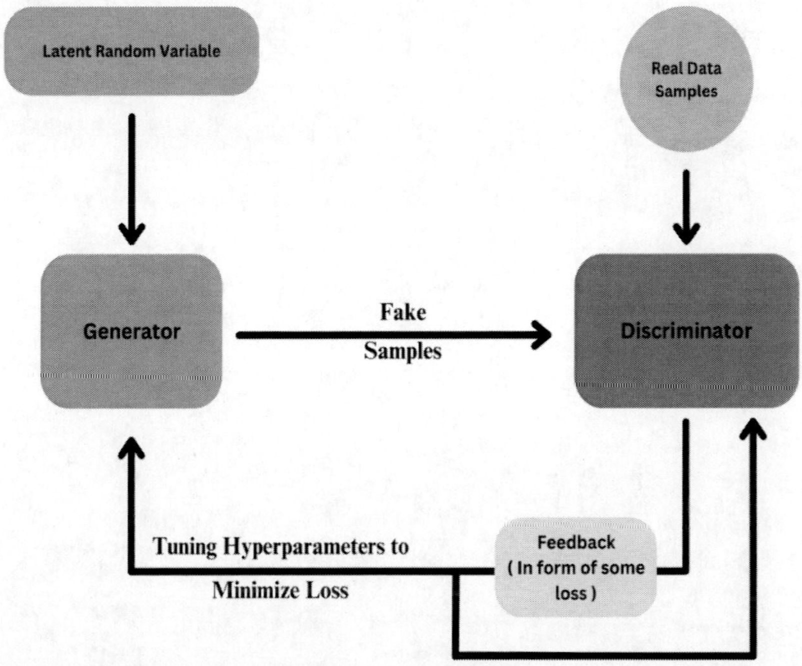

Figure 3. Block diagram describing the architecture of Generative Adversarial Networks.

From the context of game theory, it can be referred to as a zero-sum game, where the two players are aiming for a reward, and the loss for one agent equals the gain for the opposition.

Figure 4 shows the timeline of the evolution of GANs from their conception in 2014. GANs were primarily developed as image data generators. Since then, several new mechanisms have been introduced to the models to improve their efficiency and boost the quality of output generated. Model-appropriate evaluation metrics such as Inception Score, t-SNE plots, Train on Synthetic Test on Real etc have also been introduced [1-7].

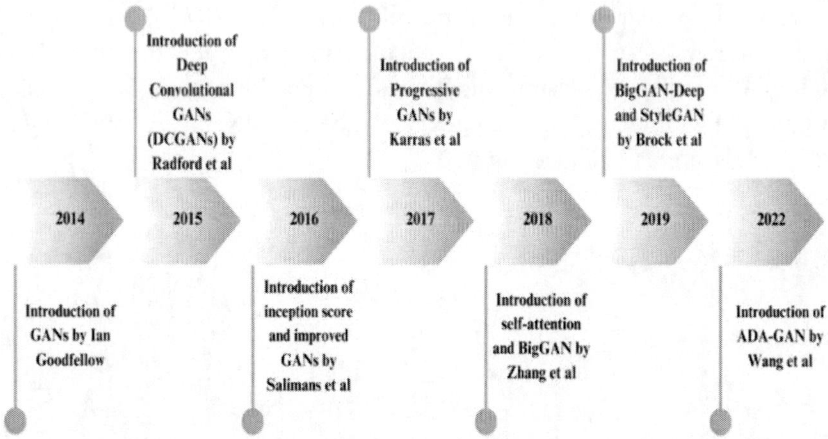

Figure 4. Timeline showing the evolution of image-based GAN models.

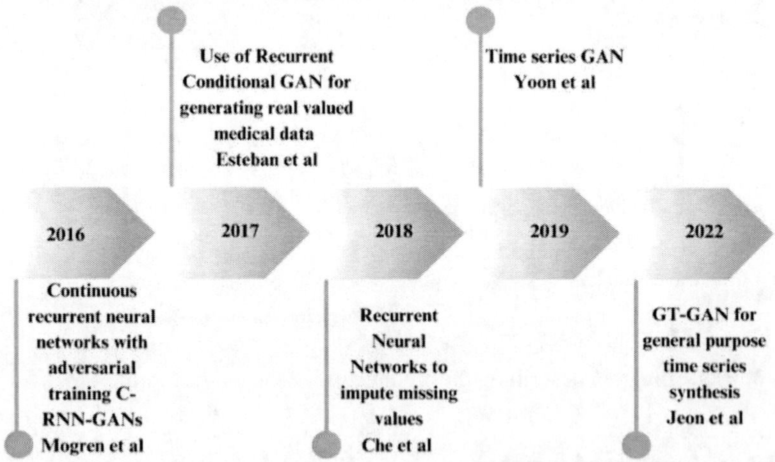

Figure 5. Timeline showing the evolution of time-series GAN models.

In addition to image-GANs, time-series-based models have also been developed, which primarily work to generate synthetic sequences, impute missing values, generate medico-synthetic data etc. Time-series GANs are also used for finance, prediction, forecasting, classification, biosignal synthesis etc. The evolution of time-series GANs is shown in Figure 5 [8-12].

Types of GANs

There are different variants of generative adversarial networks. Some of the popular variants are listed below:

Deep Convolutional GAN (DCGAN)

Deep Convolutional GANs (DCGANs) use convolutional neural networks (CNNs) to construct both the generator as well as the discriminator. The use of CNN as a generator helps the model capture the spatial mapping and patterns in image data, because of which they are used to produce high-quality image data. CNNs use batch normalisation to take care of the vanishing gradient issue and improve the overall convergence of the model. Using strided convolutional layers in the discriminator allows the model to capture the high-level features leading to the prevention of overfitting. These models generate realistic images such as faces, 3D objects etc.

Conditional GAN (cGAN)

Conditional GANs provide both random noise vector and conditioning variable, which governs the nature of the output. This conditioning variable can introduce or prevent the appearance of a certain feature(s) in the output images. Here, the discriminator also uses the conditioning variable as an input to improve its efficiency. CGANs are typically used for image generation, translation of low-resolution images to higher resolution and video prediction.

Information Maximizing GAN (InfoGAN)

Information Maximizing GAN (IMGAN) aims to utilise the degree of similarity between real and generated images as feedback to improve the generator's performance. An information maximisation network is added, maximising the mutual details between the random noise and output images. This network measures the information the generated images contain about the provided input vector and uses the backpropagation technique to give it back to the generator to improve its quality. The maximisation of information is carried out by the addition of regularisation term to the loss function.

Auxiliary Classifier GAN (ACGAN)

Auxiliary Classifier GAN (ACGAN) uses an auxiliary classifier GAN in addition to the GAN to predict the label of the image generated by the model. The presence of the classifier also encourages the generator to produce a diverse range of images belonging to several labels, compared to the traditional GAN.

Recurrent Conditional GAN (RCGAN)

RCGAN generates sequential data such as time series or natural language text. RCGAN consists of an additional RNN network. This network generates a hidden state sequence that encodes the temporal dependencies present in the output sequence. This hidden state sequence is used to compute the loss function, which includes both binary classification loss and sequence loss. The presence of the RNN network leads to the generation of more realistic and coherent sequences.

WaveGAN

WaveGANs are used for generating audio waveforms. This model uses a convolutional neural network as the discriminator. The training of both the blocks is done using a gradient descent optimization algorithm. The loss function used is binary cross entropy for the discriminator and feature-matching loss for the generator. The latter helps the generator to produce waveform that shares certain same statistical properties with the input audio. This GAN is used for high-quality audio production, speech synthesis, sound design etc.

Evaluation of Existing GAN Networks

Table 1. Table comprising details about different image and time-based GANs

Authors	Type of GAN	Methodology	Outcome
Brock et al. (2018) [6]	Image GAN	GAN with mini-batch stochastic gradient descent 'Spectral Normalisation'	Generated High Quality images on ImageNet, CelebA-HQ, LSUN bedroom datasets

Authors	Type of GAN	Methodology	Outcome
Che et al. (2018) [10]	Time GAN	Recurrent neural network GAN	Generated series by inputting missing values
Esteban et al. (2017) [9]	Time GAN	Recurrent conditional GAN	Generated real-valued medical data for analysis
Jeon et al. (2022) [12]	Time GAN	General purpose time series synthesis	Generate time series data using multi-scale approach
Karass et al. (2017) [4]	Image GAN	Progressive growing GAN modelling	Produce low to high-resolution images with better stability and variation
Mishra et al. (2022) [13]	NeuroGAN/Image GAN	GAN model with attention mechanism	Image reconstruction from EEG signals
Mogren et al. (2016) [8]	C-RNN-GANs	Combination of recurrent neural networks and GANs	Speech synthesis and music generation
Salimans et al. (2016) [3]	Image GANs	Inclusion of feature matching, minibatch normalisation, virtual batch normalisation techniques	Generation of high-quality images and stable convergence
Wang et al. (2022) [7]	Image GAN	GAN inversion method to generate images with desired attributes, new perceptual loss function introduced	High quality images generated with fine-grained details reserved from original image
Zhang et al. (2019) [5]	Image GAN	Self-attention mechanism layer with spectral normalisation	High quality images generated on CIFAR-10 and ImageNet datasets

Different types of Image-GANs and Time-GANs have been discussed in Table 1 along with their methodology and major outcomes, such as overall performance, results etc.

Methodology

Data Collection

Data is the currency of Artificial Intelligence. So, it is imperative to collect good data with minimal noise and artefacts. The data we will be dealing with in this context is Electroencephalogram. In order to capture the various frequencies (Theta, Delta, Alpha, Beta and Gamma waves) present in EEG waveforms, an appropriate Sampling Frequency should be set, as per the Nyquist Theorem to avoid aliasing. The data should be voluminous, comprising various trials based on designed protocol. To remove any artifacts or in order to get additional information, different parameters such as Electrooculogram (EOG), Electrocardiogram (ECG) etc can be recorded simultaneously as well. The protocol should be designed based on desired inclusion and exclusion criterion. Post screening, based on the research laboratory ethical committee, informed consent should be taken from all participants. Arrangements should be made to maintain data privacy and ensure minimal risk of data leak.

Data Pre-Processing

Bio signals are recorded with the objective of capturing only the physiological signal under consideration. However practically, data is contaminated due to several reasons such as electromagnetic interference (50Hz power line in India), muscle artefacts, motion artefacts, superimposition of EOG and ECG waves. It is therefore important to clean the data before working with it. One technique to deal with EEG data cleaning is to apply Independent Component Analysis (ICA). ICA performs removal of noisy components by assuming they are statistically independent of the original EEG waves. So, these unwanted components can be removed, and the rest of the components are used to backpropagate the 'clean EEG'. This can be done manually or implemented as an AI algorithm. Apart from this, outlier detection, averaging of trials, data normalisation can be done to reduce any experimental bias.

GAN Models

Time-Series GANs

Time-series GAN networks can be applied for producing sequential data such as synthetic medical data (in case of insufficient or low-quality data). The typical framework, evaluation metrics and challenges are discussed below and can be seen in Figure 6. An instance where time-series GAN can be applied is to augment the low-quantity medical data, e.g., bio signal synthesis and sensor measurement values etc. In this section, we will be discussing about application of time-series GAN by keeping in mind the EEG signal. We can generate new synthetic EEG data for data augmentation and use them for further analysis.

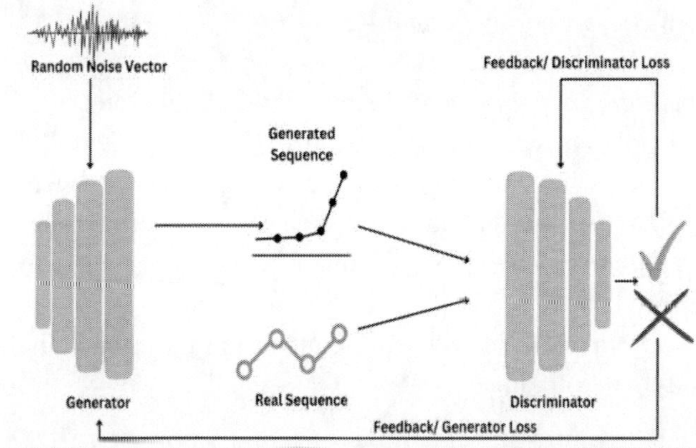

Figure 6. Illustration of how time-series GAN network works.

Application of Time-Series GAN

The data must be pre-processed according to the requirements of the GAN model architecture. These pre-processing steps may include reshaping the data, inputting the missing values in data, and scaling the data to bring the values to the same scale with various scalers such as MinMax Scaler or Standard Scaler. Data scaling is also used to remove any bias that might be present.

After the pre-processing part is done, data selection can be done. This can be done by selecting data with less noise. This is done in order to remove excess variations present in data. Various smoothening techniques can also be applied to data, such as applying Simple Moving averages (SMA) which smoothens out fluctuations in data by capturing the trend. Next, the GAN

Model architecture should be defined. It can be done with either PyTorch or TensorFlow in a Python environment.

The main components of GAN, i.e., Generator and Discriminator, must work in an adversarial manner to produce good results. The Generator network must learn to produce realistic samples that can pass as real data. It takes random noise as input and produces a time-series sequence. Both networks can be designed using LSTMs, GRUs, CNNs and RNNs or combinations of all these networks.

For Time-Series Data Augmentation, several techniques have been used, such as TimeGAN, RCGAN, C-RNN-GAN, Teacher Forcing (T-Forcing), WaveNet, WaveGAN etc. It is observed that TimeGAN performs better than other techniques on a few benchmarks. (Yoon et al, 2019). The authors of TimeGAN successfully kept the temporal dynamics of the signal intact. TimeGAN is made of four units mainly, i.e,

- *Embedding network* maps each time series into a latent space representation,
- *Generator network* takes a sequence of random vectors sampled from a normal distribution and produces a generated time series,
- *Discriminator network* discriminates between real and generated time series and,
- *Recovery network* maps the generated time series back to the original time series domain.

Model Evaluation

The quality of an AI model can be determined by evaluating its performance after computing several loss functions. The metrics for TimeGAN are *visual metrics*, consisting of Principal Component Analysis (PCA) plot and t-distributed stochastic neighbour embedding (t-SNE) plot, and Train on Synthetic Test on Real (TSTR) metrics which aim to improve the performance in terms of whatever the score was when the AI model was fit on the real training data. There are two other metrics:

- *Discriminative score:* which is the post-hoc classification error,
- *Predictive score:* which is the mean absolute error.

Challenges and Limitations

There are several challenges encountered upon using time-series data in GAN models, which have listed below

- *Quality and Quantity of Data:* TimeGAN requires a sufficient amount of high-quality time-series data to understand the underlying data distribution and maximise the similarity between actual and output data. If the data is noisy or incomplete, it may be difficult for TimeGAN to learn the true data distribution and generate accurate synthetic data,
- *Data Complexity:* Time-series data can be complex and heterogeneous, making it difficult for TimeGAN to capture all the underlying patterns and dependencies in the data. In some cases, it may be necessary to pre-process the data or use other techniques to reduce the complexity of the data before applying TimeGAN,
- *Tuning hyperparameters and the architecture*: TimeGAN has several hyperparameters that need to be carefully selected and tuned for the dataset in hand. Tuning appropriate model architecture and hyperparameters can greatly affect the performance of TimeGAN in generating accurate synthetic data.

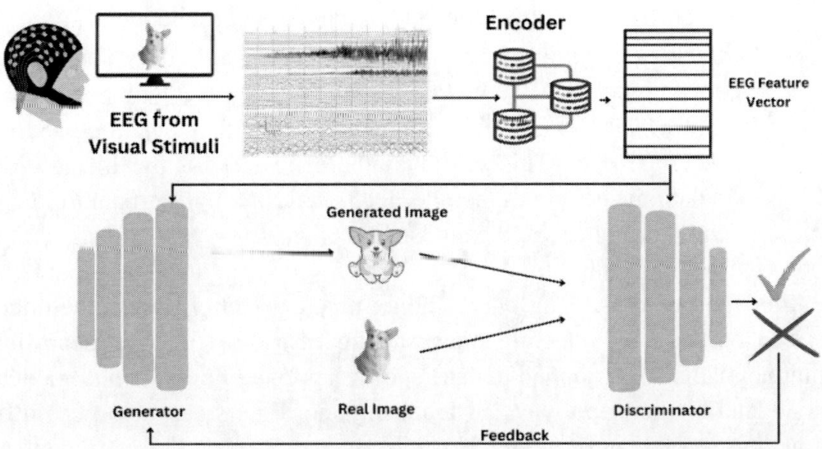

Figure 7. Illustration of how Image-generator GAN network works. EEG recordings are taken from the subject upon viewing visual stimuli. The EEG signals are encoded and fed to generator-discriminator networks for image reconstruction.

Image GANs

Image GAN networks can be applied to produce image data from signal or image input provided to the model. The typical framework, evaluation metrics and challenges are discussed below. Image GAN can be applied to perform image reconstruction from provided EEG data upon viewing several visual stimuli, as seen in Figure 7. Image GANs have been used to mimic the result of visual perception (discussed above) or model the mental imagery mechanism i.e., how 'mental images' are produced in our mind.

Application of Image GAN

The image data must be pre-processed according to the requirements of the GAN model architecture. These pre-processing steps may include

- *Resizing the Image Data:* GANs have a longer training time, especially on large images. The computational requirements of training can be reduced by adjusting the image size., It is preferred to resize the images to a smaller size which depends on the specific model architecture, typically to m×m pixel size.
- *Normalize pixel values:* The pixel values of images should be normalized to ensure that they are within a suitable range for the Image GAN model. This generally involves scaling the pixel values between -1 to 1 or 0 to 1, depending on the specific model.
- *Centering of Images:* The images should be centred by subtracting the mean pixel value across all images in the dataset.
- *Data augmentation:* Certain augmentation methods can be used on the original data. This improves the efficiency of the ImageGAN model. Some examples include Horizontal flipping, Vertical flipping, rotation, brightness and contrast changing, etc.

After the pre-processing part is done, image selection should be done. This can be done by selecting images with less noise. Various denoising techniques can also be applied to data, such as applying filters such as median filter, bilateral filter, and wavelet denoising, etc. Filters can help get rid of spatial noises such as Random Noise, Salt and Pepper Noise as well as Random Noise. Next, the GAN Model architecture should be defined with suitable deep learning frameworks.

Now, the main components of GAN, i.e., Generator and Discriminator, must work in an adversarial manner to produce good results. During training, fake images are generated from random noise by the generator. Generative Adversarial Networks (GANs) for images typically use convolutional neural networks (CNNs) as the fundamental blocks. They are well-suited for image processing tasks because of their ability to learn higher dimensional features and patterns in image data.

A generator network typically comprises several transposed convolutional layers (also known as "deconvolutional" layers) that learn to up sample the input noise into an image in the case of Image-based GANs. Batch normalisation layers are also commonly used to improve training stability and speed up convergence. A discriminator network, mainly consisting of multiple convolutional layers with one or more fully connected layers, is generally a binary classifier that distinguishes between real and fake images. The output of the discriminator is a single scalar value that represents the probability of the image belonging to the original dataset.

Several techniques have been used for Image Data Augmentation, such as DCGAN, StyleGAN, BigGAN, PatchGAN, WGAN-GP, etc. It is observed that the aforementioned types of GANs for images produce good results, subject to the benchmarks. For example, DCGAN performs better on MNIST, CIFAR-10 and CelebA than other GAN models, whereas StarGAN can perform multi-domain image-to-image translation, allowing a single generator to produce images in multiple domains (e.g., hair colour, age, and gender).

Model Evaluation

The quality of an AI model can be determined by evaluating its performance after computing several loss functions. Some metrics and losses are often used for assessing image-based GAN models:

- *Inception Score (IS):* It is a statistic that evaluates the performance of an image classifier trained on produced pictures to assess the diversity and quality of the images generated. It is computed by taking the entropy of the classifier's predictions and dividing it by the KL divergence between the predictions and the uniform distribution.
- *Frechet Inception Distance (FID):* It is a statistic that assesses the similarity between the distribution of produced pictures and the distribution of real images calculated by comparing the mean and covariance of features derived from an Inception model that has already been trained. The Wasserstein distance is a loss function employed specifically in WGAN models to stabilise the training of GANs. It calculates the difference in probability distributions between actual and produced pictures.

- *Adversarial Loss:* The primary loss function used in GANs which aims to increase the picture quality by evaluating the probability distribution difference between real and fake images. It is usually paired with other losses, such as the reconstruction loss or the perceptual loss.
- *Reconstruction Loss:* In a reconstruction job, the loss is measured as a difference between the output and input images. It is frequently used in conditional GANs to enforce image-to-image translation across domains.
- *Perceptual Loss:* A loss function that calculates the difference in features retrieved from produced and actual pictures by a pre-trained image classifier, often used to increase picture quality and realism in StyleGAN and other GAN models.

Challenges and Limitations

Despite Image-based GAN models' many triumphs in producing high-quality and diversified pictures, some various obstacles and limits must be addressed, such as:

- *Computational Requirements:* Image-based GAN models are frequently computationally costly, necessitating big datasets and sophisticated hardware to achieve cutting-edge performance, which can make training and deploying Image-based GAN models problematic in resource-constrained contexts.
- *Limited Interpretability:* Image-based GAN models are frequently employed as black-box generators that generate pictures based on complicated and non-linear transformations of input noise. Understanding how the generator maps input noise to output images and interpreting the underlying patterns and characteristics of the produced images can be difficult.
- *Dataset Bias:* Image-based GAN models may be vulnerable to biases and artefacts in the training dataset, resulting in overfitting or poor generalisation to unknown data. It might be difficult to verify that the training dataset is representative of the intended distribution and that biases in the output pictures are minimised.

Future of GANs

The current state of the GANs has shown extraordinary results so far. Image-based GAN models have been extensively used for generating high-resolution images, realistic synthetic images, and generative art. From a healthcare management perspective, they particularly show promise as they can help practitioners with better disease management, as seen in Figure 8. They can be utilised to understand or predict disease progression, identify new biomarkers and even chart personalised treatment plans. GANs can be used to evaluate the person's health, levels of different biomarkers and treatments can be designed as per an individual's need. An example of this could be evaluating the levels of various digestive hormones, and, accordingly, develop dietary plans to manage conditions such as obesity, intolerance towards certain food groups etc.

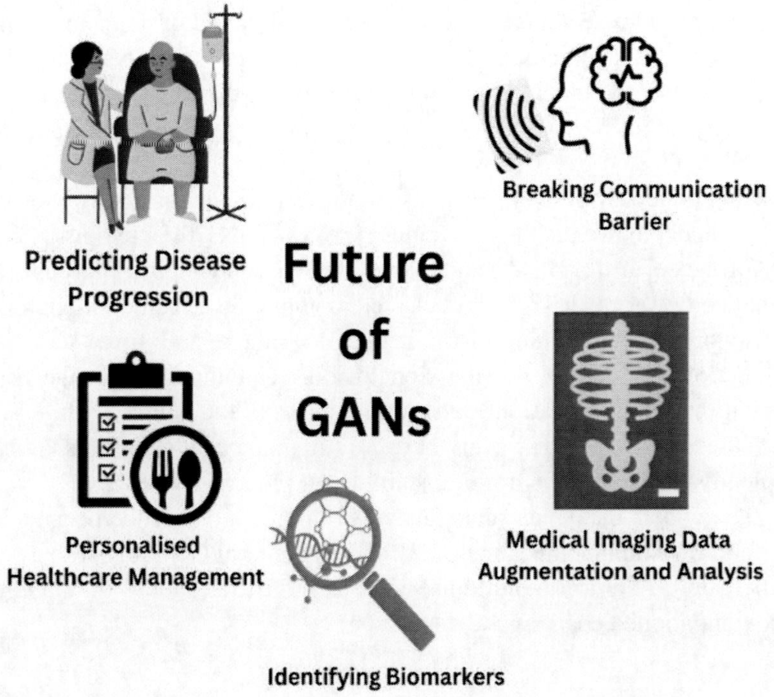

Figure 8. Future of GANs in the healthcare industry.

Owing to their ability for data augmentation, they can be used in scenarios with limited data to perform a more robust analysis of medical images. Modelling mental imagery for people with various mental health issues can also help bridge communication barriers. Time-series data also shows promise for imputing missing values or generating sequences, typically dealing with seizure prediction, heart health analysis etc. With further improvement, they can be used for early disease detection, personalised weight (and overall health) management plans, and the generation of medico-synthetic data for further analysis.

Conclusion

A thorough analysis of the existing state of Generative Adversarial Networks has already shown significant progress in various fields, such as speech synthesis, natural language processing, generative virtual art etc. They show promise to aid researchers in revolutionising the field of medical science and healthcare management. experimental results that are superior to those of earlier traditional machine learning methods. In the introduction, we gave a summary about bio-signal recording modalities, and how such medical data can be replicated by GAN was discussed later. A brief summary of various existing generative AI models was also given. Since our goal was to discuss GANs in depth, we discussed various types of GANs, their evolution and their performance in the Background Section. We conducted a thorough search, picked a few popular GAN models, and compiled the methodologies used for the two most important GAN networks: image and time series in the Methodology Section. For the Conclusion and Future Scope, we listed the limitations and evaluation metrics encountered and utilised while working with these networks. However, there are still many challenges that GANs face, typically improving the training stability and model convergence, overfitting of the model, data bias, data unavailability, ethical concerns and lack of methods to examine the authenticity and diversity of GAN-generated data. We anticipate GANs to revolutionise various industries should they address the abovementioned challenges.

Disclaimer

None

References

[1] Goodfellow, I., Pouget-Abadie, J., Mirza, M., Xu, B., Warde-Farley, D., Ozair, S., &Bengio, Y. (2014). Generative adversarial nets. *Advances in neural information processing systems, 27.*

[2] Radford, A., Metz, L., & Chintala, S. (2015). Unsupervised representation learning with deep convolutional generative adversarial networks. *arXiv preprint arXiv:1511.06434.*

[3] Salimans, T., Goodfellow, I., Zaremba, W., Cheung, V., Radford, A., & Chen, X. (2016). Improved techniques for training gans. *Advances in neural information processing systems, 29.*

[4] Karras, T., Aila, T., Laine, S., &Lehtinen, J. (2017). Progressive growing of gans for improved quality, stability, and variation. *arXiv preprint arXiv:1710.10196.*

[5] Zhang, H., Goodfellow, I., Metaxas, D., &Odena, A. (2019). Self-attention generative adversarial networks. In *International conference on machine learning* (pp. 7354-7363). PMLR.

[6] Brock, A., Donahue, J., &Simonyan, K. (2018). Large-scale GAN training for high fidelity natural image synthesis. *arXiv preprint arXiv:1809.11096.*

[7] Wang, T., Zhang, Y., Fan, Y., Wang, J., & Chen, Q. (2022). High-fidelity gan inversion for image attribute editing. In *Proceedings of the IEEE/CVF Conference on Computer Vision and Pattern Recognition* (pp. 11379-11388).

[8] Mogren, O. (2016). C-RNN-GAN: Continuous the recurrent neural networks with adversarial training. *arXiv preprint arXiv:1611.09904.*

[9] Esteban, C., Hyland, S. L., &Rätsch, G. (2017). Real-valued (medical) time series generation with recurrent conditional gans. *arXiv preprint arXiv:1706.02633.*

[10] Che, Z., Purushotham, S., Cho, K., Sontag, D., & Liu, Y. (2018). Recurrent neural networks for multivariate time series with missing values. *Scientific reports*, *8*(1), 6085.

[11] Yoon, J., Jarrett, D., & Van der Schaar, M. (2019). Time-series generative adversarial networks. *Advances in neural information processing systems*, *32.*

[12] Jeon, J., Kim, J., Song, H., Cho, S., & Park, N. (2022). GT-GAN: General Purpose Time Series Synthesis with Generative Adversarial Networks. *Advances in Neural Information Processing Systems*, *35*, 36999-37010.

[13] Mishra, R., Sharma, K., Jha, R. R., & Bhavsar, A. (2022). NeuroGAN: image reconstruction from EEG signals via an attention-based GAN. *Neural Computing and Applications*, 1-12.

Chapter 10

Deep Learning for the Closed Loop Diabetes Management System

Deepjyoti Kalita[1], MTech
Hrishita Sharma[1], MTech
Ujjal Naskar[1], MS (Pharm)
Bikash Kumar Mishra[1], BTech
Jayanta Kumar Panda[2], MD
and Khalid B. Mirza[1,*], PhD

[1]Department of Biotechnology and Medical Engineering,
National Institute of Technology, Rourkela, Odisha, India
[2]SCB Medical College and Hospital, Cuttack, Odisha, India

Abstract

The prevalence of diabetes, a chronic metabolic disease, is considered to reach 463 million individuals globally. In order to improve the care for diabetes, digital health has been extensively implemented recently. To better manage this chronic disease, a tone of data has been generated as a result. Blood sugar levels rise as a result of diabetes, which damages the pancreas's beta cells and reduces the volume of insulin released. Traditionally, the levels of the blood glucose are measured with a fingerstick before manually injecting insulin to treat diabetes. Modern alternatives like insulin pumps including the continuous glucose monitoring devices, which are much simpler and more automated, are replacing them. In addition to the analyzing also improving our information of which deep learning algorithms perform very well with

* Corresponding Author's Email: deepjyoti_kalita@nitrkl.ac.in, baigm@nitrkl.ac.in.

In: Building Intelligent Systems Using Machine Learning and Deep Learning
Editors: A. Kumar Sahoo, C. Pradhan, B. Shankar Prasad Mishra et al.
ISBN: 979-8-89113-342-6

glycemic data, this study seeks to establish a relationship between insulin pump settings and glycemic management. This has led to the widespread adoption of deep learning process, a novel type of machine learning, which gives encouraging results. In this chapter, we have described a full extensive and detailed analysis of deep learning implementations in diabetes. After conducting a thorough literature search, it was discovered that this method is effective in three crucial areas: the detection of diabetes, glucose control, and the identification of different complications for diabetes. It should be noted that among the analyzed literature, numerous deep learning architectures and frameworks have surpassed conventional machine learning methods to attain state-of-the-art performance in various numerus tasks relevant to diabetes. The inadequacy of data accessibility and the model interpretability are two significant flaws in the research that is already out there, which we highlight in the interim. These challenges can be quickly solved because of too deep learning's rapid developments and the expansion of data sources, enabling the extensive application of this technology transition in clinical contexts.

Keywords: diabetes, glucose control, deep learning, machine learning, glycemic management, insulin pump

Introduction

Diabetes is the class of chronic metabolic diseases brought either due to insufficient insulin production or insufficient insulin action. For complex pathophysiology of the disease, the International Diabetes Federation (IDF) predicts that there will be almost people of 463 million with diabetes globally in 2019. Half of these patients are still undiagnosed [1]. The next ten years are expected to see a marked rise in the prevalence of diabetes worldwide [1]. Because of this, diabetes prevention and treatment have had a considerable negative impact on the healthcare systems, national economies and the individual medical expenses, especially in middle- and the low-income countries [1].

Overview

The three subgroups of diabetes that make up the majority of cases are type 2 diabetes (T2D), type 1 diabetes (T1D), and gestational diabetes (GDM) [2].

For a longer period, type 2 diabetes sufferers resist insulin's typical effects and moderately reduce the ability for manufacturing the enough of the hormone. Patients with T2D have access to various treatment alternatives [2]. They frequently get drugs that enhance insulin secretion or absorption in the early stages of the condition, but eventually, they need to be given external insulin doses [2]. T1D patients, on the other hand, have substantial limitations in their ability to produce insulin. Thus, they must only utilize exogenous insulin to control their blood sugar (BG) [2]. For the treatment of T1D patients, either the continuous and subcutaneous insulin insertion (CSII) using a pump or multiple daily injections (MDIs) are required [2]. GDM is treated in a manner akin to T2D. Yet, because of how insulin and placental hormones interact, it only shows up during pregnancy [2].

Diabetes requires patients to follow a number of self-care routines, many of which are quite difficult for them: carefully planning meals, monitoring carbohydrate intake, exercising, monitoring blood glucose levels, and daily activity modification. Long-term consequences may take years to manifest if the suggested therapy is not followed, and their effects are not always apparent immediately. Because of this, managing diabetes is difficult, and therapeutic options must allow for a variety of medical markers as well as lifestyle-connected different tasks that need to be changed to enhance the life's quality for diabetic patients [3].

Closed Loop Diabetes Management System

Over the past ten years, the creation of the artificial pancreas (AP) or the *closed-loop* diabetes (CLD) management system, as well as adoption of the new technologies like CGM devices, have fundamentally altered the way that diabetes is controlled [3]. These developments, along with the use of the data gathered using these cutting-edge tools, have also led to the integration of new data-gathering techniques. A technology called a closed-loop diabetes management system, commonly called an "artificial pancreas," is made to automate insulin delivery to persons with type 1 diabetes. Utilizing cutting-edge algorithms, the system combines CGM devices and the insulin-pump technique to automatically alter insulin delivery in real-time in feedback to changes in the user's blood sugar levels [3].

The primary goal of a closed-loop system is to give precise glucose control and lessen the strain of day-to-day diabetes management. It aids in lowering the danger of severe hypoglycemia (low blood sugar) and improves glycemic control, essential for lowering the long-term problems related to diabetes [3]. The CGM system consistently monitors the blood sugar levels and governs how much insulin amount or volume is needed to keep them within the targeted range. The appropriate amount of insulin is then administered by the insulin pump; this dosage is continually adjusted in response to changes in the patient's blood glucose levels. The system can incorporate components like mealtimes and exercise to further improve glucose management [3]. A CGM system is generally regarded as extensive improvement in the oversight of T1D, offering users greater glucose regulation and an improved life quality, as shown in Figure 1. When a CGM sensor is used to extract the glucose value from interstitial fluid (ISF) [3], the control algorithm will estimate the amount of insulin that will be injected and at what time. As a result, the insulin amount is then delivered to the human body via the insulin pump unit. Hence, a CLD system uses a CGM sensor to assess blood glucose levels continuously, cutting-edge algorithms to compute the correct insulin dosage, and an insulin pump for delivering the insulin to achieve optimal sugar level control.

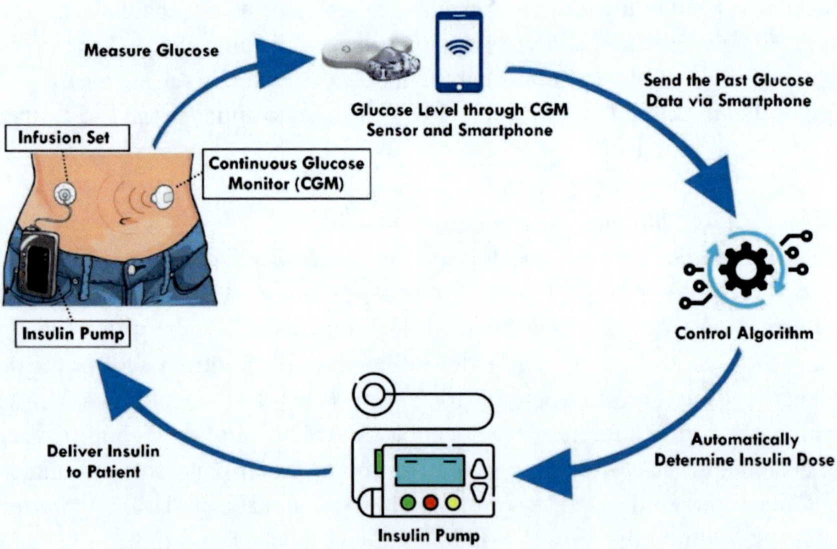

Figure 1. Overall Block Diagram of Closed Loop diabetes management system.

Role of Deep Learning in Closed Loop Diabetes Management System

A closed-loop diabetes control system, commonly referred to as an "artificial pancreas," can be developed with the utilization of deep learning [4]. A closed-loop system automatically controls the supply of insulin to a diabetic person based on their blood glucose levels in real-time. Deep learning can be used in this situation in several different ways, including:

1. Glucose Forecasting: Using a person's prior glucose measurements, insulin dosages, and meal details, a deep neural network can be trained to predict their future blood glucose levels. The optimal insulin delivery can subsequently be decided upon using this forecast.
2. Insulin Dose Prediction: Using a deep learning model, it is possible to learn the ideal insulin dosage needed to lower a person's blood sugar level to a desired range. The model generates the recommended insulin dose using the user's historical blood glucose readings, insulin dosages, and meal information.
3. Control of glucose levels: A deep reinforcement learning system can be utilized to manage the glucose levels of a diabetic person. Based on feedback from the person's glucose levels, the algorithm learns the best insulin dosing strategy.
4. Safety: By using deep learning models, harmful conditions like hypoglycemia or hyperglycemia can be quickly detected and avoided. The models can examine glucose levels and other pertinent data to alert the user or automatically change insulin delivery as appropriate.

These are just a few instances of how deep learning can create a closed-loop diabetes control system. The system may be improved to be safer, more effective, and more efficient for people with diabetes by using deep learning.

Advantage of Deep Learning over Other Machine Learning Methods

For estimating future blood glucose levels, a number of strategies have been developed recently, including machine learning models, polynomial models autoregressive exogenous (ARX) [5], autoregressive moving average (ARMA) [5] & autoregressive (AR) [5] as well as statistical models based on latent variables. Furthermore, widely used were machine learning (ML) methods which include the random forest, support vector regression, and grammatical evolution. In this discipline, deep learning (DL) is still a fresh and exciting machine learning technique. Because it can capture complicated dynamics of processes, particularly when it is challenging to retrieve the mathematical representations of a system, DL has potential. In computer vision (CV) and biomedical applications, deep learning (DL) has greatly enhanced state-of-the-art performance. Few studies have used DL for anticipating glucose levels to date. Few studies have used DL for anticipating glucose levels to date. For instance, deep layers were not used in typical dense neural networks to take advantage of their benefits. Deep learning's ability to model complex relationships, handle high-dimensional data, and provide personalized predictions makes it a promising tool for closed-loop diabetes management. So deep learning is more valuable than traditional machine learning in closed-loop diabetes management.

In the background section of this article, it will be discussed how various approaches of controlling blood glucose levels have changed over the years and how deep learning is presently used and outperforms all other approaches in terms of accuracy. In the methodology section, it is discussed how deep learning will be utilized more frequently for closed-loop diabetes treatment, incorporating physical activity with all of the currently available input parameters. In the discussion part, we have spoken about the difficulties and constraints presented by the various pieces of art that are currently in existence for the treatment of diabetes, and we have come to a conclusion.

Background

Genetics, autoantibodies, and environmental variables are the primary etiologic factors that cause diabetes. However, additional variables like gender, ethnicity and place of origin might be included in the list [6]. Interestingly, on average, T1D affects young people equally in both girls and boys, unlike the most common autoimmune disorders that preferentially impact females. Those with T1D can receive a variety of therapies, including constant subcutaneous insulin delivery with the insulin-pump or daily insulin which is fast-acting with meals along with the everyday basal insulin value. Whole metabolic normalization, however, is still not possible, and untreated diabetes can have a number of negative effects and different other diseases [6].

Diabetes Management Technology

Since the 1970s, there has been engaging in the idea of a CLD management system [6], frequently mentioned to as the artificial pancreas. The roadmap of managing the diabetes was initially initiated with the discovery of insulin by Frederick Banting in 1922 [6], as shown in Figure 2, and this journey is currently ongoing. The first insulin pump was discovered in 1962 [6], and as can be seen in the chronology of development, this led to other advancements. This system aims to autonomously control an individual's real-time insulin administrated depend on glucose levels. In the 1990s, a CGM system and the insulin pump were connected with the help of a computer program to form the prototype of a closed-loop system [6]. The CGM device would monitor blood sugar levels and transmit all information to insulin pump device, subsequently modifying insulin delivery.

The technology underlying closed-loop systems has advanced, making them more portable, dependable, and user-friendly. Today, several commercial closed-loop systems are offered on the market, and it has been demonstrated that they enhance efficient glycemic index management, lower hypoglycemia risk, and generally enhance the life quality for people with diabetes. Closed-loop systems still need to be regularly monitored and adjusted by the user because they are not a cure for diabetes. Nevertheless, they are a significant advancement in the treatment of diabetes and have a bright future.

Historically, the main monitoring technique for diabetes patients has been self-supervision of their individual blood glucose (SMBG). Yet, monitoring and treating diabetes using technology is becoming more common [7]. Insulin pumps & CGM devices are the next frontiers that must be researched and improved. CGM is a state-of-the-art diabetic technology that can detect diabetes in patients, make daily glucose monitoring easier, and guard against both mild and severe hypoglycemia. The integration of a CGM device and an insulin pump has produced algorithmically controlled pumps that stop administering insulin if it is anticipated that hypoglycemia levels will occur inside the next thirty minutes ranges or provide a supplementary insulin bolus doses to address anticipated the hyperglycemia event. These devices are referred to as hybrid *closed-loop* systems, and the use of these instruments to treat T1D is soon becoming the norm.

Different hybrid closed-loop devices have been marketed, moderately altering how T1D is treated in children and adults. This reflects how quickly this developing technology has moved from research to clinical use. One of these is the t: slim X2TM insulin pump device [7], which Tandem TM Diabetes Care introduced in 2016. It is a cutting-edge insulin pump system that can connect to the CGM sensor called Dexcom G6® [7]. The t: slim X2TM pump's Control-IQTM technology is an MPC algorithm that uses

CGM data to forecast blood glucose levels thirty minutes in the future values. To retain blood glucose levels within the normal ranges, the Control-IQTM pump automatically modifies insulin doses [7]. They stand for the top and lower limits of safe blood sugar levels. They serve as the cornerstone of the time in ranges metric (TIR), which was created in 2019 by an international group of doctors.

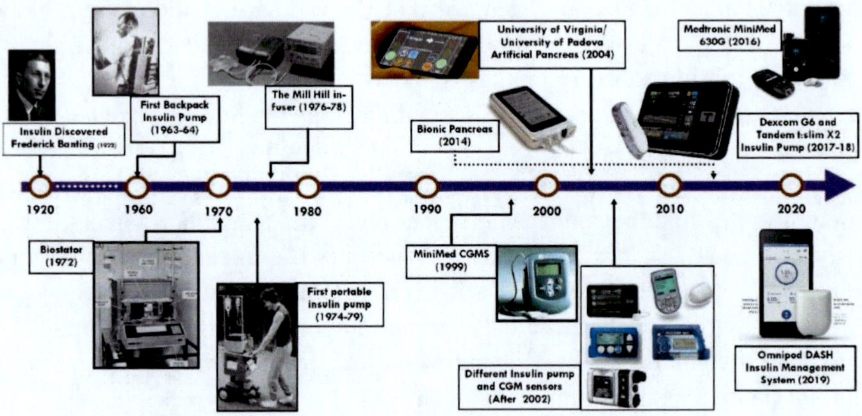

Figure 2. Timeline for the development of diabetes management technology after the discovery of insulin from the year 1921.

Use of Control Systems Algorithms in *Closed Loop* Diabetes Management System

An insulin pump with CGM sensor and a control algorithm make up the conventional CLD system. The insulin pump receives wirelessly transmitted real-time glucose measurements from the CGM. This glucose data is used by the control algorithm to determine the proper insulin supply and modify the insulin pump accordingly.

Figure 3(A) illustrates how the pancreatic and liver systems work together to regulate blood sugar levels in the human body naturally. The pancreas is a controlling factor in this situation and will regulate the release of glucagon and insulin hormones. Based on the chemical signal, the liver regulates the body's blood sugar level by acting as an actuator. A similar approach is found in Figure 3 (B control)'s system-based closed-loop artificial pancreas [7]. The control algorithm on a mobile platform substitutes the pancreas for an actuator, and the insulin pump serves as the electrical signal. The electrical signal employed here comes from the CGM sensor for glucose value.

The control algorithm can be thought of as a control system, which is a system that modifies another system's behavior (in this case, the glucose levels in the body). The control algorithm determines the required insulin supply and adjusts it as necessary using feedback from the CGM. This establishes a closed-loop system in which the input (in this case, the administration of insulin) is continuously tracked and controlled (glucose readings).

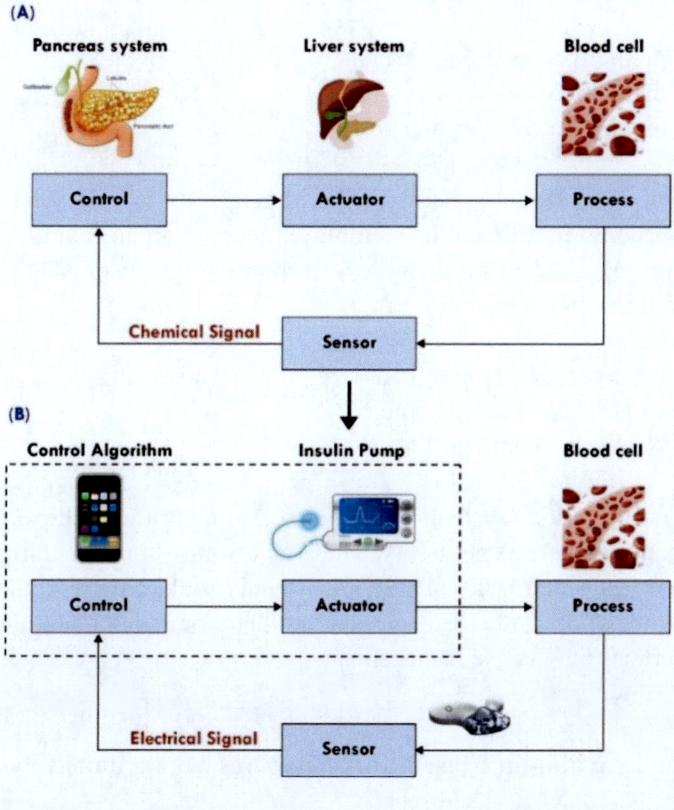

Figure 3. (A) Natural control of diabetes or blood glucose level in our body with pancreas and liver system. (B) Artificial control of blood glucose control with CGM sensor, Control algorithm running on mobile devices and insulin pump as an actuator.

Several such systems have already been created and are readily usable, and they have the great potential to enhance glucose control for persons with diabetes significantly. However, like with any medical gadget, it is crucial to use them under a doctor's supervision and pay close attention to the directions.

For closed loop diabetes management systems, numerous control algorithms have been created. Model-based and model-free algorithms are the two main groups into which these algorithms can be divided. Model-based algorithms produce predictions about future glucose levels based on existing glucose readings and insulin delivery and employ mathematical models to reflect insulin and glucose dynamics in the body. Typical model-based algorithms are as follows [7]:

1. predictive modelling (MPC)
2. State-space simulations
3. models for transfer functions

On the other hand, model-free algorithms do not rely on a mathematical model of the body. Instead, they employ a more straightforward, rule-based strategy to regulate insulin delivery in response to glucose readings. Model-free algorithms include, among others [7]:

1. Control using proportional-integral-derivative (PID)
2. Control using fuzzy logic
3. Networks of artificial neurons

Some closed-loop systems permit numerous algorithms, allowing users to switch between them as necessary. These algorithms can be modified to meet individual needs and tastes. These algorithms should only be utilized under the guidance of a healthcare expert due to their complexity and potential for diverse effects on glucose management.

Machine Learning in Closed Loop Diabetes Management System

Machine learning (ML) has recently gained popularity due to its expanding applications, particularly in the study of diabetes [7]. It is possible and desired to use artificial intelligence, and more especially machine learning, to treat diabetes in order to create efficient data management and processing tools and equipment. The lives of diabetic patients, the job of healthcare professionals, and the broader healthcare system can all be impacted and improved by these technologies [8]. The ML broadens the scope of diabetes patients' self-care, brings quick and precise judgement and adaptable follow-up for medical practitioners, and maximizes the resources of the healthcare system. There are several ways that machine learning is used in treating diabetes, from predicting and analyzing blood sugar levels to managing hypo and the hyperglycemia and improving insulin pumps. For instance, Seo et al. suggested a study that would develop a machine-learning method for forecasting postprandial hypoglycemia. Doing so is still tricky because of the dramatic glucose changes around mealtimes. With the help of a distinct feature set from data-driven method, the authors explored four machine learning models: random forest model, KNN algorithm method, SVM, and logistic regression approaches [8]. A machine learning methodology which is based on collective linear regression and the most minimal selection operator and absolute shrinkage was reported by Noaro et al. [9] in order to enhance the estimate of meal information including insulin doses in T1D managing utilizing CGM datasets in the UVa/Padova T1D simulator scenario [10]. In the year 2020, Askari et al. [11] presented an adaptable and forecasted control algorithm that would integrate disturbance prediction and pattern learning using historical data and future projections. The following year, researcher Colmegna et al. [12] conducted an *in-silico* evaluation of a linear parameter diverse control rule with a concentration on medium and intense level physical activity and the ultimate goal of minimising user intervention. In a comparative case study, Adams et al. [13] categorise blood glucose measurements using the data from the wearable sensors in people suffering from type 1 diabetes using a method called SVM and quadratic discriminant analysis algorithms. Due to this, the majority of studies concentrate on calculating blood glucose levels or determining the causes and effects of diabetes. None of them make an effort to find patterns in the relationship between basal insulin rate and glucose oscillations, particularly how insulin delivery and ongoing monitoring can affect it.

Figure 4 depicts how several machine learning or deep learning algorithms have been applied to closed-loop diabetes management. The state-of-the-art technology used a CGM Sensor to obtain patient glucose values. Also, several optional input elements that significantly impact our body's glucose level are taken into account [13]. A patient mobile application sends all data collected by various sensors to a cloud server. The doctor can monitor the patients via a web server or even a mobile application while simultaneously connected to the patient and the platform. After gathering all the input data, these data are saved on a cloud server and taught using machine learning or deep learning architecture to forecast the glucose value and insulin value that will be administered to the patient's body via an insulin pump.

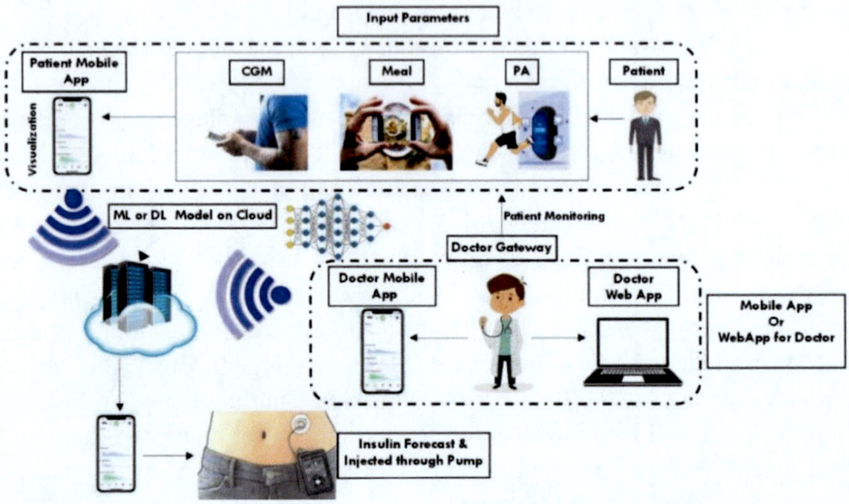

Figure 4. Overall idea of closed loop diabetes management platform based on cloud server where Machine learning or Deep learning algorithm is used as control algorithm.

Deep Learning in Closed Loop Diabetes Management System

There is yet to be comprehensive research that focuses particularly on DL applications for the diabetic patients, despite thorough analyses of the literature on AI for diabetes that included some classic machine learning techniques and statistical models [13]. A novel technique called deep learning freshly showed competitive execution in all different important aspects of diabetes, including diabetic eye diseases. Table 1 shows the different existing studies which employ various analysis criteria and deep learning architecture to manage diabetes. Thus, this research specifically examines recent advances in deep learning technology for the management of diabetes. There is yet to be comprehensive research that focuses particularly on DL applications for diabetes, despite thorough analyses of the literature on AI for diabetes that included some classic machine learning techniques and statistical models [14]. Deep learning was made possible by artificial neural networks (ANNs), which resembled the design of organic brain neurons. Iterative backpropagation is the typical method by which an ANN learns senses, albeit generalization for supervised tasks is not yet achieved. By expanding the ANN structure to DNNs, which train representations with dozens or millions of parameters and extract data features, deep learning improves generalization [14]. Throughout the past two decades, improvements in computer software including hardware infrastructures have primarily driven the development of DL by enabling DNN models to increase in size and complexity [14]. The majority of DL algorithms can be widely split into three categories: one is supervised learning, others are unsupervised learning, and reinforcement learning. For iterative model development and backward propagation for the straightforward tasks of regression and classification or separation in the process of supervised learning, where we have used the labelled input data. Convolutional neural networks (CNNs), Recurrent neural networks (RNNs) and deep multilayer perceptron's (DMLPs) are the major supervised learning based DNNs that have been discovered in the diabetes literature [14]. A lot of DNN models are constructed using the DMLP, which makes use of fully connected (FC) layers and directly connects neurons. Because to the fact that multilayer perceptron is sometimes used interchangeably with ANNs and DNNs. Deep learning has the exceptional developing potential to fiercely boost the efficacy of CLD management systems since it can offer more precise and customized glucose control, reduce the risk of hypoglycemia, and spot patterns and anomalies in glucose levels. Deep learning has been used in various studies to treat diabetes. Here are a few examples, their findings, and potential research topics for the future.

These studies demonstrate the promise of deep learning for the treatment of diabetes. Future studies could concentrate on examining the use of DL for the early diagnosis of diabetic complications as well as establishing individualized diabetes treatment techniques.

Methodology

The main goal of this study is to choose the DL technique for diabetes management as optimally as is practical with the end aim of raising the subjects' TIR (Time in Range). In order to optimize the pump, signals from the hybrid CLD system were employed in DL methods, which revealed pertinent details regarding the link between the observations and the settings.

Table 1. List of different existing studies which employ various analysis criteria and deep learning architecture to manage diabetes

Paper	Dataset	Used Model	Main Outcome
Li, Kezhi et al. (2019)	ABC4D and UVA/Padova	comprehensive multiple-layer convolutional neural network Post-processing on CNN	For UVA 10-Adults: For 30 Minutes PH: RMSE (mg/dL) = 8.88 ± 0.77 MARD (%) = 5.32 ± 0.66 Time lag (mins) = 0.83 ± 0.40 For 60 Minutes PH: RMSE (mg/dL) = 19.90 ± 3.17 MARD (%) = 10.55 ± 1.40 Time lag (mins) = 16.43 ± 4.07
Li, Kezhi et al. (2019)	UVA and Real time Patients of OhioT1D	CNN with RNN	RMSE for Simulated Data 18.87 ± 2.25 [mg/dL] in a 60-min forecasting horizon 9.38 ± 0.71 [mg/dL] in a 30-min forecasting horizon
Zhu et al. (2020)	OhioT1DM & UVA	Dilated Recurrent Neural Networks (DRNN) with the help of using tensor flow	For UVA 10-Adults: For 30 Minutes PH: RMSE (mg/dL) = 7.8 ± 0.6 MARD (%) = 4.8 ± 0.6 Time lag (mins) = 0.4 ± 0.3
Cruz-Vega et al. (2020)	167 subjects contain Plantar thermogram database	Customized 9-layer CNN	Sensitivity: 0.9167, AUC: 0.8533

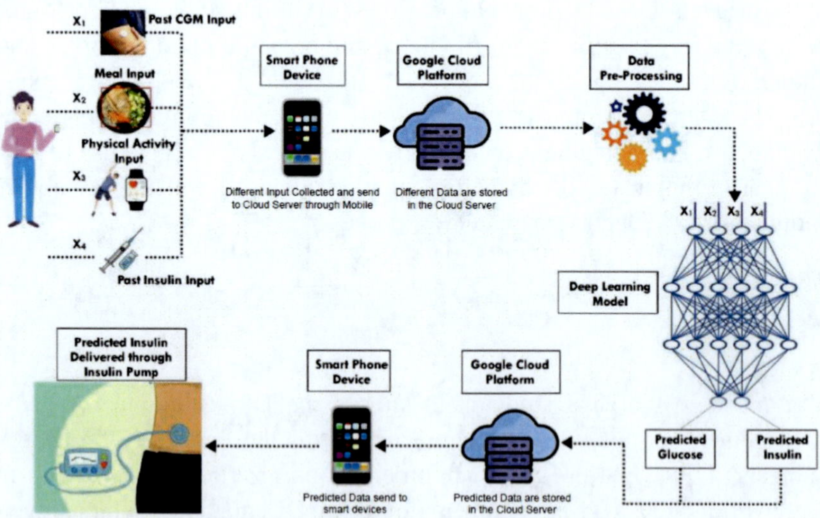

Figure 5. Closed Loop diabetes management system and its different input parameters and how it works with deep learning architecture with cloud server and smart phone platform.

Diagnosis of Diabetes

Over time, the diagnosis of diabetes has changed due to improvements in medical science and technology that have produced more precise and effective diagnostic techniques. In the past, symptoms including increased thirst, frequent urination, and exhaustion were the main criteria for diagnosis. Doctors would also use a fasting blood sugar test to check blood sugar levels, which could reveal the presence of diabetes. However, more accurate and trustworthy diagnostic techniques are now available because of the development of new technology. As an illustration, the A1C test, which gauges blood glucose levels on average over the previous three months, is now frequently used to identify diabetes. This test is beneficial for identifying diabetes in people who may not show typical symptoms [14].

Continuous glucose monitoring (CGM), which entails wearing a device that continuously measures blood sugar levels throughout the day, is another technical improvement in diagnosing diabetes. Those with diabetes who are at risk of hypoglycemia or hyperglycemia will find this strategy to be especially helpful (high blood sugar levels) [14]. Additionally, certain types of diabetes, such as monogenic diabetes, brought on by a single gene mutation, can be diagnosed via genetic testing. With new technology and diagnostic techniques, diabetes diagnosis has generally improved, enabling earlier detection and better disease management.

Technology in Glucose Management

Interstitial Fluid (ISF) is used by Continuous Glucose Monitoring (CGM) sensors as opposed to blood to obtain blood glucose levels. In comparison to tests of blood glucose, the ISF glucose values are often delayed by 10 to 15 minutes [15]. This lag is because it takes some time for the ISF's glucose to diffuse out of the blood. To account for this delay and give people access to real-time data on their blood glucose levels, glucose prediction is, therefore, necessary in the management of diabetes. Glucose prediction models can use the information from the CGM sensor to estimate blood glucose levels in real time by utilizing cutting-edge algorithms and machine learning. Patients with diabetes can use glucose prediction to plan their food, exercise, and insulin dosage. A person can eat a modest snack to raise their blood glucose level and prevent hypoglycemia, for example, if it is anticipated that they will have a low blood glucose level in the coming minutes.

Similarly, suppose someone is expected to have high blood sugar in the next few minutes. In that case, they can change their insulin dosage or increase their level of physical activity to drop their blood sugar and avoid hyperglycemia. Therefore, glucose prediction is essential for managing diabetes because it empowers people suffering from diabetes to take proactive steps to regulate their own blood sugar in targeted range and avoid the consequences of high or low blood sugar. The following section will explain how glucose prediction is made step by step with the help of the DL or ML algorithm, as shown in Figure 5.

Data Collection

For glucose prediction models to be successful and reliable, the right data must be gathered for review and testing. Considerations for data collection include the following:

a) Sampling frequency: As glucose levels can change quickly, gathering data at a frequency high enough to catch these shifts is critical. A typical sampling interval is every 5 to 15 minutes.
b) Data volume: Many data is frequently needed to train and test deep learning models. Look for a dataset that has data from a CGM sensor for at least a few weeks.
c) More information: Gathering additional information about eating habits, physical activity, medication use, and insulin dosages can aid in the development of more precise glucose prediction models that can take these things into account.
d) Ethical considerations: When gathering information from human subjects, ethical issues must be taken into account. These issues include getting informed consent, maintaining confidentiality and privacy, and abiding by all applicable laws and policies.
e) Data quality: For precise glucose prediction, data quality must be guaranteed. This entails accurate CGM device calibration, preventing electromagnetic field interference, and ensuring the data is free of mistakes and anomalies.

Preprocessing

Data must be preprocessed to eliminate noise, missing numbers, and outliers after it has been gathered. Data cleaning, normalization through MinMax Scaling, and feature engineering are steps in this process. The preprocessing part's main objective is to clean up the data, get rid of any outliers, and get it ready to feed into the neural network. Outlier identification, interpolation/extrapolation, and filtering - particularly for clinical data - are the most crucial operations to improve the data quality, in addition to the standard processes of time stamp alignment and normalization. Because of problems with calibration, measurement, data collection, and/or transmission, clinical data can contain a large number of absent or outlier data points.

Deep Learning Architecture Selection

A complicated issue requiring careful consideration of the data's features and the research topic is model selection for glucose prediction in time series data. The choice of acceptable modeling approaches can be influenced by the time series' stationary or non-stationary nature. Hence this is a crucial factor to take into account. Deep learning models can be utilized as an alternative to conventional machine learning models in glucose prediction for time series data since they can capture non-linear correlations between input variables and glucose levels.

Recurrent neural network (RNN) models, frequently used for time series prediction, are created to handle sequential data by processing each input in a time-dependent manner. RNNs, known as long short-term memory (LSTM) networks, are particularly good at simulating long-term dependencies in time series data [15]. The convolutional neural network (CNN), which is frequently employed for image identification but can also be modified for time series data, is another kind of deep learning model applied for glucose prediction [15]. A 1D CNN can extract functional predictive elements from the glucose time series, such as trends and patterns [15]. Although deep learning models for predicting glucose levels may need much training data and computer power to develop, they have shown encouraging outcomes in earlier investigations. To ensure the usefulness and generalizability of these models, it is crucial to construct and test them using the proper validation methodologies and performance indicators.

Model Training and Evaluation

The model must then be trained using the preprocessed data after being chosen. In order to reduce the prediction error, the model parameters are optimized during the training phase.

The model must be tested on a different data set after being trained to determine how well it performs. For the purposes of calculating insulin bolus and glucose prediction, the error or performance is analysed using RMSE (Root Mean Square Error) [15], MAE (Mean absolute error) [15], and MARD (mean absolute relative difference) [15]. This performance matrix can be expressed as

$$RMSE = \sqrt{\frac{1}{N}\sum_{k=1}^{N}(y_k - y_k^{/})^2} \quad (1)$$

$$MAE = \frac{1}{N}\sum_{k=1}^{N}|y_k - y_k^{/}| \quad (2)$$

$$MARD = \frac{1}{N}\sum_{K=1}^{N}\frac{|y_k - y_k^{/}|}{y_k} \quad (3)$$

Here y_k is the actual or first measurement of glucose, $y^{/}_k$ is a prediction of what will happen, and N is the total number of data points.

Model Deployment

Ultimately, the trained model can be used to provide patients with real-time glucose predictions. In order to provide individualized glucose management suggestions, this step requires linking the model with medical devices, such as insulin pumps or mobile applications. In order to maintain the model's accuracy and efficacy over time, it is crucial to continuously monitor and improve it.

Insulin Dose Forecasting

Predicting the insulin dose is a critical component of diabetes care that aids people with diabetes in improved blood sugar control. In order to maintain optimal glucose control, accurate insulin dosage is crucial. Insulin dose prediction aids in this process by considering a range of variables, including previous insulin doses, food intake, physical activity, and data from continuous glucose monitoring. Insulin dose prediction models may evaluate enormous amounts of data and produce precise predictions for insulin doses, enabling patients to receive more individualized care—through advanced machine learning methods, such as deep learning. Predicting the insulin dose helps lower the risk of diabetes complications, including chronic diseases like neuropathy and retinopathy. Insulin dose prediction can ultimately result in better patient outcomes and a higher quality of life for people with diabetes by assisting patients in maintaining more stringent glucose control.

A potent tool in closed-loop diabetes management systems is the prediction of insulin dose using deep learning techniques. A deep learning model can discover patterns and associations between these inputs using historical continuous glucose monitoring (CGM) data, insulin dosing information, heart rate, physical activity, and meal intake, and assist in adequately forecasting insulin dosages in real time.

A RNN framework, which includes a long short-term memory (LSTM) architecture, could be used to create such a system [15]. A sequence of previous time steps for the various inputs would be the model's input, and the output would be a forecast of the necessary insulin dose for the following time step [15].

Collecting and preprocessing the essential data would be the initial stage in creating such a system. This can entail gathering information from a CGM sensor, an insulin pump, a heart rate monitor, a fitness tracker, and an app for food diaries. The data would need to be cleaned and modified to make the data suitable for the deep learning model's input.

The next step would be to construct and train a deep-learning model. This would entail choosing a suitable architecture, such as an LSTM network, and determining the proper model hyperparameters. In order to forecast future insulin doses based on the input data, the model would then be trained on a collection of past data.

A closed-loop diabetes management system can incorporate the model once trained. The system continuously gathers input data from numerous sources and forecasts insulin doses in real-time using the learned deep learning model. The insulin dosages administered by the insulin pump would be updated to retain the patient's blood sugar levels within a predetermined range.

Overall, deep learning-based insulin dose forecasting can potentially increase the precision and effectiveness of closed-loop diabetes management systems. These systems must be carefully designed, validated, and monitored to ensure safety and effectiveness in clinical practice.

Role of Physical Activity

Exogenous insulin is necessary for T1D patients to survive. They must determine the proper insulin dose to inject while monitoring their blood glucose concentration (BGC) [15]. Numerous factors, including physical activity, meals, and stress, must be considered because they all impact a person's ability to use glucose and respond to insulin [15]. It can be difficult for people with T1D to accommodate physical exercise since therapy conclusions made during physical activity should think about various variables affecting blood glucose concentration dynamics (BGC). Different physical activities use variable sources of inner fuel, and they have non-identical total energy spendings, which affect BGC dynamics differently. The potential exists to better manage diabetes through various physical activity modalities using some mathematical or analytical designing to explain the usage of different energy sources [15].

The level of physical activity significantly influences the composition of energy use. Both carbohydrate and fat utilization rise when activity increases to around 60% of maximal oxygen intake ($VO_{2\,max}$) [15]. Closed-loop diabetes care, often known as artificial pancreas devices, can benefit greatly from physical exercise. Closed-loop systems do not require constant human input since they use a CGM to measure blood sugar levels and the insulin pump to give insulin automatically, depending on those levels. The following are a few ways that exercise can affect closed-loop diabetes management [15]:

- Improved glucose regulation: Exercise increases insulin sensitivity and decreases insulin resistance, which can aid in improving glucose regulation. Blood glucose levels may become more constant, making it more straightforward for the closed-loop system to maintain ideal glucose management.

Closed-loop systems use algorithms to modify insulin doses in response to CGM data. Blood glucose levels can fluctuate due to physical exercise. Thus, the algorithm may need to modify insulin dosage to account for these changes. The algorithm might restrict insulin delivery, for instance, if someone goes for a run and their blood sugar levels drop, to prevent hypoglycemia.

- Managing hypoglycemia: For patients with diabetes, hypoglycemia can be harmful due to physical exertion. Insulin supply can be reduced or stopped by closed-loop systems responding to hypoglycemia, which can assist in avoiding dangerously low blood sugar levels.
- Increasing physical activity: Closed-loop diabetes management can also include encouraging physical activity. Regular exercise helps enhance glucose control and general health, which can lower the risk of complications from diabetes.

Overall, physical activity can be very helpful in managing closed-loop diabetes by enhancing glucose control, modifying insulin dosage, controlling hypoglycemia, and enhancing general health. However, it is crucial to collaborate with a medical expert to create a specific physical activity plan that considers every person's needs and objectives.

Diagnosis Complications

Millions of individuals worldwide have diabetes, a chronic metabolic illness. While it is treatable with proper care and a lifestyle change, it can also result in catastrophic problems if neglected or improperly managed. Common side effects include cardiovascular illness, neuropathy, nephropathy, diabetic retinopathy, and foot issues [16]. Early identification and treatment are crucial to avoid or lessen the effects of these problems. Traditional diagnostic techniques, however, might take a while and are not always reliable. Healthcare professionals may make more precise and fast diagnoses using the power of deep learning and machine learning, enabling earlier interventions and better results for diabetic patients. These algorithms can assist healthcare professionals in identifying which patients are at risk for developing complications, allowing for proactive management and prevention [16]. They do this by being able to analyze massive volumes of data and spot trends. In this sense, machine learning and deep learning have the potential to completely alter how we identify and treat diabetes problems completely, ultimately enhancing the quality of life for millions of people worldwide.

Discussions

The management of diabetes may benefit from deep learning, a kind of machine learning. Deep learning algorithms can learn complicated patterns and make predictions based on vast and heterogeneous data sources more than conventional approaches like rule-based systems and statistical models. For example, deep learning can be applied to detect high-risk patients, forecast blood sugar levels and insulin needs, and customize treatment regimens. However, deep learning has its drawbacks, including the necessity for a lot of labeled data, the chance of overfitting, and the difficulty in interpreting the results. As a result, even though deep learning has enormous potential for managing diabetes, its use should be done carefully and in conjunction with more established techniques.

How Deep Learning overcome existing Techniques Technology in Glucose Management

Deep learning has shown potential in enhancing glucose control by overcoming some of the drawbacks of current methods and technology in a few ways, including:

1. Better Accuracy: DL algorithms which have been found to forecast sugar levels more accurately than conventional models. This is so that deep learning models, which conventional methods could miss, can recognize complicated and nonlinear patterns in data.
2. Personalization: Conventional glycemic management methods frequently employ universally applicable guidelines and algorithms, which may not be optimal for individual patients. By learning from a person's past glucose data, lifestyle, and medical history, deep learning models can tailor glucose treatment.
3. Real-time monitoring: Deep learning models can monitor glucose levels in real time and notify the patient or a healthcare professional when they depart from the usual range. By doing this, severe hyperglycemia or hypoglycemia may be avoided.
4. Reduced Patient burden: The burden is lessened because traditional diabetes management methods may call for repeated blood glucose checks, insulin injections, or prescription changes. Deep learning models can lessen the strain on patients by offering automated glycemic management that modifies insulin dosage and prescription schedules.
5. Integration with wearable technology: Deep learning models can provide continuous glucose monitoring and glucose management using wearable technology like continuous glucose monitors. Patients can now more simply and immediately manage their blood glucose levels.

Deep learning has the potential to significantly enhance glucose management and get beyond some of the drawbacks of current methods and equipment. More research is required to guarantee the security, precision, and dependability of deep learning models for glucose management.

Challenges and Limitations

Even though DL has increased the current research scenario in several disciplines connected to utilization in healthcare systems, diabetes still required to be highly reliable, vigorous, and compelling to keep away from security issues and provide effective treatment support. There are still a number of limitations and challenges that need to be overcome before deep learning may be further integrated in real-world therapeutic settings. Table 2 lists the five typical constraints discovered in the selected papers: data quality, data volume, feature processing, data volume and interpretability. Diabetes patient data are typically erroneous in real-world settings because of human error and sensor anomalies. The process of gathering real data can be costly and time-consuming. Datasets can be difficult to share among research teams because of data privacy laws. These factors cause several researchers to use tiny, occasionally insufficient, data. Analyzing the available data to categorize persons with diabetes presents another difficulty as an outcome of the intricacy of glucose dynamics. DL models are also opaque. Understanding why the DL frameworks construct the outcome for a specific input instance or parameter which is critical from the perspective of doctors, especially for some prime decision-creating new applications. The model is more challenging to interpret despite the DNN layers' complicated architecture effectively learning patterns from non-linear input. Thus, the trade-off between efficiency and interpretability must be taken into account when exploring deep learning for diabetes. Furthermore, it is projected that new algorithmic and hardware developments will increase the efficiency of deep learning model training [16-19].

Table 2. List of the challenges and limitations raised by the numerous works of art currently in existence

Component	Exisiting work	Explanation
Data variability	[16]	Due to the intricate dynamics of glucose, diabetes patients vary significantly from one another. Deep learning models need training data that includes a wide variety of patients to achieve better generalization, such as persons with various comorbidities and ages. Nevertheless, many datasets are frequently gathered from a particular cohort of individuals, which needs more variety and could skew the learning.
Processing of Feature	[16, 17]	The crucial problem in the feature processing method is identifying the traits that are most useful for the frameworks which will learn different tasks. Standard analyzing each and every feature value in a diabetes database may involve a large amount of technical work, yet utilizing fully automated data-driven algorithms, like as we can say PCA would ignore various physiological information and the rely also greatly on the attribute of the much-needed data. Given the improvements in data collection and physiological model development, a more thorough investigation of additional aspects and characteristics is required.
Volume of Data	[17, 18]	While training a a DL framework for difficult tasks, a lot of information or dataset is required. Collecting various data from different persons with diabetes is usually time- and money-consuming compared to other NLP and CV operations. As a result, many studies experience data scarcity during their research cycles.
Quality of Dataset	[19]	Similar to many other healthcare challenges, the majority of diabetes datasets are sparse, heterogeneous noisy, and contain some missing information. Because of the inescapable errors from CGM devices, it is impossible to expect perfect data gathering from clinical practice or everyday self-management.
Interpretability	[19]	Interpretability, or explain ability, refers to the model's ability to produce the desired result given a given set of inputs. The adoption of such systems by physicians is a crucial objective of AI applications in healthcare. Deep learning models are sometimes viewed as "black boxes" lacking model transparency since they contain numerous complicated nonlinear layers. As a result, it could be challenging to pinpoint why the model's performance suffers under specific conditions.

Opportunities and Future Technology

We anticipate considerable developments in glucose management technology in the future. Creating continuous glucose monitoring (CGM) systems that can give users access to real-time glucose level data represents one promising field of research. Moreover, these systems may use machine learning and artificial intelligence to offer individualized recommendations for controlling blood sugar levels, such as dietary changes or insulin dosage. Researchers are also looking at using implanted technologies that can continually monitor and control glucose levels without requiring constant manual input from the user, such as intelligent insulin pumps or glucose-sensing tattoos. Overall, glucose management technology has a bright future and has the ability to significantly enhance the lives of people suffering from diabetes and other illnesses connected to blood sugar levels. In Figure 6, we have shown the future technology transition which will be utilized for diabetes management. There will be considerable technological developments and a wide range of solutions for managing diabetes by 2030. Some of the most promising ones are listed below [19]:

1. Advanced Artificial Pancreas Technology: The technology for artificial pancreas has been under development for a long time and is getting more advanced over time. These gadgets are anticipated to include cutting-edge features by 2025 that enable more accurate glucose monitoring and insulin delivery. They may integrate with other technology, such as smartwatches and mobile apps, for even more precise data and immediate notifications.
2. Gene editing: It is a relatively new scientific development that has the potential to treat diabetes at its source. In the future, gene editing might allow researchers to change the genes that cause diabetes, thereby "curing" the condition. Although this technology is still in its infancy, the potential is huge.
3. Insulin pens: It have grown in popularity recently, and by 2030, it's likely that they will be considerably more sophisticated. These pens may have sensors that may automatically change dosages, prescribe dosages, and monitor blood glucose levels. Patients would find it much simpler and more convenient to manage their diabetes this way.
4. Advanced Artificial Pancreas Technology: The technology for artificial pancreas has been under development for a long time and is getting more advanced over time. These gadgets are anticipated to include cutting-edge features by 2025 that enable more accurate glucose monitoring and insulin delivery. They may integrate with other technology, such as smartwatches and mobile apps, for even more precise data and immediate notifications.

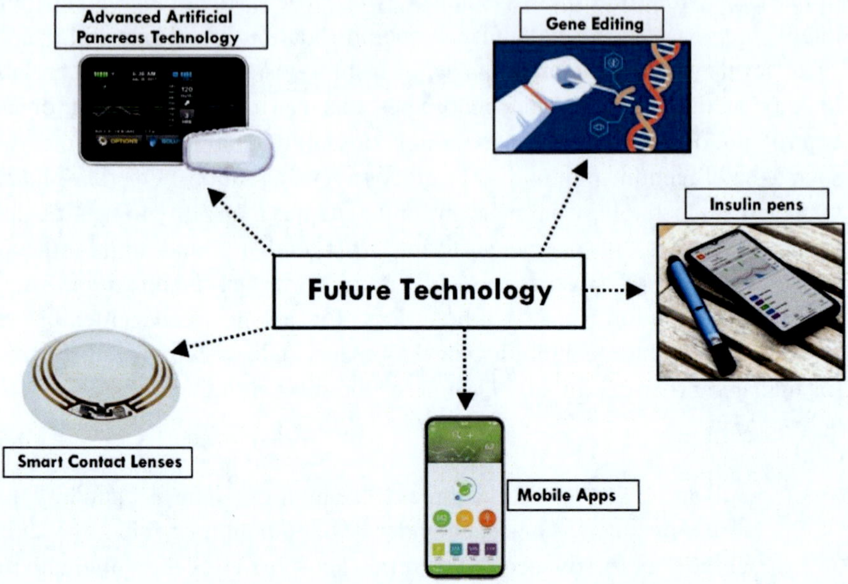

Figure 6. Future Technology for Diabetes Management and Control.

5. Gene editing: It is a relatively new scientific development that has the potential to treat diabetes at its source. In the future, gene editing might allow researchers to change the genes that cause diabetes, thereby "curing" the condition. Although this technology is still in its infancy, the potential is huge.
6. Insulin pens: It have grown in popularity recently, and by 2030, it's likely that they will be considerably more sophisticated. These pens may have sensors that may automatically change dosages, prescribe dosages, and monitor blood glucose levels. Patients would find it much simpler and more convenient to manage their diabetes this way.
7. Smart Contact Lenses: Another innovative technology that might be accessible by 2030-2040 is smart contact lenses. These glasses may potentially be able to give insulin directly to the eye while monitoring blood sugar levels. This would completely do away with the requirement for injections, making the control of diabetes far less invasive.
8. Mobile Apps: By next few years, mobile apps are projected to be significantly more sophisticated and will likely be a necessary tool for managing diabetes. Some apps might feature more advanced algorithms that can forecast changes in blood sugar, send out instant

notifications, and even give tailored advice based on a patient's individual data.

Overall, the outlook for managing diabetes is positive, and these developments are just a few instances of the numerous opportunities that lie ahead. We may hope for even more useful tools as technology develops to support individuals with diabetes in leading healthier and more satisfying lives.

Conclusion

A thorough analysis of the current state of DL technologies used in diabetes research indicates better performance by deep learning methods for *closed-loop* diabetes management. Several DNN architectures and learning methods have been employed in different fields and have produced experimental results that are superior to those of earlier traditional machine learning methods. We conducted a thorough search, picked a few studies, and compiled the most important data with a focus on three areas: diabetes diagnosis, glucose control, and diabetes-related complication diagnosis. In existing solutions, a number of issues, such as data accessibility, feature processing, and model interpretability limitations, have been noted in the different literature. By integrating the most recent developments in deep learning technology with vast amounts of multimodal diabetes management data, there is a tremendous deal of promise to overcome these obstacles in the future. We anticipate that DL technologies will be widely used in various clinical conditions and significantly advance the managing of diabetics.

Disclaimer

None.

References

[1] World Health Organization. "World Health Organization Global Report on Diabetes." *Geneva: World Health Organization* (2016).

[2] Saeedi, P., Petersohn, I., Salpea, P., Malanda, B., Karuranga, S., Unwin, N., Colagiuri, S., Guariguata, L., Motala, A. A., Ogurtsova, K., Shaw, J. E., Bright, D., & Williams, R. "Global and regional diabetes prevalence estimates for 2019 and projections for 2030 and 2045: Results from the International Diabetes Federation Diabetes Atlas." *Diabetes research and clinical practice* 157 (2019): 107843.
[3] Tuomi, Tiinamaija, Nicola Santoro, Sonia Caprio, Mengyin Cai, Jianping Weng, and Leif Groop. "The many faces of diabetes: a disease with increasing heterogeneity." *The Lancet* 383, no. 9922 (2014): 1084-1094.
[4] Noaro, Giulia, Giacomo Cappon, Martina Vettoretti, Giovanni Sparacino, Simone Del Favero, and Andrea Facchinetti. "Machine-learning based model to improve insulin bolus calculation in type 1 diabetes therapy." *IEEE Transactions on Biomedical Engineering* 68, no. 1 (2020): 247-255.
[5] Dave, Darpit, Daniel J. DeSalvo, Balakrishna Haridas, Siripoom McKay, Akhil Shenoy, Chester J. Koh, Mark Lawley, and Madhav Erraguntla. "Feature-based machine learning model for real-time hypoglycemia prediction." *Journal of Diabetes Science and Technology* 15, no. 4 (2021): 842-855.
[6] Pham, Trang, Truyen Tran, Dinh Phung, and Svetha Venkatesh. "Predicting healthcare trajectories from medical records: A deep learning approach." *Journal of biomedical informatics* 69 (2017): 218-229.
[7] Lekha, Srinivasan, and M. Suchetha. "Real-time non-invasive detection and classification of diabetes using modified convolution neural network." *IEEE journal of biomedical and health informatics* 22, no. 5 (2017): 1630-1636.
[8] Abràmoff, Michael David, Yiyue Lou, Ali Erginay, Warren Clarida, Ryan Amelon, James C. Folk, and Meindert Niemeijer. "Improved automated detection of diabetic retinopathy on a publicly available dataset through integration of deep learning." *Investigative ophthalmology & visual science* 57, no. 13 (2016): 5200-5206.
[9] Noaro, Giulia, Giacomo Cappon, Martina Vettoretti, Giovanni Sparacino, Simone Del Favero, and Andrea Facchinetti. "Machine-learning based model to improve insulin bolus calculation in type 1 diabetes therapy." *IEEE Transactions on Biomedical Engineering* 68, no. 1 (2020): 247-255.
[10] Man, Chiara Dalla, Francesco Micheletto, Dayu Lv, Marc Breton, Boris Kovatchev, and Claudio Cobelli. "The UVA/PADOVA type 1 diabetes simulator: new features." *Journal of diabetes science and technology* 8, no. 1 (2014): 26-34.
[11] Askari, Mohammad Reza, Iman Hajizadeh, Mudassir Rashid, Nicole Hobbs, Victor M. Zavala, and Ali Cinar. "Adaptive-learning model predictive control for complex physiological systems: Automated insulin delivery in diabetes." *Annual Reviews in Control* 50 (2020): 1-12.
[12] Colmegna, Patricio Hernán, Fernando Daniel Bianchi, and Ricardo Salvador Sánchez-Peña. "Automatic glucose control during meals and exercise in type 1 diabetes: Proof-of-concept in silico tests using a switched LPV approach." *IEEE Control Systems Letters* 5, no. 5 (2020): 1489-1494.
[13] Adams, Dawn, and Ejay Nsugbe. "Predictive Glucose Monitoring for People with Diabetes Using Wearable Sensors." *Engineering Proceedings* 10, no. 1 (2021): 20.

[14] Li, Kezhi, Chengyuan Liu, Taiyu Zhu, Pau Herrero, and Pantelis Georgiou. "GluNet: A deep learning framework for accurate glucose forecasting." *IEEE journal of biomedical and health informatics* 24, no. 2 (2019): 414-423.

[15] Li, Kezhi, John Daniels, Chengyuan Liu, Pau Herrero, and Pantelis Georgiou. "Convolutional recurrent neural networks for glucose prediction." *IEEE journal of biomedical and health informatics* 24, no. 2 (2019): 603-613.

[16] Zhu, Taiyu, Kezhi Li, Jianwei Chen, Pau Herrero, and Pantelis Georgiou. "Dilated recurrent neural networks for glucose forecasting in type 1 diabetes." *Journal of Healthcare Informatics Research* 4 (2020): 308-324.

[17] Cruz-Vega, Israel, Daniel Hernandez-Contreras, Hayde Peregrina-Barreto, Jose de Jesus Rangel-Magdaleno, and Juan Manuel Ramirez-Cortes. "*Deep learning classification for diabetic foot thermograms.*" Sensors 20, no. 6 (2020): 1762.

[18] Wan, Shaohua, Yan Liang, and Yin Zhang. "Deep convolutional neural networks for diabetic retinopathy detection by image classification." *Computers & Electrical Engineering* 72 (2018): 274-282.

[19] Chakrabarty, Ankush, Francis J. Doyle, and Eyal Dassau. "Deep learning assisted macronutrient estimation for feedforward-feedback control in artificial pancreas systems." *In 2018 Annual American Control Conference (ACC)*, pp. 3564-3570. IEEE, 2018.

Chapter 11

Digital Image Spatial Feature Learning and Mapping Using Geospatial Artificial Intelligence: A Case Study

Ajay Kumar[1,*]
Jay Prakash Singh[1]
Deepjyoti Choudhury[1]
Vivek Kumar[1]
and Sunil Kumar Bisoyi[2]

[1]Department of Computer Science and Engineering, Manipal University Jaipur, Rajasthan India
[2]Postdoctoral Research Fellowship, Department of Mining Engineering, IIT (ISM) Dhanbad, Jharkhand, India

Abstract

In recent trends, geospatial-artificial intelligence (GeoAI) has provided enormous opportunities and challenges to active earth research. Theoretical advances, big data, computer hardware, and robust data processing platforms that enable the creation, training, and deployment of GeoAI prototypes quickly are the driving forces behind its rapid development. The automation of geospatial studies and artificial intelligence, particularly computer vision techniques and the most recent intelligent systems, including research and industry, has made significant strides in recent years. Besides attention to spatial contexts and ancestries

* Corresponding Author's Email: ajay3789@gmail.com.

In: Building Intelligent Systems Using Machine Learning and Deep Learning
Editors: A. Kumar Sahoo, C. Pradhan, B. Shankar Prasad Mishra et al.
ISBN: 979-8-89113-342-6

in topography or geospatial science, GeoAI can be defined as the study of intelligent computer programs that simulate human perception, spatial cognition, and realization about spatial occurrences and evolution; extend our information; and solve problems in the human natural ecosystem and their contexts. In this study, the usefulness of a manual survey is based on experience. Still, other technology serves a consoling job in a fast, systematic approach to evaluating the spatial feature using the application of GeoAI. This GeoAI-based technique has played a pivotal role in the spread of accurate measurement-based information. Besides this, the case study location at the Indian Institute of Technology, Dhanbad (IIT-DHN), Jharkhand campus, included multiple areas such as roadways, buildings, vegetation, water tanks, etc. So, it has utilized GeoAI for feature discrimination to spot linked map terrain dilemmas at reconnaissance (1:250,000) levels. It is also critical for the development and future shape of prediction.

Keywords: geospatial; artificial intelligence; geographical information system; digital image; mapping

Introduction

A geospatial field survey user or professional always prefers comfort for work and time savings. Also, geographic information systems (GIS), global positioning systems (GPS), and satellite imagery acquisition are a few examples of broad technologies for geospatial modeling and analysis. It does adhere to geographical information gathered from satellite sensors or aerial sensors. A GIS mapping offer is significantly improved by satellite imagery, and it also offers information and data to help analyze and classify for spatial evaluation and the modeling process. An earth observation-based navigational device using a constellation of 24 satellites put in orbit for coordinate collection is also utilized with GPS. Understanding land use and employing supporting data are crucial for developing countries, which frequently face significant environmental and demographic challenges. Spatial governance dramatically benefits from the practices and processes used for mapping ecological asymmetries. Over several decades, GPS systems have been extensively fitted with frame sensors, line scanning sensors, LiDAR, SAR, and other sensors in aerial remote sensing based on the latest position surveys. Geospatial artificial intelligence (GeoAI) and satellite imagery are incredibly useful for assessing such aspects as urban area mapping and GIS modeling, size, and the ecological effects of rural and urban expansion. GeoAI has used many fields in integrating, manipulating, and analyzing multisource datasets, like population, topography, and infrastructure frameworks. GeoAI's analytical capabilities have the potential to be separated into basic (classification, overlays, neighborhood actions) and advanced (modeling, interpolation) [1]. After selecting and preliminary processing layers (georeferencing, projections, enhancement, spatial adjustment, etc.), GeoAI tasks are capable of recognizing criteria-based spatial results through map algebra activities (add, subtract, multiply, divide, etc.), helping solve the spatial problems with expansion [2]. Researchers [3] critically examined the spatial analysis of features that demonstrated the characteristics of spatial development, labeled through the recognition of infrastructure and roadways. Digital geospatial maps from Google Earth or other sources are used to map spatial and built-up expansions [4].

Moreover, satellite images could be used to cover the earth with a resolution in pixels, and higher resolution images are achieved using manned aircraft specially designed for mapping [5, 6]. Besides, GeoAI, an innovation in aerial mapping, provides reliable data information (IIT-DHN campus map) that is able to rapidly map a local area from a low altitude and at a low cost with more informatics data information. Additionally, such aerial images can be utilized not only for generating local orthographic images and topographical maps but also for building three-dimensional surfaces [7]. Additionally, its rise of digital morphology in three dimensions and more prominent is required due to the growing use of multi-dimensional images in machine visualization applications [8]. More specifically, digital curves, lines, surfaces, planes, and other computer analogs of Euclid mathematical components have been the subject of a significant amount of research [9, 10]. Several different approaches have been considered [11, 12, 13]. The earliest attempts to describe digital data were computational; an image was established as the outcome of a specified method. Referring to the canonical [14, 15] is appropriate. It may be difficult to conceptually investigate the attributes of objects defined in this manner, which is a general shortcoming of this technique. In the context of a digital image, choosing a digitization method based on the requirements for accuracy, digitization model type, and digitization quality can be challenging [16 - 19].

Furthermore, the information provided by the various manufacturers of digitization systems regarding the efficacy of their methods is only sometimes consistent with the performance of the actual models. The objective focuses on using GeoAI for digital image feature learning and mapping. Also, the organization of the research article has been carried out with methodology, results, and discussion in sections.

Methodology

Background Information and Basic Observations

The integration of based on geography studies and Intelligent systems is indeed not unique [20 – 23]. Despite the importance of location vagueness, spatial heterogeneity, and dependence on spatial information, the development of spatially explicit AI systems requires spatial memory and thematic maps [24, 25]. Consequently, there is more than one way to integrate terrain and the addressing location. Any location addressing is vital for integrating or synthesizing multisource data layers, and spatial concepts and geospatial domain-specific help generate different context-specific zones are crucial for advancing GeoAI models. Also, the data portrayal or feature extraction level generally impacts several machine-learning algorithms' efficacy [26]. Thereby, besides employing spatial relations and constraints, latent feature learning or pattern recognition for spatially explicit Intelligent systems has attracted great interest in GeoAI.

The reconnaissance survey is the wide-ranged analysis of a large area that could be used as a study boundary. The purpose is to find the best options and eliminate the ones that won't work. Also, the aerial views and emerging maps could be advantageous. Thus, the study encompasses the Central Institute of Mining and Fuel Research (CIMFR), the headquarters of DGMS, and Bharat Coking Coal Limited (BCCL), all of which are located on the campus of what was formerly ISM and are now part of IIT. Academic buildings, student dorms, and staff and student apartments comprise the IIT (ISM) campus. There's a central library, a seismic observatory, a data processing lab, a gallery showcasing artifacts from the long wall mine, a remote sensing lab, and a data processing lab.

Procedure of Data Map

An urban land survey raster data map with analytical features powered by GeoAI. The Earth Observatory publishes and makes publicly available (https://earthexplorer.usgs.gov/) all raster data collected from satellite photographs created by the autonomous agency of the United States federal government responsible for the civil space program. Europe collaborated with several other nations to launch the ERS and Envisat satellites, which are equipped with a wide range of sensors and are used for satellite imaging. Several private companies also provide commercial satellite imagery. Several companies and organizations in the early 21st century made satellite imagery widely accessible by delivering low-cost, user-friendly software that provided access to satellite imagery databases.

Geoai Approach for Spatial Feature Learning and Mapping

GeoAI-based application analysis of features follows some basic procedures according to the flow chart shown in Figure 1. As of late, we have employed an intelligent system and methodology-compliant field surveying coordinates. Also, georeferencing is defined as associating something with locations in physical space [27, 28]. Commonly used in geospatial intelligent systems, it refers to assigning coordinates to features on a map or raster image of a map. In addition to landmarks, roads, places, bridges, and buildings, georeferencing can be used for anything related to a specific location—furthermore, this other data, such as the GPS mentioned above points, links to the imagery. GeoAI and georeferencing are essential to making aerial and satellite imagery, typically raster images, useful for mapping.

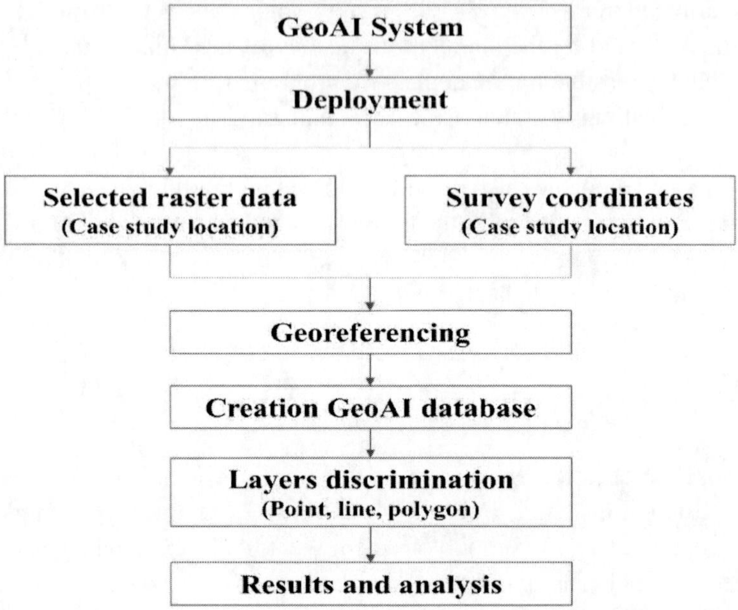

Figure 1. Adapted flowchart of GeoAI-based digital image learning and mapping.

Mapping Process Using Georeferencing

Many different types of GeoAI systems, including trustworthy and on-premises computing, can transform digital image data into a geographic control framework. The digital information can be packaged in points, lines, polygons, pictures, or 3D structures using georeferencing [29, 30]. When a GPS system logs a given location's coordinates, this is an example of georeferencing. Unique identities are also required for location-based georeferenced data. In other words, there needs to be something special about the spot where a georeferenced point is used as a benchmark. The sequence of georeferenced images begins with an attempt to construct control points, an approach to their known geographic coordinates, the acquisition of the coordinate system, and other projection parameters. It ends with the minimization of residuals. Its residuals reflected the deviation from the projected coordinates of the control points based on the geographic model constructed with the help of the control points. The next step is to provide them with robust, intelligent systems to evaluate the precision of the georeferencing procedure. In order to translate information from postal or area codes to geographic coordinates, a definitive directory or gazetteer file is often used. National mapping organizations, census bureaus, and postal services typically compile these gazetteers. These need not be more complicated than two lists: one of names and codes, the other of locations. The availability of codes and their intended use also varies by country.

Creation of Geoai Database for Spatial Features

The GeoAI database is provided for the framework of the intelligent system in prevalent data handling and storage. It establishes a centralized data repository for the storage and management of spatial data by fusing the terms "GeoAI" (spatial data) and "database" (data repository). As shown in Figure 2, it may be used in desktop, server, and mobile settings to keep GeoAI data in one place, where it can be easily accessed and managed.

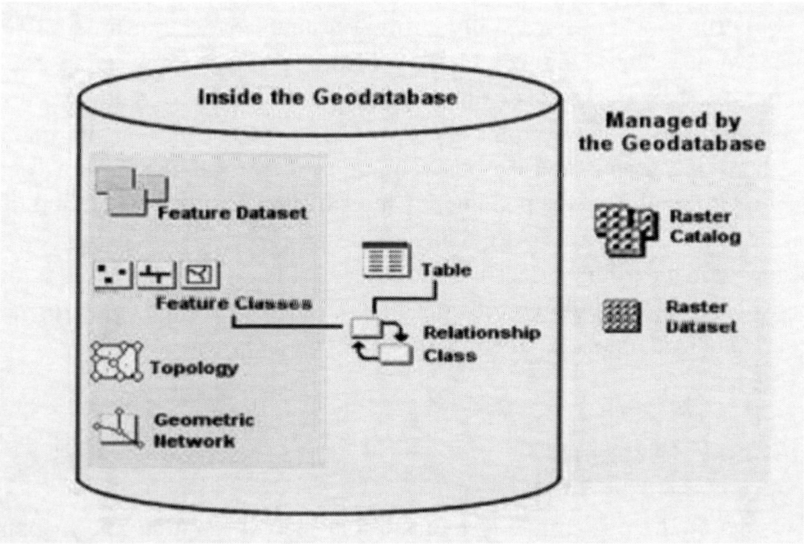

Figure 2. GeoAI database manipulation for spatial features.

While spatial database systems use indexes to quickly lookup values, the way most databases index data could be more conducive to spatial queries. Alternately, spatial databases shorten processing times by indexing data spatially. (a) quantify the world by measuring things like line length, polygon area, distance between shapes, etc., (b) spatial functions: altering preexisting features to generate new ones via crossing features, buffering existing ones, etc., (c) spatial predicates: supports yes/no inquiries on the existence of a connection between two geometries in space, (e) observer functions: inquiries which return precise information about a feature such the location of the Centre of a circle, and (d) geometry constructors: generates new geometries, typically by specifying the vertices (points or nodes) which define the shape.

Learning and Mapping of Raster Data Map

Learning and mapping are visual organizers that emphasize learning, competencies, and prominent beliefs. Also, the map illustrates the crucial data to be realized and precisely how the distinct learning sections are coupled. Whether carried from raster data originals that have been scanned or captured digitally, a topographical instrument like a scanner, or a 3D scanning device to obtain precise dimensions from a physical object. Further, the primary technique for storing images in a format suitable for transmission and computer processing is digitization. A geographic intelligent system's use of raster or vector images to create digital representations of geographic features, i.e., the production of electronic maps, relies on digitizing both traditional paper maps and graphs and various geographical and satellite imaging data. Also, it additionally has the potential to describe the procedure of adding files or data to GeoAI databases. Although technically incorrect, this usage derives from the term's earlier correct use to describe the step of the process that involves digitizing digital converter sources, like printed pictures and brochures, before uploading them to the target GeoAI database.

Result and Discussion

The results of the present study indicate that GeoAI learning and mapping have significantly shifted their focus toward digital images. The digital image that suggests that GeoAI learning should go beyond the simple steps that introducing a GeoAI intelligent system to instructional activities would automatically provide automatic learning, and mapping helps identify and discuss these design approaches. Given an overview of current GeoAI intelligent systems that offer virtual terrain mapping and feature extraction. Summary of findings Significant improvements in 3D visualization and animation have been made in 3D geospatial. However, there is still a deficiency in 3D capabilities such as 3D geo-object creation and management (querying), 3D structures and manipulation (e.g., 3D overlay and 3D buffering), and 3D analysis (e.g., 3D shortest route). This is due, in part, to the differences between 3D and 2D data. As a result, there are still obstacles to overcome in 3D data organization, 3D object reconstruction, representation, and navigation of big 3D models.

Occurrence of the Final Report

Depicted study site IIT-DHN campus findings include the names, lengths, areas, and widths of the campus boundaries (Table 2), roads (Table 3), and water tanks (Table 4).

Table 2. The campus boundaries

Object_ ID	Material	Width	Shape_ Length
1	Cont. track	8	1674.988073
2	Cont. track	7	770.187332
3	Cont. track	7	450.139228
4	Cont. track	6	76.398388
5	Cont. track	7	1015.972031
6	Cont. track	7	237.363331
7	Cont. track	6	198.020254
8	Cont. track	6	139.538479
9	Cont. track	6	294.497341
10	Cont. track	7	157.462692
11	Cont. track	6	84.897521
12	Cont. track	6	160.178165
13	Cont. track	7	114.060324
15	Kachha road	6	277.638938

Table 3. Roads

Object_ ID	Name	Shape_ length	Shape_ Area
3	Mining Dept.	713.073028	4236.730858
4	Old ground	283.585899	5872.3069
5	Upper ground	411.671007	12016.361872
6	Lower ground	529.066942	18971.073677

Table 3. (Continued)

Object_ ID	Name	Shape_ length	Shape_ Area
7	Senior academy hostel	192.785495	1966.27625
10	EDC	293.804994	4066.384215
11	Diamond	495.497694	3266.258655
12	Jasper	729.215352	9098.635859
13	New library	198.718759	2481.759207
14	Geodetic	170.284858	1776.008384
15	Petroleum dept.	141.989909	1108.179008
16	library	71.453066	311.495277
17	New lecture hall	312.702247	2286.909915
18	Tennis play ground	113.208006	711.801519
19	Volleyball &Basket ball ground	198.777078	2291.411571
20	swimming pool	230.211554	2187.822918
21	Student activity center	243.062965	3480.265478
22	emerald	328.740393	5556.103553
23	amber	753.685824	8189.543393
24	Sapphire	383.210448	8355.657097
26	civil dept.	272.355579	3087.815713
27	Research scholar hostel	135.756863	1188.683014
28	workshop	189.221775	1148.780326
29	Mining machinery	380.083543	2403.270315
30	fuel &mineral	226.5299	1142.499848
31	computer science dept.	177.837577	1244.349071
32	management dept.	139.827444	876.412859
33	hospital	112.468416	795.946427
34	Ruby hostel	56.200323	200.47823
35	Teachers colony	110.703443	525.214796
36	geophysics dept.	87.134405	392.874418
37	EC& Environment dept.	211.313095	1314.889919
38	Long wall	151.042898	1060.617686

Table 4. Water tanks

Object_ ID	Name
157	Watertank1
158	Watertank2
160	Watertank3
161	Heritage tree

Conclusion

An implementation of a GeoAI-based rendering of the study site (the IIT-DHN Campus in Jharkhand, India) was created, and study findings were generated based on it. Analysis of geospatial features, coordinate transformation from ground control point to raster data map, georeferencing, GeoAI database used to store spatial features, digitization of raster data map, and description research after work is complete are all components of field-based modeling on the geospatial intelligent system. In the modern world, it is particularly useful in terms of workload in the domains of area modeling and surveying, as well as for the day-to-day reasons of mapping. Additionally, a GeoAI-based interface was developed in order to manage the parameters of the model and integrate candidate locations and demand nodes as point data. In addition to this, it provides transit agencies with the decision-making tools necessary to determine which stations are unnecessary and should be eliminated, as well as which ones should be maintained because of their strategic importance. Therefore, the geospatial interaction coverage model offers an alternative strategy for modeling the effectiveness and redundancy of public transport. On the other hand, it is of great assistance when it comes to interpreting points of view, and it also makes maps instructive.

References

[1] Malczewski, Jacek. "GIS-based land-use suitability analysis: a critical overview." *Progress in planning* 62, no. 1 (2004): 3-65.

[2] Berry, Joseph K. "Cartographic modeling: The analytical capabilities of GIS." *Environmental modeling with GIS* 58-74 (1993).

[3] Ye, Xiuzi, Hongzheng Liu, Lei Chen, Zhiyang Chen, Xiang Pan, and Sanyuan Zhang. "Reverse innovative design—an integrated product design methodology." *Computer-aided design* 40, no. 7 (2008): 812-827.

[4] Nor, Amal Najihah M., Ron Corstanje, Jim A. Harris, and Tim Brewer. "Impact of rapid urban expansion on green space structure." *Ecological Indicators* 81 (2017): 274-284.

[5] Mangan, Alan P., and Ross T. Whitaker. "Partitioning 3D surface meshes using watershed segmentation." *IEEE Transactions on Visualization and Computer Graphics* 5, no. 4 (1999): 308-321.

[6] Benkő, Pál, Ralph R. Martin, and TamásVárady. "Algorithms for reverse engineering boundary representation models." *Computer-Aided Design* 33, no. 11 (2001): 839-851.

[7] Shean, David E., Oleg Alexandrov, Zachary M. Moratto, Benjamin E. Smith, Ian R. Joughin, Claire Porter, and Paul Morin. "An automated, open-source pipeline for mass production of digital elevation models (DEMs) from very-high-resolution commercial stereo satellite imagery." *ISPRS Journal of Photogrammetry and Remote Sensing* 116 (2016): 101-117.

[8] Maga, A. "Digital Morphology: The Final Frontier." İstanbul AntropolojiDergisi/ *Istanbul Anthropological Review* (2021).

[9] Brimkov, Valentin E., and RenetaBarneva. "Applications of digital geometry to surface reconstruction." *Int. J. Comput. Vis. Biomech 1*, no. 2 (2016): 163-172.

[10] Shelden, Dennis Robert. *"Digital surface representation and the constructibility of Gehry's architecture." PhD diss.*, Massachusetts Institute of Technology, 2002.

[11] Wood, Joseph. *The geomorphologicalcharacterisation of digital elevationmodels.* University of Leicester (United Kingdom), 1996.

[12] De Smith, Michael John, Michael F. Goodchild, and Paul Longley. *Geospatial analysis: acomprehensive guide to principles, techniques and software tools.* Troubadorpublishingltd, 2007.

[13] Wheatley, David, and Mark Gillings. *Spatial technology and archaeology: the archaeological applications of GIS*. CRC Press, 2013.

[14] Piegl, Les A., and Wayne Tiller. "Parametrization for surface fitting in reverse engineering." *Computer-Aided Design* 33, no. 8 (2001): 593-603.

[15] Barbero, Basilio Ramos. "The recovery of design intent in reverse engineering problems." *Computers &Industrial Engineering* 56, no. 4 (2009): 1265-1275.

[16] Razdan, Anshuman, and MyungSooBae. "A hybridapproach to feature segmentation of triangle meshes." *Computer-Aided Design* 35, no. 9 (2003): 783-789.

[17] Dai, Dangdang, Xianpei Wang, Jiachuan Long, Meng Tian, Guowei Zhu, and Jieming Zhang. "Feature extraction of GIS partial discharge signal based on S-transform and singular value decomposition." *IET Science, Measurement &Technology* 11, no. 2 (2017): 186-193.

[18] Kumar, A., Srivastava,V., Kumar,R.,Vardhan, A., Kumar, L."A *GIS based application and analysisfeatures of land survey of urban area of raster data map*", vol.5, (2014): ISBN 978-81-908989-6-5.

[19] Varady, Tamas, Ralph R. Martin, and Jordan Cox. "Reverse engineering of geometricmodels." *Computer-aided design* 29, no. 4 (1997): 253-330.

[20] Smith, T. R. "Artificial Intelligence and ItsApplicability to Geographical Problem Solving." *Professional Geographer* 36.2 (1984):147–158.

[21] Couclelis, H. "Artificial Intelligence in Geography: Conjectures on the Shape of Things to Come." *Professional Geographer* 38.1(1986): 1–11.

[22] Openshaw, S. "Some Suggestions concerning the Development of Artificial Intelligence Tools for Spatial Modelling and Analysis in GIS." *Annals of Regional Science* 26.1 (1992): 35–51.

[23] Janowicz, K., S. Gao, G. McKenzie, Y. Hu, and B. Bhaduri. "GeoAI: Spatially Explicit Artificial Intelligence Techniques for Geographic Knowledge Discovery and Beyond." *International Journal of Geographical Information Science* 34.4 (2020): 625–636.

[24] Kuhn, W. "Core Concepts of Spatial Information for TransdisciplinaryResearch." *International Journal of Geographical Information Science* 26.12 (2012): 2267–2276.

[25] Zhu, A. X., G. Lu, J. Liu, C. Z. Qin, and C. Zhou. "Spatial PredictionBased on Third Law of Geography." *Annals of GIS 24.4* (2018): 225–240.

[26] Bengio, Y., A. Courville, and P. Vincent. "Representation Learning: A Review and New Perspectives." *IEEE Transactions on Pattern Analysis and Machine Intelligence* 35.8 (2013): 1798–1828.

[27] Hill, Linda L. *Georeferencing: The geographic associations of information*. Mit Press, 2009.

[28] Graça, João, and Silva JNdOe. *"GeoSharding: Optimization of data partitioning in sharded georeferenced data bases." PhD diss*., PhD thesis, Instituto Superior Técnico, 2016.

[29] Ghosh, Triparna, Anupam Chattopadhyay, Gyan Verma, Srijan Srivastava, Arindam Sarkar, and Dipanjan Bhattacharjee. "Digital mapping and GIS-based spatial analyses of the Pur-Banera Group in Rajasthan, India, withspecialreference to the structural control on base-metalmineralization." *Journal of Structural Geology* 166 (2023): 104762.

[30] De Donatis, Mauro, Mauro Alberti, MattiaCipicchia, Nelson Muñoz Guerrero, Giulio F. Pappafico, and Sara Susini. "Workflow of digital field mapping and drone-aidedsurvey for the identification and characterization of capable faults: The case of a normal fault system in the monte nerone area (Northern Apennines, Italy)." *ISPRS International Journal of Geo-Information* 9, no. 11 (2020): 616.

About the Editors

Dr. Abhaya Kumar Sahoo is currently working as an Associate Professor in the School of Computer Engineering at Kalinga Institute of Industrial Technology (Deemed to be University) in Odisha, India, where he completed his B.Tech, M.Tech, and Ph.D. He has received the Founder's Gold Medal and Chancellor's Gold Medal in M. Tech. He has eleven years of teaching experience and one year of industry experience. His favourite teaching subjects include big data, operating system, web technology, computer organization, and databases, and his main areas of research include data analytics, recommender system, data security, and data mining. In addition to having published more than thirty-five research papers in national and international conferences and journals, he has published more than ten chapters in different reputable books. He was the Odisha State Student Coordinator for the Computer Society of India from 2019-2020. Dr. Sahoo received the CSI Young IT Professional Award in 2013 and the Best Faculty Award for good academic performance in 2013 and 2014. He is a life member of various national and international professional societies in the field of engineering and research, such as CSI, IAENG, CSTA, and IET.

Dr. Chittaranjan Pradhan holds a doctorate and master's and bachelor's degrees in computer science and engineering. He currently works as an Associate Professor in the School of Computer Engineering at Kalinga Institute of Industrial Technology (Deemed to be University) in Bhubaneswar, Odisha, India. Dr. Pradhan has sixteen years of academic teaching experience and more than seventy publications in peer-reviewed journals, edited books, and conferences of national and international repute. He has published several books with LAP Lambert, IGI Global, Elsevier, and others. His research areas include information security, image processing, deep learning, and multimedia systems, and he is a member of various national and international professional societies in the field of engineering and research, such as IET, IACSIT, CSI, ISCA, IAENG, and ISTE.

Dr. Brojo Kishore Mishra received his Ph.D. in computer science from Berhampur University in 2012 and worked at several reputable private engineering colleges and state universities for more than seventeen years. He is currently a Professor and Head of the Department of Computer Science & Engineering at the National Institute of Science and Technology (NIST) in Berhampur, India, and also works as Joint Secretary of IEEE Bhubaneswar sub-section. He has published more than 130 publications in international conferences, journals, and online books (indexed by SCI, SCIE, SSCI, SCOPUS, DBLP) and has fourteen edited books, two authored books, two patents, one copyright, and four book series. He has successfully guided one Ph.D. research scholar and currently guides six research scholars. He has served in the capacity of keynote speaker, program chair, proceeding chair, publicity chair, and as an advisory board member of many international conferences. He is also a life member of ISTE and CSI and a senior member of IEEE.

Dr. Bhabani Shankar Prasad Mishra received his B.Tech. in computer science and engineering from Biju Pattanaik Technical University in Odisha (2003), his M.Tech. in computer science and engineering from Kalinga Institute of Industrial Technology (2003), his Ph.D. in computer science from F.M. University in Balasore, Odisha, India (2011), and his Post Doc from the Soft Computing Laboratory at Yansei University in South Korea (2013). He currently works as a Professor in the School of Computer Engineering at Kalinga Institute of Industrial Technology in Bhubaneswar, Odisha, India. His research interests include pattern reorganization, remote sensing, data mining, soft computing, big data, and machine learning. He has published more than ninety research articles in reputed journals and conferences, edited more than five books, and has one patent. Under his guidance, twenty M.Tech and two Ph.D. scholars have already been awarded. His h-index is 12. Dr. Mishra was the recipient of the Gold Medal and Silver Medal during his M.Tech for the best postgraduate in the university.

Index

A

B

C

D

E

F

G

H

I

K

L

M

N

O

P

R

S